WITHDRAWN

Extraordinary World

SUPERPOWER

Heroes, Ghosts, and the
Paranormal in American Culture

M. KEITH BOOKER

University of Nebraska Press

Lincoln and London

Superpower: Heroes, Ghosts, and the Paranormal in American Culture by M. Keith Booker was originally published in hardcover as *Red, White, and Spooked: The Supernatural in American Culture* by Praeger Publishers, an imprint of ABC-CLIO, LLC, Santa Barbara, CA. Copyright © 2009 by M. Keith Booker. Paperback edition by arrangement with ABC-CLIO, LLC, Santa Barbara, CA. All rights reserved.

Manufactured in the United States of America

∞

First Nebraska paperback printing: 2010

Library of Congress Cataloging-in-Publication Data
Booker, M. Keith.
[Red, white, and spooked]
Superpower: heroes, ghosts, and the paranormal in American culture / M. Keith Booker.
p. cm. — (Extraordinary world)
Previously published under title: Red, white, and spooked: the supernatural in American culture, 2009.
Includes bibliographical references and index.
ISBN 978-0-8032-3289-1 (pbk.: alk. paper)
1. Mass media and culture—United States. 2. Popular culture—United States. 3. Motion pictures and television—United States. 4. Supernatural. 5. Supernatural in motion pictures. I. Title.
P94.65.U6B66 2010
700'.45873—dc22
2009048720

For Adam, Skylor, and Benjamin

CONTENTS

INTRODUCTION: CULTURE OF LONGING—
THE SUPERNATURAL IN AMERICAN CULTURE

In his 2001 Hugo Award–winning fantasy novel *American Gods*, British author (but U.S. resident) Neil Gaiman metaphorically dramatizes some of the central conflicts in American culture. Writing with the insights of an outsider who nevertheless has extensive firsthand knowledge, Gaiman treats readers to the most memorable literary tour of Americana since that given to us by another displaced European, Vladimir Nabokov, in *Lolita* (1955). In particular, Gaiman imagines a battle between the old gods of mythology and the new gods of modern commerce and technology (representing such contemporary powers as the Internet, the media, credit cards, and cheap plastic) that takes the various gods and the ex-convict protagonist, Shadow, to various sites around the country. These locations (e.g., Las Vegas, Wisconsin's House on the Rock, and the Rock City tourist attraction near Chattanooga, Tennessee) are what pass for holy sites in America, but they are in fact thoroughly secular attempts at fabricating special places in a land devoid of true magic. Meanwhile, the old gods, led by the Norse deity Odin, seem decidedly overmatched in their struggle against the new gods of modern capitalism, who are after all much more at home in America. Odin explains to Shadow that America's churches have about as much spiritual significance as dentists' offices and that the best that Americans can muster in terms of true "places of power" are roadside attractions such as models made from beer bottles or gigantic bat houses. Thus, whereas in other parts of the world people might feel themselves being drawn to places where they could discover that part of themselves that is truly transcendent, in America they go to attractions like Rock City and the House on a Rock. (Big-time tourist attractions such as Disney World, conversely, are for Odin purely commercial enterprises that lack even the feeble magic of the smaller roadside attractions, although the original Disneyland might have a bit of supernatural power associated with it.) At these vaguely holy roadside sites, visitors then "buy a hot dog and walk around, feeling satisfied on a level they cannot truly describe, and profoundly dissatisfied on a level beneath that" (p. 118).

The doubleness described here is crucial to my arguments in this book about the prominence of supernatural and superhuman elements in American popular culture; like all popular culture (but in a particularly obvious way), these elements are designed to provide satisfaction within the status quo but also to address a (largely unconscious) dissatisfaction with the way things are. It is my argument that the evident fascination with the supernatural in American popular culture arises largely from an attempt to satisfy utopian longings that result from the lack of genuinely supernatural elements in day-to-day American life. In this sense, my argument is heavily influenced by Fredric Jameson's observation in *The Political Unconscious* that the continuing popularity of "magical" narratives (which he tends to group under the rubric of "romance") in a modern world notably bereft of magic can be explained by a persistent desire for dimensions of life that go beyond the day-to-day, rationalized routine of modern capitalism. In the modern capitalist world, Jameson argues, "romance now again seems to offer the possibility of sensing other historical rhythms, and of demonic or Utopian transformations of a real now unshakably set in place" (p. 104). It is my argument that supernatural narratives in American culture tend to be dominated by a desire that is structurally similar to the consumerist desires that drive contemporary capitalism. As a result, such narratives tend merely to reinforce the hold of capitalist ideology on the minds of those who consume these narratives. Indeed, as Linda Degh has convincingly argued, magic has become an important tool of marketing in recent years (pp. 54–79). However, Jameson's suggestion of the utopian potential of such narratives thus usefully complicates such insights by providing a reminder that the structural similarity between consumerist desire and the longing for magic in the modern world does not prevent supernatural narratives from indicating at least a few glimmers of other worlds beyond that of the capitalist present.

Meanwhile, Jameson's own argument refers to the crucial early-twentieth-century insight of pioneering sociologist Max Weber that capitalist modernization has stripped the world of magic. Importantly, Weber argues that the world views of Protestantism and of capitalist modernity share numerous important characteristics and that Protestantism is a rationalized form of religion that lacks the reliance on magic of many other religions, including Catholicism. Thus, given that American Christianity has from the beginning been dominated by Protestantism, the proclaimed religiosity of Americans, from Weber's perspective, would in no way be inconsistent with Gaiman's characterization of the United States in *American Gods*. Indeed, the thorough secularization of religious experience that lies at the heart of the America of *American Gods* is precisely the sort of phenomenon described by Weber, who believes that the growth of Western capitalism (aided by the spread of Protestantism) has led to a thoroughly rationalized view of the world, in which every aspect of life (including religion) is understood through and regulated by scientific principles, leading to a sense of reality that is completely stripped of any sense of wonder and magic.

Weber's analysis and my analysis of American culture in this volume are thus both consistent with Gaiman's characterization, in *American Gods*, of the United States as a place of "negative sacredness," although Gaiman's novel also draws especially heavily on the related perception that the United States is a bastion of modernity, devoted to technological and economic innovation and therefore inhospitable to tradition (p. 430). "This is a bad land for gods," declares Shadow. "The old gods are ignored. The new gods are as quickly taken up as they are abandoned, cast aside for the next big thing" (p. 538). Of course, this declaration echoes the observation made by Karl Marx and Friedrich Engels in *The Communist Manifesto* (back in 1848) that, under the innovation-driven system of capitalism, "all fixed, fast-frozen relations, with their train of ancient and venerable prejudices and opinions are swept away, all new-formed ones become antiquated before they can ossify. All that is solid melts into air, all that is holy is profaned, and man is at last compelled to face with sober senses, his real conditions of life, and his relations with his kind" (p. 476).

Gaiman's perception that capitalist modernity has rendered the United States hostile to traditionalist forms of religious thought thus seems quite consistent with even the earliest Marxist critiques of capitalism. Meanwhile, *American Gods* itself participates in a long fascination with the supernatural in American culture, even if the basic premise of the book seems at first glance to imply that Americans have little use for the supernatural, preferring instead to concentrate on more practical (and profitable) matters. One of my principal arguments in this text, however, is that popular fascination with the supernatural in the United States is not merely consistent with the fundamental rationalist materialism of American society but also is in fact largely a product of that materialism. American life, I shall argue, is so devoted to a rationalist pursuit of material gain that it is indeed stripped almost entirely of magic, resulting in a widespread longing to believe in something greater and spiritually richer than the mere quest for money. Furthermore, I shall argue that this longing for the supernatural is (not coincidentally) structurally quite similar to the consumerist desires that drive contemporary capitalism. Both longings are fundamentally unfulfillable and unending because, by definition, they are based on a desire for more than what one currently has—no matter how much one already has. I should again like to argue that there is at least a partial back-and-forth, cause-and-effect relationship here. The functioning of modern consumer capitalism requires the presence of a reasonably affluent population of consumers whose longing to consume never ends, thus continuing to drive consumption. Americans thus live in an environment that is saturated with cultural energies that are designed to reinforce this sort of unending economic desire, which then informs all other aspects of American life as well, including attitudes toward religion and the supernatural. At the same time, religious longings that were already in place at the end of the nineteenth century helped to fuel the explosive growth in American consumer capitalism that began at that time and that has continued to this day.

The long history of fascination with the supernatural in American culture is part of the subject of the current text. After all, from its very beginnings, American literature has included strong elements of the supernatural, from the religion-driven writings of colonial Puritan authors such as John Winthrop and Cotton Mather, to early stories such as Washington Irving's "Rip Van Winkle" (1819) and "The Legend of Sleepy Hollow" (1820), to the Gothic tales of Edgar Allan Poe, published in the 1830s and 1840s. Supernatural elements remained strong in the work of such now-canonical authors as Nathaniel Hawthorne, whose Romantic tales of hauntings and witchcraft were much influenced by the Puritan tradition. Even the hulking presence of Herman Melville's Moby-Dick clearly acquires metaphysical dimensions far beyond the mere fact of its physical size and power, while the formal eccentricities of *Moby-Dick* (1851) distance it from the realist tradition as well.

In fact, one would be hard pressed to find any major form of American culture that has not included strong elements of the superhuman and supernatural throughout its history, although this phenomenon (like most other aspects of American life) has accelerated in the past few decades. Some cultural forms are natural vehicles for the presentation of such elements, as in the case of comic books and, more recently, graphic novels, which have tended to be dominated by superhero narratives and often involve supernatural motifs as well. Similarly, it might not be surprising that fantasy films involving supernatural adventures have come to dominate the American box office in recent years, given a long cultural history in which the products of the Hollywood film industry have conventionally been marketed as "movie magic." Television, not traditionally a strong medium for supernatural programming, has also recently seen a marked increase in the prevalence of programs involving supernatural or superhuman themes, partly because such programs have been made more viable by the increasing quality and decreasing cost of computer-generated special effects. Even popular music has long drawn on supernatural themes for material, including such classic albums as *Ghost in the Machine* (1981), by the British group[1] The Police, and Santana's *Supernatural* (1999). Prominent individual songs containing supernatural references or imagery includes such diverse works as the rock classic "Sympathy for the Devil" (1968), by the Rolling Stones; Charlie Daniels Band's 1979 country crossover "The Devil Went Down to Georgia"; the 1983 glam/heavy metal hit "Shout at the Devil," by Mötley Crüe; or the recent "Supernatural Superserious" (2008), by the alternative rock band R.E.M. All of this is not to mention the strong influence of gospel on country music, or the paranoid tradition of declaring rock and roll to be the devil's music, part of a Satanic plot to suborn America's youth. For example, rumors that various rock songs contain Satanic messages if they are played backwards (Led Zeppelin's 1971 classic "Stairway to Heaven" might be the most prominent example) have become widespread urban legends over the years. Meanwhile, groups such as Black Sabbath have responded with glee to these charges of Satanic inspirations behind rock music by overtly building occult and horror themes and motifs into their music and their identities as performing artists.

Supernatural and superhuman elements are so prominent in American culture that it would be impossible to discuss them all in detail in a single volume. In this text I focus primarily on film and television to make the amount of available material a bit more manageable, while acknowledging the relevance of fiction, comic books, music, and other forms as well. I also pay especially close attention to film and television from the past 10 to 15 years, when superhuman and supernatural elements have become increasingly prominent. In the years 1998 to 2008, for example, the top nine grossing films at U.S. box offices were all supernatural fantasies, science fiction, or superhero movies. Meanwhile, there has been an explosion of superhuman and supernatural programming on American television in the past few years, beginning with crucial forerunner series such as *The X-Files* (FOX, 1993–2002) and *Buffy the Vampire Slayer* (WB, 1997–2001; UPN, 2001–2003), and extending to recent hits such as *Lost* (ABC, 2004–) and *Heroes* (NBC, 2006–). In addition, 2007 and 2008 alone saw the renewal and continuation of such programs as *Smallville* (CW), *Kyle XY* (ABC Family), *The Ghost Whisperer* (CBS), *Medium* (NBC), *The 4400* (USA), and *The Dead Zone* (USA)—although the last two ostensibly ended multiyear runs during that period. Even more new programs with such themes debuted in 2007 and 2008, including *Journeyman* (NBC, about a man who can travel through time), a remake of the classic series *The Bionic Woman* (NBC), *Eli Stone* (ABC, about a lawyer driven by supernatural visions), *Pushing Daisies* (ABC, about a man whose touch can bring the dead to life), *The Dresden Files* (SciFi, about a wizard who helps the police to solve unusual cases), *Moonlight* (CBS, about a vampire private detective), *New Amsterdam* (Fox, about an immortal New York City cop), *John from Cincinnati* (HBO, about a young man with supernatural abilities who visits a California surfing community and who may be the second coming of Christ), *Reaper* (CW, about a young man who is forced to work as a bounty hunter for the devil), and *Saving Grace* (TNT, about a police detective aided by an angel). Even "reality" television has now moved into the supernatural arena with shows such as *Ghost Hunters* (SciFi channel, 2004–) and *Paranormal State* (A&E, 2007–).

Perhaps the most representative work of recent American popular culture to deal with the supernatural is the appropriately titled *Supernatural*, which premiered on the WB network in the fall of 2005 and moved over to the CW network for its second season when that network began operation in 2006. The series has remained there since, a fourth season having been announced as of the completion of the third season in May 2008. Interestingly, *Supernatural* creator Eric Kripke has listed *American Gods* as being among the most important influences on the series, which is an almost encyclopedic compilation of motifs that have been featured in supernatural television over the years. In particular, the series deals quite centrally with a variety of supernatural conspiracies, many potentially leading to apocalyptic consequences, but does so in a hip, self-consciously postmodern fashion that signals a lack of real anxiety about such conspiracies, even as the interest in such conspiracies signals other anxieties about the real world.

Much of the attitude toward supernatural evil in *Supernatural* is reminiscent of *Buffy the Vampire Slayer*, which joins *The X-Files* as the two most obvious predecessors of the show. *Supernatural* relates the adventures of twenty-something brothers Sam and Dean Winchester (played by Jared Padalecki and Jensen Ackles, respectively), who travel the country in Dean's classic 1967 Chevy Impala on the hunt for various supernatural bad guys. The two were raised by their father, John (Jeffrey Dean Morgan), to be such hunters after their mother was killed by a demon when Dean was four and Sam was still an infant. John has been on the trail of that demon ever since, battling (and usually killing) various other supernatural foes along the way. Dean has followed very much in his father's footsteps, although Sam had hoped to have a more normal life. As an added twist, through most of the first season the sons are also looking for their father, who has disappeared while on a hunt, causing Sam to drop out of college and join Dean on the road, spurred on by the fact that the same demon that killed their mother also kills Sam's live-in girlfriend, Jessica (Adrianne Palicki), in the untitled pilot episode (September 13, 2005).

Supernatural can be extremely dark and very scary, and it doesn't shy away from viscerally powerful horror. Similar to *Buffy* and *The X-Files*, however, it mixes this darkness with a consistent thread of humor (especially by means of Dean's constant wise-cracking), never taking itself too seriously despite the sometimes very grim nature of the material being presented. Late in Season Two, the humor of *Supernatural* comes even more to the fore with the introduction of self-parodic ludic episodes. In "Tall Tales" (February 15, 2007), a Trickster demigod invokes a series of clichéd urban legends to bring gruesome deaths to a variety of ne'er-do-wells, ironically commenting on the use of such legends throughout the series. Most of the humor, however, comes from the fact that the events of the episode are told in flashback, with Sam and Dean alternating as narrators, each presenting comically exaggerated versions that seek to make the narrating brother look good and the other brother look ridiculous. In "Hollywood Babylon" (April 19, 2007), meanwhile, the brothers travel to Hollywood on vacation but become involved in the making of a Hollywood horror movie, which allows the episode to lampoon such movies—and Hollywood movies in general. Then again, some of this humor is self-directed, because *Supernatural* itself participates in much the same genre. In one bit of ironic self-commentary, the director of the horror movie in question is real-world film director McG (Joseph McGinty Nichol, played here by Regan Burns), who also happens to be an executive producer of *Supernatural*—but who is treated here as comically inept.[2]

Among other things, this episode, while having a good deal of fun with the bad writing and hackneyed plots that often haunt horror movies, allows *Supernatural* to pay homage to some of its own important predecessors, including *Poltergeist* (1982) and *The Evil Dead* (1981), and also tosses in an allusion to the Kripke-scripted *Boogeyman* (2005). The episode also allows Dean to display his encyclopedic knowledge of such films, which is part of his seemingly limitless knowledge of American popular culture (especially from the 1970s) as a whole. With its young protagonists and its classic-rock soundtrack, *Supernatural* is self-consciously hip, pitched to a relatively young audience. Much of this hipness derives from its engagement with other works of popular culture, especially through Dean's tendency to compare the situations in which the brothers find themselves to situations from popular films—or in his tendency to adopt aliases (e.g., John Bonham and David Hasselhoff) derived from well-known figures from film, television, or popular music. The series is allusive in other ways as well, as in frequently casting actors known for their appearances in other examples of supernatural television, thus placing itself in the company of those series. In addition to the fact that Ackles had played recurring roles in both *Dark Angel* and *Smallville*, guest stars in individual episodes of *Supernatural* include William B. Davis from *The X-Files*; Amber Benson from *Buffy the Vampire Slayer*; Julie Benz from *Buffy*, *Angel*, and *Roswell*; Mercedes McNab from *Buffy* and *Angel*; Emmanuelle Vaugier from *Smallville*; Tricia Helfer from *Battlestar Galactica*; Teryl Rothery from *Stargate SG-1*; and Meghan Echikunwoke, Samantha Ferris, and Conchita Campbell, all from *The 4400*. Perhaps the most striking example of this sort of allusive casting, however, occurs in the second-season episode "The Usual Suspects" (November 9, 2006; the title itself alludes to a popular 1995 film of that title), which features a middle-aged Linda Blair (still best known for her childhood appearance in *The Exorcist* in 1973) as a police detective. At one point in the *Supernatural* episode, the brothers decide that the woman played by Blair looks oddly familiar, and, if there is any doubt that the two are stepping outside the fictional frame to comment on Blair's earlier appearance in *The Exorcist*, Dean then quips that he has a sudden craving for pea soup—referring to the notorious projectile-vomiting scene in *The Exorcist*.

Supernatural also quite openly acknowledges its awareness of its debt to predecessors such as *The X-Files* and *Buffy*. In the first-season episode "Hell House" (March 30, 2006), two comically inept would-be ghost hunters finally encounter a real ghost and ask themselves, "WWBD: What would Buffy do?" These same ghost hunters reappear in the third-season episode "Ghostfacers" (April 24, 2008), in which they are making a reality TV show that seems suspiciously similar to shows such as *Ghost Hunters*. In "The Usual Suspects," Sam and Dean argue over which of them is Mulder and which is Scully, acknowledging the program's debt to *The X-Files*. Even in the pilot episode, Sam and Dean walk past two FBI agents, and Dean addresses them as Agents Mulder and Scully. In fact, Dean is always ready with the quip, whereas Sam is more intense and serious: one of the models for the two young men was the duo of Luke Skywalker (in the case of Sam) and Han Solo (in the case of Dean) from *Star Wars* (1977). In any case, the difference in personality between the two brothers is a key element of the show, sometimes leading to conflicts between them but always enriching their relationship and making it more interesting for viewers.

Supernatural partakes of a variety of other traditions in addition to horror films and supernatural television. For example, in the way that Sam and Dean are constantly on the move, existing on the fringes of polite society, the series clearly participates in the literary tradition of the picaresque. In fact, the two are outlaws of a sort, constantly (and illegally) impersonating various authority figures (including law enforcement officers) in the course of their investigations of the supernatural. They support themselves largely by credit card fraud and other nefarious means learned from their father, who has lived a similar life. Dean, meanwhile, allows himself to be pronounced officially dead after he is presumed killed in the early episode "Skin" (October 18, 2005), which is quite convenient, given that he is also wanted for murder after a shapeshifter commits a killing while in the guise of Dean in that episode.

In "The Usual Suspects," Dean is arrested but regains his freedom, although he subsequently becomes the object of a nationwide manhunt when the authorities realize that he is alive. This situation places the brothers even more on the margins of polite society, and for a time they even have their own personal FBI special agent (played by Charles Malik Whitfield), who is charged with hunting them down. The brothers are arrested in Arkansas in the episode "Folsom Prison Blues" (April 26, 2007)—but only because they have set up their own arrest so that they can infiltrate a haunted prison at the request of a prison guard, who later helps them to escape.

The Winchester brothers' hunt for the demon that killed their mother provides a continuous plot arc for the first season of *Supernatural*, which otherwise plays very much like a sequence of monster-of-the-week episodes from *The X-Files*. The supernatural world of the series seems peopled particularly by various sorts of demons, but it also includes a virtual catalog of other kinds of supernatural monsters, including most of the traditional types of such monsters, such as ghosts, vampires, and werewolves, as well as more specialized creatures from American folklore and urban legend. The cosmology of the series seems vaguely Christian, although Christianity itself wields very little actual power in the world of *Supernatural*. The brothers themselves (especially Dean) do not generally seem at all religious, despite all the supernatural power they have encountered. In "Nightmare" (February 7, 2006), the brothers impersonate priests, one of the many disguises they employ in the course of their investigations—although Sam is in fact quite unhappy with this particular imposture. When Christianity and Christian symbols do appear in the series, they tend to be no match for the dark forces to which they are presumably opposed. In the episode "Faith" (January 17, 2006), the brothers encounter a preacher who seems to be a genuine faith healer, only to discover that he is actually (without his knowledge) employing demonic and not godly powers to do his work. In "Salvation" (April 27, 2006), a woman possessed by a demon kills a priest in a church, laughing off his suggestion that she cannot come into the church because it is hallowed ground. Crosses have no effect on the vampires the Winchesters encounter in "Dead Man's Blood" (April 20, 2006), whereas traditional weapons such as holy water are of only limited value against the various monsters of the series. Although some demons find holy water painful (but not deadly), other, more powerful, demons are completely unaffected. In the first-season finale, the Winchesters reunite with their father and finally encounter the yellow-eyed demon (Fredric Lehne) that killed their mother. They discover that holy water has no effect on this particularly nasty demon, who simply mocks it, asking with considerable sarcasm, "You think something like that's gonna work on something like me?" The demon reacts similarly when Dean issues a holy threat after it possesses the body of the senior Winchester. "Let him go or I swear to God . . ." proclaims Dean, to which the demon merely sneers, "What are you and *God* gonna do?" In fact, God does nothing, although the sons are able to save their father but only at the expense of letting the demon escape—and then apparently kills them all in a cataclysmic auto accident as the first season reaches its shocking conclusion. It is revealed early in Season Three, however, that the yellow-eyed demon was none other than Azazel himself, pulling the series more within the orbit of Christian mythology.

One of the ways in which Sam resembles Luke Skywalker is in the fact that he seems to have been born a Chosen One with special psychic powers that are only beginning to emerge in his early adulthood. This gradual emergence provides part of the continuous plot arc that binds together the first season, although Sam's abilities do not really become a major element of the program until the second season. In this season, we gradually learn of a budding war between demons and humans, in which those with special powers such as Sam could be fated to fight as soldiers on the side of the demons. As the second season begins, we find that Sam and his father are actually recovering nicely from their injuries in the auto crash that ended Season One. Dean, however, lies dying, causing the father to make a deal with Azazel: John Winchester agrees to give up his own life in return for that of his son. The demon accepts the deal, which adds a dark twist to Dean's character in subsequent episodes. Suspecting (and eventually discovering) the deal made by his father, a brooding Dean is tormented by the realization of his father's sacrifice.

In addition, just before his death, the father warns Dean (although we do not learn the content of the warning until several episodes later) that he has to keep an eye out for Sam—and not just in the usual big-brother way he has been doing throughout Sam's life. In particular, he warns Dean that Sam (here in an echo of the *Star Wars* story, not of Luke Skywalker but of Luke's father Anakin) might be in danger of going over to the dark side. If that happens,

John warns, Dean must kill his brother, a mission that adds still more weight to the heavy burden that Dean already carries, while also laying the foundation for the main plot arc of the second season. This plot arc does not really become clear until the final two episodes toward which many of the earlier episodes then retrospectively appear to have been building.

Among other things, this arc involves the introduction of more and more information about the "hunter" culture in which the Winchesters participate, which consists of a loosely aligned network of individual persons who are dedicated to tracking and killing demons, spirits, vampires, and other kinds of evil supernatural creatures. Particularly aligned with the brothers is hunter Bobby Singer (Jim Beaver), a former ally of John Winchester who comes to the aid of John's sons in several episodes. Also particularly important among the other hunters the brothers encounter is Gordon Walker (Sterling K. Brown), who specializes in slaying vampires. In the episode "Bloodlust" (October 12, 2006), which marks Walker's first appearance in the series, the vampire slayer remarks that he loves his life as a hunter because "it's all black and white. There's no maybe. You find the bad thing; you kill it. Most people spend their lives in shades of gray." Walker's expressed desire for easy and absolute moral distinctions mirrors a desire that seems to inform numerous examples of supernatural film and television. Walker's ruthless dedication to eradicating his supernatural foes often blurs the boundary between good and evil, however, and sometimes puts him at (violent) odds with the brothers. Indeed, in "Bloodlust," the vampires that he hunts turn out to be benevolent, having resolved to live off of the blood of cattle so that they can forgo attacks on humans. Walker wants to kill them nevertheless: He has a special hatred for vampires because his own sister was bitten by one, subsequently becoming a vampire that Walker had to kill. The brothers intervene on the side of the "good" vampires, but the episode as a whole seriously complicates the simple good versus evil dichotomy that Walker had found so comforting.

As the war with evil gradually approaches in Season Two, *Supernatural* sometimes addresses religious questions in a more serious (if ultimately non-committal) way. Particularly crucial to this turn in the series is the episode "Houses of the Holy" (January 2, 2007). Here, a series of innocent people suddenly commit murders, claiming that they have been ordered to do so by an angel that appeared before them. When the brothers investigate, Dean scoffs at the very notion of angels, but Sam takes it very seriously. Indeed, much to Dean's surprise, Sam admits to a belief in God and angels, saying that he prays every day. Later, Dean reacts even more cynically when he learns that the "angel" has appeared before Sam, similarly instructing him to be prepared for a sign that he must kill someone to prevent them from doing something awful. Describing the experience with the angel, Sam says that a feeling "like peace, like grace" washed over him in the presence of the angel. "Okay, ecstasy boy," responds Dean. "Maybe we'll get you some glow sticks and a nice Dr. Seuss hat."

It turns out, however, that Dean has a special reason to be skeptical about angels. Their mother had been a great believer in angels, and the last thing she had expressed to Dean before her horrible death was her faith that angels were watching over them. "She was wrong," Dean bitterly concludes. "There was nothing protecting her. There's no higher power. There's no God. There's just chaos and violence and random unpredictable evil that comes out of nowhere and rips you to shreds." Subsequent events in the episode, however, throw both brothers into confusion, leaving Sam questioning his faith and leaving Dean questioning his lack of faith. It turns out that Dean was right about the "angel": Sam eventually discovers that the apparition that appeared to him and the others was not an angel at all, but the misguided spirit of a murdered priest that only thinks it is an angel. When Dean pursues the man that the spirit commanded Sam to kill, however, he finds that the man is indeed about to commit a heinous crime, which Dean is able to prevent. The man's subsequent weird death then leaves Dean wondering if it had been God's will for the man to die.

The supernatural war motif finally comes to a head in the final two-part episode of Season Two. In this episode, the yellow-eyed demon manages to employ a human minion to open a gate into hell that had been rendered inaccessible to demons, thanks to the work of nineteenth-century inventor and industrialist Samuel Colt. In fact, Colt figures prominently in the mythology of *Supernatural*, having also fashioned a special revolver that is the only weapon in existence capable of killing the yellow-eyed demon. The series thus adds Colt, already something of an American legend because of his innovations in the design and manufacture of firearms, to the catalog of myths and legends on which it draws. With the help of John Winchester, who emerges from hell with other spirits and demons when the gate is opened, the special revolver does indeed kill the yellow-eyed demon in the final episode of the second season, thus bringing to an end the quest that had driven the first two seasons. By this time, however, a virtual army of demons has been released through the hellgate, giving the brothers and other hunters plenty to do in Season Three. Moreover, in these final episodes of the season, Sam is at one point killed, and Dean can bring him back only by making a deal with another demon: In return for Sam's life, Dean's soul will become the property of the demon after 1 year. Finding out about the deal, Sam (who now seems to have lost his psychic powers) vows to find a way to extricate Dean from this Faustian deal, thus adding another plot element for the third season.

Various events mark the third season, which is loosely tied together by the continuous plot arcs of the battle against the released demons and the fight to save Dean. For example, in "Fresh Blood" (November 15, 2007), Gordon Walker returns, determined to kill Sam, whom he has concluded is the Antichrist, set on bringing about the Apocalypse. Instead, Sam kills Walker, but only after the vampire hunter has himself been turned into a vampire. Season Three also sees the introduction of two important new female characters, as the series continues its search for an effective female lead. The first is a beautiful blonde demon named Ruby (Katie Cassidy), who becomes an ally of the brothers in their struggles against other demons, for purposes of her own. The second, Bela (Lauren Cohan), is a charming, sexy, and ruthless British thief (somewhat reminiscent of Gwen Raiden in *Angel*, but without superpowers) who specializes in stealing supernatural relics and selling them to the highest bidder. Her own projects often put her at odds with the brothers, although they sometimes become allies as well. As the season draws to a close, we learn that Bela's soul has also been contracted to the same demon who holds the contract on Dean. In the final episode, Bela and Dean are apparently both killed and their souls sent to hell. No details are provided, however, because the season ends here, leaving viewers to wait for Season Four for the rescue (at least of Dean) that presumably will come.

That Season Four is indeed forthcoming makes *Supernatural* a relative success among American television series, especially those on marginal networks such as the CW. Although the series has never attracted a huge audience (partly because it *is* on the CW), it does seem to have an unusually loyal and devoted fan base among the coveted 18-to-34-year-old demographic. Its appeal can, I think, be traced to several factors. First, the Winchester brothers are compelling heroes, made more so by the chemistry between the two of them, which allows them to be both individualist outlaws and figures of genuine community, answering two seemingly contradictory fantasy longings at once. This series also responds to a longing for adventure that seems especially strong in recent American popular culture, presenting the brothers with challenges and opportunities that go far beyond any that might be encountered in the workaday world of contemporary capitalism. Finally, the series, through its elaboration of various (potentially apocalyptic) supernatural conspiracies, responds to a popular contemporary fascination with such conspiracies that seems related to a longing for order that results from the chaos and confusion of life in the early twenty-first century.

Supernatural thus provides at least some fantasy fulfillment of three major types of longings that are crucial to American cultural representation of the supernatural and the superhuman: (1) the American cultural fascination with narratives of adventure, which often take their adventurers into supernatural territory; (2) the American fascination with heroism and heroes, who often turn out to have supernatural or superhuman abilities; and (3) the prominence in American culture of narratives involving confrontations with supernatural evil, often told in a paranoid mode that involves vast supernatural conspiracies that threaten to end human existence as we know it. These three types of longings provide the structure for my arguments in this text, which devotes one extensive chapter to each of them.

In these chapters, I argue that all three of these fascinations are functionally similar to (and, at least since World War II, partly driven by) the consumerist desires that are central to contemporary capitalism. Chapter 1, focusing on the American longing for adventure, looks at the way in which American culture has so often employed narratives of grand, epic adventure that take their protagonists into worlds that clearly go beyond the bounds of reality, often into the supernatural. In recent years, this particular fascination has led to colossal box-office success for film franchises such as the *Lord of the Rings* trilogy, the *Harry Potter* films, the three *Pirates of the Caribbean* films, and the three *Shrek* films. Noting that the first two of these four franchises have their origins in British, not American, culture, I also discuss the aspects of this film phenomenon that are distinctively American, including a discussion of the ways in which *Pirates* and *Shrek* differ from *Lord of the Rings* and *Harry Potter*.

The second major part of this study, focusing on the longing for heroism, looks at the extraordinary fascination with heroism that informs American cultural history, paying particular attention to the prominence in American culture of hero figures who are in one way or another superhuman. From the tall-tale heroes who grew largely in conjunction with nineteenth-century frontier narratives, to larger-than-life comic-book superheroes, to the more recent trend toward humanized superheroes on film and television, American culture is filled with examples of heroes who defend the rest of us against dangers too severe for normal humans to overcome. This chapter traces the historical development of American ideas of heroism and discusses the ways in which this history helps to tell the larger story of American history as a whole. For purposes of more detailed illustration, this second part looks in special detail at several specific phenomena in American culture, including the evolution of the frontier hero into antiheroes such as the hard-boiled detective; such figures then provide the basis for the rise of the recent subgenre of vampire detective narratives. This chapter also discusses the recent prominence of several different types of superheroes, including female, teenage, and mutant superheroes.

Finally, Chapter 3 discusses narratives involving confrontations with supernatural or superhuman evil, often couched (especially in recent years) in terms of vast conspiracies designed to destroy the American way of life—or human life altogether—in a final apocalypse. These narratives, I note, are part of a paranoid tendency in American culture that dates back at least as far as the Puritan obsession with Satan in early New England, accompanied by a concern among the Puritans that their experiment was under constant surveillance from observers who did not necessarily wish the Puritans well. In this chapter, however, I argue that the recent fascination with the theme of vast evil conspiracies designed to bring about the Apocalypse is at least partly related to a longing to find patterns in and to make sense of a world that otherwise seems overwhelmingly complex and confusing.

Together, these three sections help to indicate some of the most important ways in which superhuman and supernatural elements have been featured in American culture over the years, especially in film and television. They also provide some historical context and theoretical basis for an understanding of why such elements would be so popular. My concluding chapter then turns to a brief discussion of the significance of the prominence of superhuman and supernatural elements in American popular culture and to an elaboration of the implications of these cultural products for those who consume them.

One

NOT JUST A JOB: THE LONGING FOR ADVENTURE IN AMERICAN HISTORY AND AMERICAN CULTURE

The Reagan-era U.S. Navy recruiting slogan "It's Not Just a Job; It's an Adventure" is probably one of the best-remembered slogans in advertising history and also one of the most telling. During a time in American history famed for its devotion to capitalist profit seeking, the slogan showed an understanding of the fact that many young Americans might welcome an opportunity to escape, at least for a time, the capitalist rat race and seek adventures rather than pay raises. The slogan thus captured something very real about the special context of the 1980s, when an unprecedented devotion to the dogged pursuit of economic success also triggered an unprecedented (even if largely unconscious) uneasiness about the emptiness of life under capitalism. This uneasiness, meanwhile, was exacerbated by a sense of something lost, a sense that the glorious quest for adventure that had once been so central to the American national endeavor had now been replaced by a banal scramble for fancier cars and bigger houses.

This same sense of loss permeates American culture throughout the twentieth century, although it did reach new levels in the 1980s.[1] This loss has been particularly dramatic given the way that American history has not simply been informed by a fascination with and quest for adventure, but it has, to a very real extent, itself been figured as a grand adventure, with the national identity of the United States deriving in large measure from a sense of being engaged in a wondrous enterprise. The great political documents of American history—the Declaration of Independence, the Constitution, the

Gettysburg Address—are filled with expressions of this notion of a national mission that is a magnificent enterprise, breaking new ground in the annals of human history so that human beings can at last live free. Much of this rhetoric, of course, is common to the Western Enlightenment, in which the American Revolution was firmly rooted. Much of it, however, especially in the extent to which the rhetoric appeals to superhuman powers and principles, is particular to the United States—sometimes seeming almost paranoid in its constant reminders, from Puritan leader John Winthrop's "city upon a hill" sermon forward, that the whole world is watching what takes place in the United States, looking for evidence that the American national mission is either blessed or damned.

One could argue that the history of the United States begins with the initial voyages of Columbus, which themselves were surely among the great adventures of Western history, as were the subsequent exploration and colonization of the Western hemisphere. Furthermore, a sense of adventure was clearly central to the gradual spread of the United States across North America through much of the nineteenth century. Indeed, if one accepts Frederick Jackson Turner's influential thesis (dating back to 1893), that the existence of a frontier waiting to be explored and conquered was central to the evolution of the national consciousness of the United States, then it seems clear that a quest for adventure is one of the crucial driving forces in U.S. history. Importantly, adventure in this sense has usually been envisioned on an epic scale: A sense of magnitude and importance—combined with a sense of a special mission in the world—has been fundamental to the cultural identity of the United States from Winthrop's sermon onward (and remains a major element of American political rhetoric to this day).

By the time of Winthrop's voyage to New England, America itself had long been viewed by at least some Europeans as a New World of hope and opportunity, invested with precisely the sort of magic that had been draining out of European life since the late Middle Ages. One recalls here the accounts of early travelers, including Columbus himself, that related the sighting of a variety of marvels in the New World. These tales of wonder must now be processed through our retrospective knowledge that the voyages of explorers such as Columbus ultimately led to the destruction of what has been estimated at as much as 95 percent of the Native American population (Diamond, p. 211).[2] From the beginning, therefore, the "magic" of the New World has been problematic. Nevertheless, a belief that American history itself was a grand, divinely ordained adventure has been crucial to the national identity of the United States from the seventeenth-century Puritan settlements onward. The loss of such a belief in the modern world thus creates a particular sense of longing for what has been lost.

VOYAGES OF DISCOVERY: AMERICAN ADVENTURE FROM COLUMBUS TO JEAN-LUC PICARD

In viewing Columbus's accounts of the New World, we must keep in mind that Columbus was encountering a precapitalist America and that his perceptions of that America arise from a medieval Catholic perspective. Columbus's sense of the magical potential of the New World is thus perfectly consistent with Weber's arguments about the lack of magic in Protestantism, which involve a strong distinction between precapitalist and capitalist perceptions of the world and between rationalist Protestantism and traditionalist Catholicism. Indeed, as a thoroughly medieval (and Catholic) man, Columbus was in many respects remarkably ill suited to understand the newness of the world that unfolded in front of him on his first encounter with America. When Columbus arrived in the New World, he experienced an encounter with Otherness, with a hitherto completely unknown culture, that went beyond anything previously recorded in human history. As Stephen Greenblatt notes, all previously recorded encounters between Europeans and alien cultures were informed by at least a sprinkling of prior knowledge and contact. In contrast, Columbus's encounter with the peoples of the New World was thoroughly new and entirely unanticipated, so much so that he and the Europeans who followed him had great difficulty attaining a clear cognitive grasp of the "incommensurability, the astonishing singularity" of what they were experiencing (p. 54).

Faced with this inability to process the "radical otherness of the American lands and peoples," the early European explorers of the Americas reacted the only way they knew how: They "used their conventional intellectual and organizational structures, fashioned over centuries of mediated contact with other cultures" to interpret the new in ways that made it seem more familiar (Greenblatt, p. 54). Even when they seem accurate, Columbus's accounts (which have themselves been the object of much textual controversy) are remarkably oblivious to the fact that he was undergoing an unprecedented encounter with strangeness. Moreover, Columbus's accounts often go beyond the bounds of credibility (as when he reported seeing mermaids off the coast of Haiti), whether for rhetorical effect or simply because Columbus, out of sheer unfamiliarity with the region, could not adequately process and interpret what he saw.

Most famously, Columbus initially mistook the Caribbean islands he encountered for the Asian East Indies. His level of incomprehension of what he experienced in the Americas went well beyond that fundamental misunderstanding, however. Indeed, as Greenblatt has demonstrated, Columbus seems to have interpreted everything he experienced in the New World through the optic of Old World discourses. He was particularly good at projecting onto Native Americans the thoughts and responses he expected of them, even though they had no way to communicate such ideas to him. In short, Columbus displayed the kind of inability to appreciate the material reality and genuine difference of other peoples and other cultures of a kind that would go on to inform the entire European colonial enterprise and that continues to haunt Western interactions with the rest of the world to this day.

Granted, Columbus and other early European explorers of the Americas typically augmented their accounts with expressions of wonder at the marvelous things they saw; however, Greenblatt convincingly demonstrates that, far from suggesting an appreciation of the authentic newness of the experiences of these explorers, these expressions were part of a rhetorical strategy comfortably situated within preexisting medieval European discourses. The lack of any real appreciation on the part of Columbus and those who followed him of the newness of what they were encountering is almost staggering considering that they were undergoing an experience of real-world cognitive estrangement of a kind unprecedented in Western history. Then again, Columbus had no experience with the genuinely new, something medieval European society was uniquely ill equipped to comprehend.

Conversely, however medieval Columbus's mind might have been (and however genuine he might have been in his protestations that his main motivation for exploration and colonization was the spread of Catholicism), the voyages of Columbus certainly mark an important historical landmark in the downfall of medieval Catholicism and the rise of capitalist modernity. After all, the exploitation of the material wealth of the American colonies would ultimately supply much of the capital that was necessary for the building of Western capitalism. In *The Conquest of America*, Tzetan Todorov also sees the colonization of the Americas as part of a large historical process that went into the building of the mindset of modern capitalism. Columbus, Todorov demonstrates, managed to get support from the Spanish crown for his initial voyage by arguing that he might be able to obtain great riches that could subsequently be used to finance an expedition to wrest Jerusalem from its current Islamic rulers (p. 11). Subsequently, the urge to win new souls over to Christianity was a powerful driving force for the Spanish colonization of the Americas. In the long run, however, the urge to obtain wealth became an end in itself, so that by the middle of the sixteenth century, the atrocities that continued to be committed against Native Americans were driven more by a lust for gold than by Christian evangelism. For Todorov, therefore, the conquest of America not only provided financial support for the bourgeois cultural revolution back in Europe but also gave that revolution an ideological boost by helping to bring out in the Spanish conquistadors an unprecedented "subordination of all other values" to a "passion for gold," thus heralding the "modern mentality" (pp. 142–143). Meanwhile, this modern mentality involves not only a passion for gold but also a tendency toward massacre in the pursuit of gold. As Todorov puts it, "The 'barbarity' of the Spaniards has nothing atavistic or bestial about it; it is quite human and heralds the advent of modern times" (p. 145).

There is a question of cause and effect here, and the bourgeois cultural revolution in Europe was clearly underway well before Columbus undertook his first voyage to the Americas. Indeed, Todorov ultimately concludes that the "modern" tendencies he describes in the Spanish treatment of America were already firmly ingrained in sixteenth-century Spanish society; the American adventure did not produce this new attitude so much as offer ideal circumstances (the availability of riches to be gained and of a vulnerable native population to be exploited in the interest of that gain) for it to flourish. What might be most important, however, is that beneath this apparent sea change in values lies a fundamental continuity: a hostility toward and lack of respect for the Other. If Columbus began his voyage as a Quixotic quest to garner resources that would help to break the power of an alien Islam in the Middle East, his successors continued the rape of America by ravaging an alien Native American population, so that this initially medieval Catholic project became the forerunner of the entire bourgeois project of colonialism.

If Columbus was a pioneering voyager, he was also a literary pioneer of sorts, his journals serving (at least in retrospect) as the forerunner of an important new genre of European literature. Given the excitement generated in Europe over the discovery and colonization of the Americas from the fifteenth to the seventeenth century, it should come as no surprise that one of the most interesting and vibrant literary phenomena of this period involved the new genre of travelogues detailing trips to the Americas. Similarly, given that the exploration of the Americas involved an encounter with the new for which the European mind was exceedingly ill prepared, it is not surprising that these tales of travel were often filled with accounts of remarkable sightings, filled with expressions of awe and wonder.

Most of these travelogues presented themselves as true accounts, although they spilled over into the realm of fiction as well. For example, it is no coincidence that a new, modern form of utopian fiction arose soon after Columbus's discovery of the Americas—or that the utopian realms envisioned by writers such as Sir Thomas More and Francis Bacon are actually set in the Americas. More founded the modern utopian genre with *Utopia* (1516), the work that gave the genre its name. Whereas More's text is rhetorically complex and contains a great deal of satire and other modes that go beyond the simple description of an imaginary ideal world, it is still significant that the utopia he described is set on an island off of South America. Bacon's *New Atlantis* (1627), meanwhile, stands not only as an important marker in the rise of science as a discourse of authority in Western thought but also places its utopian realm on an island in the Americas, on which the narrator and his companions accidentally land after being blown off course in a storm.

The echoes of Columbus's accidental discovery of the Americas are clear in this motif, which also recalls what is probably the most famous literary text to have been inspired by accounts of travel to the New World of the Americas, Shakespeare's then-recent *The Tempest* (1611). As Charles Frey notes, critics have been relating elements of Shakespeare's play to the exploration and colonization of the Americas at least since the eighteenth century, when it was demonstrated that the reference to "Setebos" in the play is apparently a reference to a god worshipped by the native inhabitants of South America, as reported in Richard Eden's account of the voyage of Magellan past the southern tip of the continent. Perhaps more importantly, Edmond Malone argued as early as 1808 that Shakespeare derived the title and numerous incidents in his play from accounts of a 1609 storm that caused the shipwreck in the Bermudas of the *Sea Venture*, a British ship headed for the Jamestown colony.

In fact, there were numerous accounts of this shipwreck and of the subsequent experiences of the company in the Bermudas and of their later safe passage to Virginia. These accounts include at least three that Shakespeare seems to have read before writing *The Tempest*: a letter sent in July, 1610, to a noblewoman in England by William Strachey, one of the passengers on the wrecked ship; an account written by another passenger, William Jourdain, entitled *A Discovery of the Bermudas* and published in October, 1610; and a pamphlet commissioned by the Council of Virginia entitled *A True Declaration of the Estate of the Colonie in Virginia*, published in November, 1610. Critics have found numerous echoes of these accounts in *The Tempest*. For my purposes here, it is important to note how Shakespeare's disturbing depiction of the lowly Caliban echoes contemporary accounts of Native Americans while also noting the importance of magic (through the offices of the sorcerer Prospero) to Shakespeare's play. Thus, *The Tempest* contains elements of magic and of contempt toward the Other that would go on to form central elements of much of the culture of the United States. Indeed, Ronald Takaki has seen Shakespeare's play as expressing much the same racialist ideology as that which would inform the Puritan settlements in North America (pp. 24–50).

Accounts of travels in America would also provide the starting point for other narrative forms. For example, Jonathan Swift's *Gulliver's Travels* (1726) gains much of its energy from satirizing these accounts, while the whole emergent genre of the novel took important inspiration from accounts of travels in the Americas, which added an element of adventure that saved the realist novel from mere tedium. Thus, Daniel Defoe's *Robinson Crusoe* (1719), often seen as the first modern novel, details the adventures of its title character, centering on a shipwreck in the Caribbean that leaves him stranded on a deserted island. Works that could easily be classified as novels had already taken the New World of the Americas as a setting, as in Aphra Behn's *Oroonoko* (1688), the key action of which also takes place in the Caribbean (the sugar plantations of which were at that very time fueling the rise of capitalism in Europe).

Behn's title character is an African king (dragged to the New World in slavery) whose nobility is greatly emphasized, possibly to the point of stereotype. In any case, his fate provides a literary reminder that, for the millions of Africans brought to the Americas in chains, then forced to work on plantations as slaves, coming to America was far from a glorious adventure. The same goes for the Native Americans who were displaced or exterminated in the European conquest of the New World. Fueled by the religious justification that Native Americans were irredeemable minions of Satan, the New England Puritans began the grisly genocidal process that eventually led to the conquest of territory all the way to the Pacific Ocean. This conquest was itself figured as a mighty adventure (quite often as one undertaken on behalf of God, almost in the mode of the medieval Crusaders, with infidel Muslims replaced by heathen Indians), however grim and murderous it might have been in reality.

By the time Turner was articulating his thesis about the importance of this expansionism to the American national consciousness, however, the frontier had essentially been conquered, implying that a major source of the energy and vitality that had driven American history had been removed. It might be no coincidence, then, that consumer capitalism came onto the scene with an explosive period of growth that began roughly as the process of taming the West was coming to a close. In *Land of Desire*, William Leach presents an excellent account of the growth of consumer capitalism in the early twentieth century, noting some of the vigor and energy that were poured into the building of brands, labels, and distribution chains—energies that formerly had gone into taming the frontier. Leach also notes how these energies were reflected in the American culture of the day, in a widespread fascination with the exotic (and with the adventurous possibilities of capitalism itself), as exemplified in the work of L. Frank Baum. Richard Slotkin, in *Gunfighter Nation*, identifies the early-twentieth-century work of Edgar Rice Burroughs as also indicative of a diversion into culture of those energies that had formerly gone into taming the frontier.

The author of two series of colorful adventure novels featuring the exploits of John Carter on Mars and of Tarzan in darkest Africa, Burroughs was one of the most commercially successful authors of his time, suggesting that his work answered a widespread desire for such adventure among the American populace. In particular, both of Burroughs's series seemed perfectly designed to allow readers to imagine the reopening of the now-closed American frontier, but without the real dangers and hardships that life on the actual frontier had posed.

Burroughs's work is informed by a nostalgic return to the days before capitalist routinization had stripped the world of adventure and magic. For example, Tarzan is presented as noble primarily because of his superior English aristocratic bloodlines. The rightful Lord Greystoke, he is inherently superior not only to the savage cannibals he constantly encounters in Africa but also to the vulgar capitalists he encounters in America. Like the later hero, Superman, he is devoted to truth and justice, but he remains safely aloof from and above the American Way, at least as long as that way is equated with the workaday world of the scramble for money. Tarzan thus represents idealized standards of conduct (and racial superiority) that look back to precapitalist times.

The Tarzan books also suggest a nostalgia for empire. For one thing, the idea of imperial expansion offered an obvious possibility for renewal of the frontier and thus a presumed resuscitation of the American spirit. For another, it was the empire that made Great Britain great, and if America looked to Britain for models of glory, then the notion of empire was necessarily central to those models. Of course, the Africa patrolled by Tarzan was already thoroughly colonized by European powers, leaving no room for American expansion there. By the time of Burroughs's first Tarzan novel, *Tarzan of the Apes* (1914), there were few places on the entire earth still available for colonization. For that, Burroughs had to look beyond earth, which he did in the Mars stories, which are even more overtly imperialistic than the Tarzan stories. Here, Burroughs "projected the American imperial (and protective) zeal into outer space, making of Mars what Theodore Roosevelt had made of the western hemisphere, a ward of the United States" (Seelye, p. xiii). As Slotkin puts it, Burroughs, in books such as *A Princess of Mars* (first published in serial form in 1911), essentially adapted the format and ideology of the Western to a Martian context, complete with the attendant glorification of violence and (white) racial purity (*Gunfighter*, pp. 195–211).

Burroughs's fiction indicates a widespread American desire for escape into a less rationalized world in the early twentieth century, and the popularity of the film adaptations of his Tarzan books in the 1930s suggests (not surprisingly) that this desire was still just as strong in the Depression years. Meanwhile, this escapist desire is even more central to the Oz books of Baum, which (thanks largely to the central role played by the 1939 film *The Wizard of Oz*) have garnered an even more important place in modern American cultural history. In fact, "Over the Rainbow," the crucial song from that film, might in fact be taken as the theme song of this modern American longing for something beyond the mundane world of modern capitalism.

Clearly escapist works such as *The Wizard of Oz* (or even the glitzy, spectacle-filled musicals of the 1930s) have often been dismissed as politically retrograde because they provide a respite from contemporary reality that might tend to make that reality more bearable—and to make consumers of such cultural forms less likely to take action to change the status quo. Richard Dyer has offered a spirited (if not entirely convincing) argument, however, that musicals in particular have a strong utopian dimension, arguing that such feel-good works of pure entertainment present viewers with "what utopia would feel like rather than how it would be organized" (p. 20). Meanwhile, even so estimable a figure as Ernst Bloch (the leading Marxist utopian thinker of the twentieth century) was a devoted reader of the German Western and adventure writer Karl May; further, Bloch notes the genuine (politically powerful) utopian potential to be found in the adventure story, which he sees as a modern version of the fairy tale. Bloch grants that such stories, like fairy tales, have an escapist quality; they are "castles in the air par excellence" (p. 369). For Bloch, however, such stories nevertheless suggest the possibility of a better golden world of "happiness which penetrates from the night to the light" (p. 369).

Baum's work is all about happiness, although it is a happiness that is always already commodified. Noting that Baum had a prominent career as a pioneer in the design of store window displays before he became a popular writer, Leach identifies Baum's *The Wonderful Wizard of Oz* (1900) and its sequels (Baum wrote thirteen Oz sequels, as well as nine other fantasy novels, whereas other authors wrote still more Oz sequels) as key markers of the rise of consumerism at the beginning of the twentieth century. Characterizing Baum's book as an all-American boosterist fairy tale that lacks the darkness of its European predecessors, Leach notes the way in which the positive tone of the book assured its early readers that the dramatic changes occurring around them should be welcomed, rather than feared. Moreover, although some have seen the book as a critique of capitalism, Leach sees no trace of such critique in a book that "far from challenging the new industrial society, endorsed its values and direction" (*Land*, p. 251).[3] The Wizard himself is a sham and a humbug whose power arises not from genuine magic but from the kind of chicanery that is the stuff of advertising, promotion, and, of course, window dressing. The Wizard is ultimately a positive figure, however; he rules the Emerald City wisely and well, and he is able to help Dorothy and her entire entourage achieve everything they desire. The Emerald City itself is a bit of fakery: Everything in it appears to be the color of money, but only because the entire population has been tricked into wearing green glasses at all times. But no matter. The illusion is a benevolent one that helps the inhabitants to have happier lives. The message seems to be clear: The new prosperity of American consumer capitalism could be partly a matter of smoke and mirrors, but those who go along with the deception can have wonderful lives.

Baum's message was well received. His book was vastly popular, conveying (along with the other works it spawned) the feel-good message that all you have to do is believe in yourself and in the system and all will be well. Granted, in the first book Dorothy does seem to prefer the drab grayness of Kansas to the lure of the Emerald City, but later in the sequence she abandons this attitude and moves once and for all to the consumerist utopia of the green metropolis, taking Uncle Henry and Auntie Em along with her. Once there, they live in splendor, with all their dreams fulfilled. In 1939, of course, Baum's work became a central icon of American popular culture once and for all, with the release of a lavish Technicolor film version (directed by Victor Fleming with the aid of producer Mervyn LeRoy) that contrasted with the bleakness of the Depression in much the same way that the Emerald City contrasted with the drabness of Kansas (to which Judy Garland's Dorothy nevertheless willingly returns to rejoin her family and friends). "There's no place like home," the film reminds us, suggesting meanwhile (unlike Baum's books) that Oz might have been just a dream, not a real alternative world. The reassuring intentions of this film are clear, and they are effectively achieved, which might be why the film is still much viewed and beloved.

Writers such as Baum and Burroughs, and showmen such as Buffalo Bill Cody, capitalized on the thirst for adventure that drove early consumer capitalism by making adventure itself a slickly packaged, highly marketable (but safely contained) commodity. It is also the case, however, that numerous events in American history have been powerfully influenced by the ongoing quest to find a replacement for the grand adventure that had been supplied by the conquest of the frontier in the nineteenth century. Most immediately and directly, of course, the expansionism that had moved the effective boundaries of the United States across the North American continent was simply diverted into imperialist adventures overseas. It is no accident that America's brief flirtation with overt global imperialist expansion began in the 1890s, just as the domestic frontier had been declared closed. The Spanish-American War is probably the clearest marker of this phenomenon, whereas the desire to become a colonial power on a par with the great colonial empires of Britain and France became a major factor in American political life during the Progressive Era. Rudyard Kipling's notorious turn-of-the-century poem "The White Man's Burden" is, we should recall, about *American* imperialism, not British, intended to encourage his pal Teddy Roosevelt to get on the imperialist bandwagon.

The rhetoric of adventure was used extensively to promote the highly controversial U.S. involvement in World War I, variously labeled the "Great War" and the "War to End All Wars." Others, however, disturbed by this involvement and by the repressive turn in American domestic policies that accompanied it (including brutal suppression of dissent), saw the U.S. involvement in this war as an end to the American adventure and as a harbinger of a more restrictive future.[4] Indeed, visions of adventure and magic played a smaller role in American culture in the years immediately after World War I than in any previous period.

Adventure and magic made something of a comeback in American culture in the grim Depression decade of the 1930s, but largely as a counter to and escape from the reality of American history rather than as an accompaniment to it. Indeed, one might see this decade as a crucial turning point in the history of American adventure narratives, although it is probably better seen as the culmination of a turn that began with the closing of the frontier at the end of the nineteenth century. The consumerist boom of the first three decades of the twentieth century provided a sort of substitute form of adventure, so that works such as Baum's Oz novels could be taken as dramatizations of that new adventure. By the time of the 1939 film version of Baum's novel, however, there were no real adventures to be had, so the best one could hope for was to return safely home. Indeed, the Depression seemed to mark the collapse of consumerist expansionism as a whole, so that the most adventure-filled works of the decade had little correspondence with reality but instead retreated into escapist entertainment.

For example, science fiction (mostly in the form of stories in pulp magazines) was coming into its own in the 1930s and often featured large-scale galactic adventures in the form that came to be known as "space opera," but these adventures had little connection with contemporary reality. Meanwhile, other than monster movies such as James Whale's *Frankenstein* (1931), the American science fiction film genre of the 1930s was largely confined to low-budget serials, such as those featuring Flash Gordon and Buck Rogers as the protagonists. These serials were based on popular syndicated comic strips, and they definitely had a comic-strip quality to them. Produced in episodes of 15 to 20 minutes in length, each serial ran for 12 to 15 episodes that were shown weekly in theaters in an attempt to attract young audiences. By today's standards (or, for that matter, the much lower standards of the 1930s), the special effects of these serials were extremely crude. To a generation of young Americans, however, they offered thrilling images of other planets and other times that presented an exciting alternative to a dreary Depression-era world that was drifting toward global war.

In particular, these serials envisioned the future as a time of adventure and excitement, far different from the dreary decade in which they were produced. Other entertainments of the 1930s recapitulated the adventures of the past, as if new adventures were no longer imaginable. Thus, the Western, although born as a film genre in Edwin S. Porter's *The Great Train Robbery* (1903) and thus essentially as old as narrative film itself, really came into being in its modern form in the 1930s. Among other things, technological advances took the Western out of the studio and into the panoramic landscape of the West itself, enabling the production of films that captured some of the sense of adventure that had informed the original taming of the West. The Westerns of the decade tended strongly toward narratives of this taming, with upright heroes battling savage Indians and other obstacles on their way toward making the West safe for upstanding (white) Americans.

John Ford's *Stagecoach* (1939), shot on location in Utah's Monument Valley (scene of numerous subsequent Westerns as well), can be taken as the classic case of the 1930s Western in its fully developed form. The film that made John Wayne a major star, *Stagecoach* also established many of the conventions and motifs that would become staples of the Western genre. The plot is based on the journey, in many ways the archetypal American form. In particular, it follows a single stagecoach and its passengers as they travel cross-country through an Old West landscape that is itself a main attraction of the film. Meanwhile, the trip is made especially treacherous by the recent activities of Geronimo and his renegade Apaches in the area. The Apaches, depicted as savage and senseless killers, eventually do attack, although the cavalry arrives at the last moment, saving the day and leading the stagecoach safely (except for one dead passenger) to its destination in the town of Lordsville.

This simple plot is supplemented by considerable character development, and the real strength of the film is its gradual introduction of the passengers and the relationships among them. The passengers constitute a virtual cross section of the margins of frontier society. Two of them, the drunken physician Doc Boone (Thomas Mitchell) and Dallas, a lady of questionable virtue, are on the stage because they are being run out of their former town as undesirables by the sanctimonious biddies who make up the local Law and Order League. One passenger, Mr. Gatewood (Berton Churchill), is a corrupt bank manager, who is absconding with his bank's funds, seeking also to escape an upcoming examination of the bank's books by government investigators. Also aboard is the rather sinister Hatfield (John Carradine), a gambler and former Confederate soldier, who will be killed by the Apaches. The most respectable passengers are Mr. Peacock (Donald Meek), a traveling liquor salesman everyone mistakes for a Reverend because of his appearance, and Mrs. Mallory (Louis Platt), who has just come West to join her husband, a cavalry officer.

Just after leaving town, the passengers are joined by the film's protagonist, the Ringo Kid (Wayne), whose horse has gone lame and who wants to get to Lordsville to take revenge on the evil Luke Plummer (Tom Tyler) and his two brothers for killing the Kid's father and brother. Indeed, the Kid has escaped from prison to take this revenge, a fact that causes Marshall Curly Wilcox (George Bancroft), who is riding shotgun on the stage, to declare him under arrest, even though Wilcox knows that the Kid is a good man. Along the way, it is revealed that Mrs. Mallory is pregnant; in fact, she gives birth at one of their stops. It is also revealed that Hatfield has been fascinated by Mrs. Mallory ever since serving in her husband's regiment in the Civil War.

However, the principal relationship that evolves on the trip is that between Dallas and the Ringo Kid. Having already been insulted by the Law and Order League, Dallas finds that her reputation follows her and that she is repeatedly slighted and abused on the trip. Only the gallant Kid stands up for her, insisting that she receive the treatment due a lady. Eventually, these two outcasts from polite society fall in love and begin to envision a possible life together. Unfortunately, they still face important obstacles. After they reach Lordsville, the Kid must first face the deadly Plummer brothers, which he does successfully, gunning them down in a battle that is the dramatic climax of the film. In the town he also realizes that Dallas has been a prostitute, but nevertheless, to her surprise, he reiterates his marriage proposal. She accepts and agrees to wait for him on his ranch in Mexico while he serves the remainder of his prison sentence. Fortunately, this wait becomes unnecessary when Wilcox contrives to allow the two of them to escape across the border together (despite their being nowhere near Mexico at the time).

The film thus ends on a note of redemption as Dallas and the Kid, despite their checkered pasts, are allowed another chance at happiness. In some ways, then, *Stagecoach*, in its treatment of the passengers as a microcosm, is a classically American story about the building of community. Conversely, the film's utopian ending somewhat obscures the fact that the redemption achieved by the film's two central characters can only be achieved by fleeing the United States for the more hospitable climes of Mexico, suggesting that true freedom is difficult to achieve amid the growing routinization of life in the United States. This interpretation would make *Stagecoach* the forerunner of later "waning of the West" films, such as *The Professionals* (1966), *The Wild Bunch* (1969), and *Butch Cassidy and the Sundance Kid* (1969), in which the protagonists must move south of the border in search of frontier adventure. The most overt commentary on American routinization in *Stagecoach* occurs in Gatewood's complaints about growing government regulation of and interference in business. Given Gatewood's motivation for this complaint, his comments are obviously undercut, and the implication of this scene is clearly that a certain amount of government regulation of business is a good thing indeed. In 1939, this is a suggestion that can be taken as an endorsement of Roosevelt's New Deal policies, while it also foreshadows the critique of capitalism in later films depicting the waning of the West, such as *McCabe and Mrs. Miller* (1971) and *Heaven's Gate* (1980).

It might thus be significant that some of the most memorable entertainments of the 1930s were the elaborate musicals choreographed (and sometimes directed) by Busby Berkeley—*Gold Diggers of 1933* (1933) is probably the classic example. These musicals replace genuine adventure with sheer spectacle, although even that, as Richard Dyer has strenuously argued, has a certain utopian potential. It is telling, however, that the plots of such films generally involve a quest for rather mundane (often economic or at least acquisitive) goals—getting the girl (or boy), getting a part in the musical that provides the centerpiece of the film, getting the money to stage the musical in the first place—rather than grand battles against evil or ambitious voyages of discovery. Indeed, even the musical that topped off the decade, becoming one of the touchstones of American popular culture, the 1939 adaptation of *The Wizard of Oz*, converted Baum's consumerist fantasy-adventure into a heart-warming assurance that the best things in life are to be found not over the rainbow but right where you are (if you are in America), no adventures necessary.

A similar message can be found in the phenomenon of the Disney animated feature, which arose in the 1930s not only from the individual genius (and entrepreneurship) of the estimable Walt Disney but also as a response to specific historical circumstances. The rise of Disney, which began with *Snow White and the Seven Dwarfs* in 1937 and continued with *Pinocchio* in 1940, was almost exactly contemporary to the film version of *The Wizard of Oz* and responded to much the same need for reassuring escapist fantasy in a world in which the Depression continued to drag on, while American involvement in a world war looked more and more inevitable. The colorful, beautifully animated worlds of the Disney films represent an infantilization of American fantasy that indicates the growing difficulty of taking seriously the possibility that our own world could be similarly beautiful and morally simple, with good ultimately and inevitably triumphing over evil. In this light, "When You Wish upon a Star," the classic theme song of *Pinocchio* (sung, we should remember, by an animated insect hobo), seems more a cry of desperation than a statement of confidence in the power of wishes. The emphasis on wishing in this and so many other Disney songs of the period clearly reflects the longing for something better that informed the American consciousness during the dark years of the Depression, which still was exerting its effect on the economy in 1940 and would not truly be lifted until the production boom that followed the U.S. entry into World War II.

The years of World War II saw a brief reflowering of the American national rhetoric of adventure as wartime propaganda (predictably) focused on depiction of the American war effort as a noble mission to combat evil. Frank Capra's near-legendary *Why We Fight* propaganda films are probably the best known example of this turn in American culture during the war, but pro-war sentiments were prominent in other areas as well. Hollywood filmmakers, at the urging of the U.S. government, made numerous pro-war and anti-Nazi films, some of which—such as *Mission to Moscow*, *Song of Russia*, and *The North Star*—were specifically designed to generate public support and sympathy for the Soviet Union, America's most important ally against the Nazis. All of the films mentioned were released in 1943, when the Soviets were engaged in a life-or-death struggle with the invading Germans, a struggle that ultimately crippled the German army, paving the way for the eventual Allied victory. These films typically depicted the Soviets as a heroic people engaged in an epic battle against savage foes and are clearly calculated to draw on positive associations in the American consciousness with epic adventure, casting the Soviets in the role usually reserved for the United States.

The United States, of course, continued to occupy that role as well. Positive depictions of the Soviet war effort were an exceptional case amid a barrage of representations in film and other media (comic books were an especially important venue for pro-war propaganda) that made it seem as if the United States was essentially fighting alone against hordes of evil and savage foes. Thus, Tom Engelhardt notes that the discourse of "victory culture," which had earlier been used to promote the genocidal assault on Native Americans, was revived and repeated during World War II, especially in support of the American war in the Pacific, thus extending the narrative of violent triumph (usually over a savage racial Other) that had sustained the American national identity for a century and a half. Indeed, racialized depictions of the Japanese as vicious, simian subhumans during World War II are some of the most strik-ingly and overtly racist images to have been produced by mainstream Ameri-can culture in the twentieth century.

According to Engelhardt, however, this narrative of triumph ceased to func-tion with any effectiveness in the postwar years. In fact, Engelhardt argues that narrative in general becomes difficult to maintain in postwar American cul-ture, a characteristic that clearly anticipates the rise of postmodernism, with its famously fragmented and inconclusive narratives, in this period. This frag-mentation of narrative also suggests hard times for epic adventure, which thrives on simple, clear-cut, continuous plots, of which the quest narrative is the leading instance.

America in the new postwar world had to present itself as a global de-fender of peace and freedom, which seriously compromised the value of the national narrative of violent victory over anyone who was different. In addi-tion, for Engelhardt, three specific Asian events contributed to this collapse of the American national narrative. First, the atomic bombing of Hiroshima and Nagasaki made the notion of racial extermination all too real: "Here was a victory in no sense previously imagined, for it was victory as atrocity" (p. 56). Indeed, Engelhardt argues that, in the American imagination, the unimagin-able violence of the final victory over Japan threatened to conflate American actions in the war with the atrocities committed by the German Nazis, and thus to undermine the American myth of noble victory in war (p. 57). More-over, this particular atrocity also threatened to come home to roost, as the subsequent Cold War convinced a generation of Americans that they might very soon be on the other end of the atomic stick. The possibility that Amer-icans might be defeated in the coming nuclear conflict grew all the more real after the next two Asian events cited by Engelhardt, which saw the Chinese communists sweep to victory in their own country in 1949 and then help to fight the United States to a standstill in Korea a few years later.

In short, those nonwhite hordes (usually in the form of American Indi-ans) who had for so long been routed routinely by small bands of virtuous white settlers on American movie screens, were apparently not so easily dis-patched after all, a lesson that the Vietnam experience would soon drive home all the more. Meanwhile, the 1950s also saw an era of explosive growth in con-sumer capitalism in some ways even more spectacular than the original rise of consumerism in the first three decades of the twentieth century. The con-sumerism of the 1950s, no longer supported by an effective national victory culture, tended to create at least as much anxiety as pleasure. Affluent Amer-icans had achieved everything they ever dreamed of, only to find the dream empty, leading to a feeling of "entrapment in abundance" (Engelhardt, p. 88).

As I have discussed in more detail in *Monsters, Mushroom Clouds, and the Cold War*, even "successful" Americans of the 1950s were caught in a crushing double bind of alienation and routinization. On the one hand, they were terrified of being different, of not living up to the images of normality constantly beamed into the new television sets in their suburban living rooms. On the other hand, they were terrified of losing their individuality altogether, thus joining the series of anonymous and interchangeable cogs that made up the gears of the corporate machine. Meanwhile, there were lurking and potentially ominous reminders that not all Americans were so affluent, not to mention most of the population of the rest of the world. White, middle-class Americans thus came increasingly, in the long 1950s, to think of their world as an island of prosperity and tranquility surrounded by a threatening sea of poverty and turmoil, similar to those bands of pioneers who had long circled their wagons to fight off savage Indian attacks on American movie screens.

Of course, despite such complications, propaganda remained a major mode of American culture after the Second World War as well, as the United States moved directly from actual combat against fascism to ideological combat against communism. Meanwhile, with the anticommunist propaganda machine running around the clock and around the globe, the U.S. population itself was inundated with an unprecedented barrage of both political propaganda and commercial propaganda—in the form of a vast increase in advertising output that accompanied the dramatic expansion of American consumer culture in the 1950s, an expansion that was itself greatly facilitated by the rise of television as the greatest medium yet for the conveyance of political and commercial messages.

The combination of fears about the Cold War and a growing pressure to conform to the middle-class norm made the 1950s a difficult decade for adventure in U.S. culture. Indeed, the explosive growth of consumer capitalism in the 1950s brought with it a crushing sense of alienation and entrapment on the home front, even as the specter of nuclear destruction haunted the American mind, rendering warfare, that time-honored locus of American adventure, decidedly unromantic. The romance of commodities can be a powerful force, as Marx had already understood a century earlier, but the dancing and singing soap bubbles of television commercials clearly lacked epic scope and any sense of glorious mission. To a large extent, however, what passed for adventure in the 1950s shifted from content to style. Technology limited the ability of television to portray grand adventure in those early years, but the medium was new enough to be an adventure in itself. The broadcasting of moving pictures through the air seemed like a kind of magic—just as moving pictures themselves had seemed magical to their first audiences half a century earlier. Meanwhile, in an attempt to counteract the growing popularity of television, the film industry turned to more spectacular productions, employing brilliant color, wider screens, and stories and casts of epic scope, in an attempt to deliver to filmgoers something they could not get from television. Westerns grew much grander, with considerable emphasis on panoramic views of the Western landscape. Also part of this same phenomenon were the self-consciously big (especially compared with the small, rounded black-and-white screen of the typical 1950s television) biblical epics of the decade, the most successful of which were Cecil B. DeMille's *The Ten Commandments* (1956) and William Wyler's *Ben-Hur* (1959), both starring Charlton Heston. These big-budget spectacles no doubt gained some traction from the religiosity of the 1950s, but what they really helped to do was turn religion into big-time entertainment, a strategy that the most successful purveyors of religion had understood for decades, although not quite at this level of budget and audience. Of course, one reason why these films were so entertaining was that they told familiar and comforting stories, but they also presented audiences with thrilling spectacles (sometimes involving supernatural events) that took them out of the gray-flanneled, conformist world of the 1950s and into a world of magic. These spectacles were thrilling for their sheer scope, completely apart from any religious message they might have conveyed.

The biblical epic remained a popular genre into the 1960s, with such films as Nicholas Ray's *King of Kings* (1961), the first major sound film actually to show the face of Jesus Christ (played by Jeffrey Hunter) on the screen, and George Stevens's ultra-expensive *The Greatest Story Ever Told* (1965), this time with Max von Sydow as a Christ unable to attract sufficient audiences to make back the film's $20-million-plus budget, thus effectively ending the era of the big-budget biblical epic, which was in any case beginning to seem more and more irrelevant in the increasingly politicized 1960s. Probably the most adventurous pop cultural genre of the 1960s was the spy drama, epitomized by the James Bond films (beginning with *Dr. No* in 1962 and still running as a film franchise as of this writing), which featured stirring music, science fictional gadgetry, over-the-top villains, and a healthy dose of titillating sexuality. All this was in support of the stirring exploits of a larger-than-life hero, no doubt made more exotic by the fact that he was British (and, at least in the Connery era, had a colorful Scottish accent) rather than American.

Similarly, the New York–born Patrick McGoohan (who grew up in Ireland and England) sported an Irish accent as the ultra-cool John Drake in the British ITV series *Danger Man* (broadcast after the first season as *Secret Agent* in the United States). This series ran off and on for three full seasons from 1960 to 1966, plus a two-episode mini-season in 1968. Meanwhile, Roger

Moore played Simon Templar in the British ITC television series *The Saint* (1962–1969) with enough British suavity to gain him a later turn as Bond. Indeed, partly because of the special success enjoyed by the Bond franchise, American audiences of the 1960s came to associate espionage heroism with suave Britishness. American television did enter the fray with such programs as *The Man from U.N.C.L.E.* (1964–1968) and *Mission: Impossible* (1966–1973). These programs (especially the latter) were largely celebrations of properly used technology and efficient planning that lacked the romance of the Bond films. The British might have produced more romantic spy dramas than the Americans, but that was partly because they seemed to take the genre less seriously than did their American counterparts. The early Bond films already contained numerous self-consciously campy elements, while the most successful of all British television spy dramas, ITV's *The Avengers* (1961–1969), overdid the conventions of the genre, including Patrick Macnee's character, John Steed, who became more and more dandified over time, eventually becoming a virtual parody of the suave characters played by Connery, McGoohan, and Moore. Meanwhile, one of the most interesting (although short-lived) of all 1960s spy dramas was *The Prisoner*, which ran on ITV for a single seventeen-episode season in 1967 and 1968. Strange, disturbing, surreal, and claustrophobic, *The Prisoner* was a sort of rejoinder to the films and TV series that presented the spy game as great adventure, depicting it instead as tedious, dangerous, and potentially soul destroying.

The real adventure in America in the 1960s, of course, involved the growth of broad-based (though youth-centered) oppositional politics, including the antiwar, civil rights, and women's movements. These movements were often conceived as adventures, bringing with them a "new world" rhetoric that often resembled early European descriptions of America during the colonial era, but now with a specific attack on the mind-numbing conformity brought about by capitalist routinization. Thus, these insurgent movements showed some of the same fascination with adventure that had long informed the mainstream ideology of the United States. For example, much of the rhetoric of the "Port Huron Statement," issued by the Students for a Democratic Society in 1962 and something of a manifesto for the radical oppositional student political movements of the 1960s, could have been taken straight from the Declaration of Independence in its expressed fascination with adventure. This document certainly deviates from the monuments of American history in important ways, perhaps most centrally in its refusal to appeal to God (the word "God" does not appear at all in the text) for its authority. The authors of this statement (it was drafted by Tom Hayden) do not repudiate the historic sense of American adventurism so much as excoriate the powers that be for having retreated from the American adventure in the interests of conservatism, conformity, and bureaucratic efficiency. In this atmosphere, college students are taught not to take risks or agitate for change but to accept whatever is offered to them under the status quo:

> Almost no students value activity as a citizen. Passive in public, they are hardly more idealistic in arranging their private lives: Gallup concludes they will settle for "low success, and won't risk high failure." There is not much willingness to take risks (not even in business), no setting of dangerous goals, no real conception of personal identity except one manufactured in the image of others, no real urge for personal fulfillment except to be almost as successful as the very successful people. Attention is being paid to social status (the quality of shirt collars, meeting people, getting wives or husbands, making solid contacts for later on); much too, is paid to academic status (grades, honors, the med school rat-race). But neglected generally is real intellectual status, the personal cultivation of the mind.

Furthermore, the statement goes on to suggest that America's meekly conformist campuses are merely microcosms of the society at large:

> That student life is more intellectual, and perhaps more comfortable, does not obscure the fact that the fundamental qualities of life on the campus reflect the habits of society at large. The fraternity president is seen at the junior manager levels; the sorority queen has gone to Grosse Pointe: the serious poet burns for a place, any place, or work; the once-serious and never serious poets work at the advertising agencies. The desperation of people threatened by forces about which they know little and of which they can say less; the cheerful emptiness of people "giving up" all hope of changing things; the faceless ones polled by Gallup who listed "international affairs" fourteenth on their list of "problems" but who also expected thermonuclear war in the next few years: in these and other forms, Americans are in withdrawal from public life, from any collective effort at directing their own affairs.

Some, the statement goes on, "regard this national doldrums as a sign of healthy approval of the established order—but is it approval by consent or manipulated acquiescence?"

American consumer culture underwent distinctive changes in the 1960s, at least partly in response to the sense of adventure that pervaded the student movements of the 1960s. These changes led to a decidedly hipper and groovier form of capitalism (or at least of capitalist marketing), although Thomas Frank has questioned the order of cause and effect here, suggesting that to an extent, the supposedly subversive counterculture was actually created—or at the very least urged on—by corporate strategies designed to open markets for new, hipper consumer products as capitalism itself evolved into a new phase. As a result, the counterculture of the 1960s might best be "understood as a stage in the development of the values of the American middle class, a colorful install-ment in the twentieth century drama of consumer subjectivity" (p. 29). This stage then led to "a new species of hip consumerism, a cultural perpetual mo-tion machine in which disgust with the falseness, shoddiness, and everyday op-pressions of consumer society could be enlisted to drive the ever-accelerating wheels of consumption" (p. 31).

Frank is interested primarily in advertising and marketing, although he notes the arguments of Mark Crispin Miller that American television has of-ten broadcast seemingly countercultural messages in the interest of supporting the existing capitalist power structure. Miller notes that "TV would seem to be an essentially iconoclastic medium, and yet it is this inherent subversive-ness toward any visible authority that has enabled TV to establish its own total rule—for it is *all* individuality that TV annihilates, either by not conveying it or by making it look ridiculous" (p. 324). Perhaps it is thus not surpris-ing that the countercultural adventure of the 1960s did not really translate into adventurous television programming; however, there was at least one ma-jor effort in the decade to build on adventure traditions such as the frontier Western in ways that directly reflected the political concerns of the decade. That effort was the original *Star Trek* series, which ran on NBC from 1966 to 1969. As signaled by the opening declaration that the Starship *Enterprise* and her crew intend "to boldly go where no man has gone before," this was to be adventure in the grand mode, clearly looking back to the early voyages of discovery of Columbus and others. *Star Trek* is also very much a frontier narrative that seeks to recapture some of the sense of adventure involved in the taming of the West—but in a more politically correct way that would preclude campaigns of conquest and colonization. Instead, the explorers sent out by the Federation of Planets are on voyages of discovery designed to learn about the galaxy in which we live and potentially to invite other advanced civilizations that they might encounter to join as equal partners in the Fed-eration. Meanwhile, the "Prime Directive" given by the Federation of Planets to the explorers featured in *Star Trek* dictates that they are forbidden to in-terfere in any way in the development of cultures that are less advanced than their own.[5]

The original *Star Trek* was not a highly successful series when it was first broadcast, perhaps suggesting that it was a bit ahead of its time and that mass audiences were not yet ready for its utopian messages. Until late in the decade, the 1970s were even less adventurous in American culture as a whole. This decade, dominated in the national consciousness by attempts to come to grips with the disastrous American experience in Vietnam and the Watergate revelations that followed soon afterward, was actually one of the richest in American film history. The cinematic high points of the decade, however, tend to be such things as Roman Polanski's resurrection of the film noir in *Chinatown* (1974) and Robert Altman's exploration of the dark and violent impulses of America and American culture in *Nashville* (1975). Francis Ford Coppola's first two *Godfather* films have a kind of epic grandeur, although their location of potential utopian energies in the close-knit collectivities of organized crime families does little to allay the emphasis on corruption and violence that informed other films of the decade. In any case, the movement from *The Godfather* (1972) to *The Godfather: Part II* (1974) suggests that even organized crime families (with the emphasis on family) were giving way to capitalist rationalization and corporate-style management.[6]

Fantasy-adventure films were almost nonexistent in the early 1970s, although Disney did continue to foray into worlds of magic with such films as *Bedknobs and Broomsticks* (1971). Walt Disney had died in 1966, and most of the films of the 1970s (marked by an increasing tendency to mix live-action with animation) were minor efforts compared with the classic Disney films of earlier decades. Not surprisingly, given the relatively dark mode of most of the 1970s, the decade did prove to be a rich one for horror films, many of them low-budget efforts that nevertheless clearly captured the national mood better than funny animals or flying beds did.

In the wake of the success of films such as *Planet of the Apes* and Stanley Kubrick's *2001: A Space Odyssey* (both released in 1968), science fiction films also made something of a comeback in the early 1970s, with a cycle of films that strove for relevance and artistic seriousness, perhaps reflecting the influence of the New Wave that marked the science fiction stories and novels of the period. But the science fiction films of the early 1970s typically reflect the era's growing skepticism and increasing sense that the new and better world envisioned by the political movements of the 1960s did not seem that different from the old and darker world that had preceded it. In 1971 alone, several films projected a dystopian future, including Kubrick's *A Clockwork Orange* (1971), Wise's *The Andromeda Strain* (1971), and Boris Sagal's *The Omega Man* (1971). Other dark visions of the future followed, including Douglas Trumbull's *Silent Running* (1972), Richard Fleischer's *Soylent Green* (1973), Norman Jewison's *Rollerball* (1975), and Michael Anderson's *Logan's Run* (1976).

All of this, however, began to change in the late 1970s, in a movement back toward the comforts of traditional fantasy. The groundbreaking animation of Ralph Bakshi was important here, including an attempt to unite fantasy and science fiction in *Wizards* (1977) and an even more ambitious attempt to bring J.R.R. Tolkien's *Lord of the Rings* (or at least the first half of it, until money problems shortened the project) to the big screen. The killer application of late 1970s fantasy, however, was ostensibly a science fiction film, George Lucas's *Star Wars* (1977), which self-consciously looked back to the optimistic science fiction of the 1930s, while introducing several classic romance and fantasy elements as well.

Star Wars, of course, triggered a whole subgenre consisting of its own (five) prequels/sequels and numerous imitators, although none of the latter came close to the *Star Wars* franchise in mythic resonance or cultural impact. Of course, *Star Wars* was much about technology as magic, although the most important technology was not wielded by the characters in the film but by George Lucas and the film's makers. The film helped to bring about a special-effects revolution that, together with its huge financial success, ushered in a sort of golden age in American science fiction film in the late 1970s and early 1980s, a period that saw the release of such important films as *Close Encounters of the Third Kind* (1977), *Star Trek: The Motion Picture* (1979), *Alien* (1979), *E. T. the Extraterrestrial* (1982), *Blade Runner* (1982), and *The Terminator* (1984). This same period also saw the release of the first two *Star Wars* sequels: *The Empire Strikes Back* (1980) and *The Return of the Jedi* (1983)—films that would ultimately be joined by *The Phantom Menace* (1999), *Attack of the Clones* (2002), and *Revenge of the Sith* (2005). *Star Wars* also took the phenomenon of merchandising to unprecedented levels, as a seemingly limitless array of related books, toys, and various kinds of collectibles produced even more income than did the blockbuster films themselves. In America, myth sells, as it should, given the close connection between consumerist desire and the desire for grand mythic adventure that escapes the humdrum everyday world of modern capitalism.

The success of *Star Wars* and other science fiction films in the 1970s and 1980s was also crucial to bringing the genre back to television, where it had been a minor presence since the cancellation of *Star Trek* in 1969. In particular, 1987 saw the debut of *Star Trek: The Next Generation* (*TNG*), a series that would last for seven years and ultimately become even better known (at least to the new generation of viewers that it brought to the franchise) than the original series. Partly because it lasted longer and thus had more time to develop, *TNG* is even more clearly an exercise in mythmaking than the original *Star Trek* had been. Like its predecessor, it is built on the basic motif of an intrepid band of adventurers exploring the galaxy and encountering the unknown, thus drawing on the mythic resonances of the colonial/frontier narratives that are so central to American cultural history. Granted, *TNG* makes good use of the advances made in special-effects technology during the previous decade to produce the kind of compelling look that its contemporary audiences (accustomed to such technology in science fiction film) demanded, but the real secrets to the success of *TNG* were its compelling characters, the relationships among them, and the vividly imagined future world in which the adventures of these characters take place.

In general, the future world presented in *TNG* is consistent with that presented in the original *Star Trek*. Earth once again is the center of the United Federation of Planets (which continues to expand, adding new planets), humanity is again at the center of the universe, and high technology has combined with the enlightenment gained from contact with other species to produce a time of peace and prosperity on earth. In the tradition of utopian science fiction dating back at least to the work of H. G. Wells, *TNG* envisions a global government that oversees this idyllic future earth, although this monolithic government is extremely tolerant of diversity. We even learn in the episode "Attached" (November 8, 1993) that the Federation is extremely hesitant to admit any planets that do not have a unified world government, the existence of such a government being taken as a necessary sign of an advanced state of civilization.

TNG fills in numerous details concerning the future history of earth, including the fact that the second half of the twenty-first century had been marked by global nuclear destruction that virtually drove humanity back into barbarism. In the two-hour inaugural episode, "Encounter at Farpoint" (September 28, 1987), Captain Jean-Luc Picard (Patrick Stewart) and his crew members are placed on trial by a godlike superhuman entity known as Q; in the resulting proceedings, we learn that the savage-seeming court in which they are tried is like something from the "mid-21st century. The post-atomic horror." Conversely, partly because of the lessons learned in this holocaust (and also, we eventually learn, because of lessons learned from the Vulcans after first contact with them), such global conflict would be unthinkable in the twenty-fourth century. Thus, when Q impersonates a Cold War–era military officer, exhorting the *Enterprise* to return immediately to earth to fight "commies," Picard responds, "What? That nonsense is centuries behind us!" Q responds that this might be the case, but that humanity is "still a dangerous, savage, child race."

Picard is able (at least partly) to convince Q otherwise, and we learn in *TNG* that the human race has indeed come a long way since the antagonisms of the Cold War. For example, the high level of technology and the low level of political tensions on earth have produced a sort of material paradise in which all needs are met virtually without the use of human labor, thus freeing up humans for more fulfilling activities, such as exploring the galaxy on a starship. With all material needs met at the touch of a replicator button, there is no need for such things as money, and the series even occasionally jokes about the quaintness of the very concept of currency.

Capitalism has no place in this future world. In "The Neutral Zone" (May 16, 1988), the *Enterprise* discovers a derelict ship containing the frozen bodies of three humans from the twentieth century, including a former investor who wonders about business conditions in this (to him) future world. Picard responds, speaking to him almost as if he were a child, "People are no longer obsessed with the accumulation of *things*. We've eliminated hunger, want, the need for possessions. We've grown out of our infancy." When the investor, who can imagine only profit as a motive, wonders what challenges and motivates people under such circumstances, Picard replies that people are now motivated by the desire to fulfill their full potential as human beings. "The challenge," he says, "is to improve yourself, to enrich yourself."

This enrichment, incidentally, is thoroughly secular in nature. In fact, *TNG* tends to be highly suspicious of any form of organized religion, treating such practices as forms of barbaric superstition with no place in a technologically advanced society. The Federation is a sort of materialist Utopia, abundantly affluent but free of greed and competition for profits, yet still able to provide challenges and opportunities for individual growth and development. Set against these idealized conditions are the occasional alien cultures that still place an emphasis on competitive profit making. Chief among these are the buffoonish Ferengi, who live only for the pursuit of profit and the accumulation of wealth. Totally unscrupulous and entirely self-serving, the huge-eared Ferengi serve as a sort of caricature of twentieth-century capitalists. They are willing to lie, cheat, deceive, and even kill to increase their profits, and their characterization in *TNG* makes the pursuit of profit seem simultaneously silly and sinister. Furthermore, although the Ferengi can be quite dangerous, they are never really a match for the *Enterprise* and its crew, whose nonprofit ideology is thus presented as superior in both the moral and practical sense.

Some of the enemies encountered by the Federation in *TNG* are considerably more frightening, however. Central among these are the Borg, a nightmare race with numerous precedents in dystopian and horror fiction. As their name indicates, the Borg are cyborgs, composites of the organic and the mechanical/electronic. They are composed of beings from various humanoid races who have been "assimilated" into the Borg collective through the addition of numerous implants that give them powerful destructive capabilities, while also stripping them of free will and the ability to think as individual persons. In fact, there is only one collective Borg mind, shared by all of the various "drones," whose only mission is to sweep across the galaxy, assimilating any beings that might be useful as drones and any technology that might be useful to them in increasing their own capabilities.

The Borg drones are descended from several specific predecessors, ranging from Frankenstein's monster to the zombies of *Night of the Living Dead* (1968). They are, however, entirely secular and have no precedents in the realm of supernatural horror. As their appearances on *TNG* and its successor *Star Trek* series continue, they tend to get darker and creepier, looking less like robots and more like high-tech zombies. In many ways, the Borg are modeled on insects, such as bees and ants, and in the later *Voyager* series they even have a queen, analogous to queen bees. They are, however, complex and clearly derive from several sources. At an obvious level, they represent contemporary fears that human beings are gradually becoming slaves to their own technology. In their suppression of individualism, the Borg recall Western Cold War depictions of communism, and, given that individualism is one of the central values informing all of the *Star Trek* series, this trait alone makes them the virtual antithesis of the Federation. Conversely, in their insatiable drive to accumulate, the Borg recall Marxist descriptions of capitalism. This trait also sets them in direct opposition to the ideology of the Federation and *Star Trek* as a whole, both of which are quite devoted to the notion that capitalist greed and competition for wealth will be swept away in the future.

In 1994, *TNG* was terminated by its producers (creator Gene Roddenberry had died in 1991) so that the story and its cast could move into feature films, even though the series was at the height of its popularity at the time of its cancellation. The end of *TNG* also cleared the way for the ongoing growth of the *Star Trek: Deep Space Nine* series that had begun running in syndication in 1993 and for the new *Star Trek: Voyager* series that was slated to begin broadcasting in 1995. These two latest *Star Trek* series moved in significant new directions that brought them well beyond the scope and tone of the first two series. In the meantime, as I discuss in more detail in my book *Science Fiction Television*, science fiction television as a whole experienced an unprecedented period of richness and innovation in the 1990s, with series such as *The X-Files, Babylon 5, Farscape,* and *Stargate: SG-1* enjoying successful runs in a mode of epic adventure that clearly owes much to *Star Trek*. As one would expect from science fiction, such series tended to avoid supernatural themes, although they often feature alien entities with superhuman and even god-like powers. By the early years of the twenty-first century, however, all of this would change, and epic fantasies featuring strong supernatural components would suddenly become a dominant force in American popular culture, even though many of them were based on British models.

THE BRITISH INVASION: *LORD OF THE RINGS* AND *HARRY POTTER* MAKE IT BIG IN AMERICA

The success of the film version of *The Wizard of Oz* points toward the way in which the visual (and auditory—the film is also a highly successful musical) resources of film as a medium are better suited than print to a depiction of lavish visions of realities different from our own. That the film did not trigger a spate of successors going for a similar effect can be attributed to several factors, not the least of which is the onset of World War II, which led to generally diminished film budgets, encouraging the rise of phenomena such as film noir, which thrived in the low-budget world. Indeed, the very success of film noir through the 1940s might have discouraged studios from making big investments in high-gloss, high-color fantasy-adventure films. With the rapid spread of television beginning in the early 1950s, however, the world of inexpensive black-and-white productions quickly came to be dominated by the small screen. Technological and budgetary considerations meant that early television was extremely limited in its ability to portray the kind of exotic settings and large-scale action that are so crucial to fantasy-adventure tales, although some of the most beloved television programs of the 1950s did venture into the world beyond realism. These programs included such productions as *The Adventures of Superman* (which ran in syndication from 1951 to 1958) and *The Twilight Zone* (which topped off the 1950s with its premiere in October 1959, going on to run for five seasons and to become one of the hallmarks of television history).

Still, epic fantasy was clearly one thing film could do better than television, given the limited special-effects technologies available in the 1950s. Indeed, although recent advances in computer-generated imagery have made the sweeping epic more viable as a television genre, the fact remains that such epics, which often rely on a sense of grandeur and magnitude, remain best suited for the big screen. Even television series that potentially move into the realm of epic fantasy and adventure—such as *Hercules: The Legendary Journeys* (1995–1999) and *Xena: Warrior Princess* (1995–2001)—have typically done so with considerable self-consciousness, often relying as much on campy self-parodic humor as grand adventure to entertain their audiences. In addition, one of the few recent programs to seek to achieve epic scope, the Sci Fi channel's reimagining of *Battlestar Galactica* (the 1970s original of which was quite campy), is striking more for its texture of gritty realism than for its mythic undertones—although the latter are certainly there in large doses. Meanwhile, epic fantasy series have typically resided in the margins of American commercial television, airing in syndication (as with *Hercules* and *Xena*) or on cable/satellite networks (as with *Battlestar Galactica*) rather than the major broadcast networks.

Film therefore remains the central medium for epic fantasy/adventure, and such films have in fact exploded in popularity in the past decade or so. This is thanks largely to the availability of computer-generated special effects that make it possible to do justice on film to such classics of fantasy literature as J.R.R. Tolkien's *Lord of the Rings* trilogy. Indeed, the three *Lord of the Rings* films, the five (to date) *Harry Potter* films, the three *Pirates of the Caribbean* films, and the three *Shrek* films, all of which fit, in one way or another, into this category, have been among the most commercially successful franchises in film history, bringing in huge receipts that have justified the megabudgets required to make such films effectively.

That the *Lord of the Rings* and *Harry Potter* films are adaptations of British novels (although books that had an extensive American readership even before the release of the films) points to the long-term strength of fantasy as a genre of British literature. That this particular literature has long been dominated by British rather than American authors should probably come as no surprise, given its links to older traditions of medieval romance that have never really had a place in U.S. culture, which has been decidedly modern since its roots in High Enlightenment revolution. Indeed, one could argue that British fantasy takes much of its energy precisely from an opposition to what is seen as the dehumanizing and soul-destroying force of runaway American modernization. For example, Tolkien's aversion to capitalist modernity (which is, of course, epitomized by the United States) is well known, and one could argue that British fantasy in the modern form (of which Tolkien is the exemplar) began with the late-nineteenth-century work of William Morris, best known today for his vision, in *News from Nowhere* (1890), of an idyllic agrarian Utopia that, although socialist in its ideology, in many ways looks back to premodern times. *News from Nowhere* was written precisely in opposition to the utopian novel *Looking Backward* (1888), in which Edward Bellamy presents a distinctively American vision of a future Utopia built on scientific and technological progress. The more humane and genteel virtues of Morris's Utopia are, of course, much more in line with Tolkien's antimodern vision, even if the socialist Morris and the conservative Catholic Tolkien would have otherwise found little to agree on. Perhaps it is little wonder then that Tolkien, despite his political distance from Morris, cited Morris's fantasy novels of the

1890s—*The Wood beyond the World* (1894) and *The Well at the World's End* (1896) are probably the best—as an important inspiration for his own work. Morris's fantasy novels, which took their literary inspiration from the medieval romance, were the first British novels to be set in an entirely invented world and thus exercised an important influence on such world-building writers as Tolkien.

Of course, just as Morris was "inventing" the modern fantasy novel, his compatriot H. G. Wells was writing the founding works of the modern science fiction novel. By the 1950s, however, just as Tolkien and his fellow Inkster C.S. Lewis were writing what would become the dominant works of twentieth-century fantasy, science fiction had come to be almost entirely dominated by American writers, who, spurred by the American urge to modernize, were perhaps more in tune with the technological future. It is probably no accident that fantasy writers such as Lewis and Tolkien rose to prominence at a time when the "Golden Age" of science fiction writing was coming more and more to be dominated by American writers such as Isaac Asimov and Robert A. Heinlein. Roger Luckhurst has argued that, as American writers rose to prominence in science fiction, that genre came to be associated by many in Britain with the contamination, or even extinction, of indigenous British cultural traditions by American popular culture—and American-driven modernization as a whole. For Luckhurst, the association of science fiction with "Americanized modernity... is surely part of the reason that the most notable form of writing in England in the wake of the war was the more indigenous form of fantasy" (p. 123). Luckhurst argues that the writing of Lewis and Tolkien, in particular, "responds directly to the condition of modernity in England, and to what they perceived as a disastrous defeat of tradition" (p. 124).

Of course, Luckhurst's identification of fantasy as an "indigenous" form of British literature suggests precedents that date back not just to Morris, but even before, just as Morris's own reliance on medieval romance suggests much earlier roots and just as the tradition of British fantasy in general has obvious precedents in the fantasy plays of Shakespeare, or even earlier works, such as *Beowulf* or *Sir Gawain and the Green Knight*. Modern fantasy, however, is distinct in the extent to which it responds quite directly to the phenomenon of capitalist modernization, often seen as dehumanizing and dispiriting. A classic case occurs in Edith Nesbit's *The Enchanted Castle* (1907), where three English schoolchildren specifically set out in search of the kind of magical experience that has been removed from the modern world by the capitalist rationalization described by Weber. As one of them puts it, "I think magic went out when people began to have steam-engines, and newspapers, and telephones and wireless telegraphing" (p. 10). Stumbling on an enchanted castle in their wanderings, they do indeed find magic; however, this magic has trouble residing in the modern world. In the end, this magic must be largely negated—although it retains enough power to produce a romance ending in which a couple find true love and are wed, presumably to live together happily ever after.

Nesbit's contemporaries among American "fantasy" writers, such as Baum and Burroughs, were producing very different works that generally lacked nostalgia for precapitalist times, however admiring Burroughs might have been of Tarzan's British nobility. By the 1950s, American nonrealist literature was heavily dominated by the science fiction of writers such as Asimov and Heinlein, whose work is very much in tune with the American mindset. In the long run, however, these writers have failed to capture the American popular imagination in the way that fantasy writers such as Tolkien and (to a lesser extent) his friend and contemporary Lewis would do, suggesting that the works of Lewis and Tolkien respond to deep, unfulfilled longings in the American popular consciousness for something necessary to human health and happiness that is not being supplied by the economic juggernaut of American capitalism.

Like Lewis did with Narnia, Tolkien stipulates a magical world free of capitalist rationalization and routinization. Of note, however, is that he never asks his readers specifically to ponder the ways in which Middle Earth differs from our own world, and he certainly does not ask them to imagine how it might have gotten that way. Middle Earth just *is*, making it beside the point for readers to ask why. Tolkien goes far beyond Lewis in the process of building a detailed world, however. Using sheer information to create a sort of reality effect, Tolkien made good use of his background as a distinguished academic in producing the mass of information that fleshes out Middle Earth, drawing on his extensive knowledge of Anglo-Saxon, Norse, and Greco-Roman mythologies, as well as Catholicism. The density of Tolkien's description of Middle Earth probably accounts for the fact that so many readers have found Tolkien's work so compelling, despite the fact that it detracts from the fantasy effect, naturalizing the magic presented in the text to the point where cognitive estrangement is virtually excluded from the reading experience. Meanwhile, the plot of the trilogy is carefully crafted—based, as Richard Mathews has noted, on the "scriptural pattern of revelation" (p. 138)—to enhance reader involvement and to deliver satisfying resolutions in the end.

Tolkien began the creation of the elaborately detailed imaginary realm of Middle Earth in *The Hobbit* (1937) but perfected it in the seminal *Lord of the Rings* trilogy, which comprises *The Fellowship of the Ring* (1954), *The Two*

Towers (1954), and *The Return of the King* (1955). Middle Earth is an avowedly imaginary realm that bears little direct connection, real or allegorical, to our own world, even if it seeks to convey moral messages relevant to our world. In it, the intensely conservative Tolkien constructs Manichean morality plays in which good triumphs over evil—and in which there is no difficulty in distinguishing between the two terms. Meanwhile, Tolkien not so subtly reveals his own distaste for capitalist modernity and nostalgia for the Catholic Middle Ages. To this day, Tolkien's work remains highly popular with general readers, although it has long received mixed reviews from critics, many of whom have complained of the blandness of Tolkien's style, the oversimplicity of his moral vision, and the escapist and unrealistic nature of his nostalgia for earlier, presumably simpler, and better times. Nevertheless, his works of fantasy remain the standard against which all such works are still judged today, especially after the vast popularity of Peter Jackson's trilogy of films based on the original trilogy of novels.

These films, *The Fellowship of the Ring* (2001), *The Two Towers* (2002), and *The Return of the King* (2003), were among the biggest hits in film history. Although the films attempt a reasonable fidelity to Tolkien's work, they can do so largely because of the availability of advanced technologies that are in themselves contrary to Tolkien's antimodern spirit—and in ways that go beyond the obvious fact that the films' emphasis on special effects and spectacular battle scenes creates an effect that is far bloodier and more violent than the novels. Thus, the films are decidedly more American than the original novels, at least to the extent that "American" is a buzzword for technology-driven capitalist modernity and not necessarily a marker of specific national origin. Indeed, the tremendous box office success of the *Lord of the Rings* films no doubt owes something to these spectacular effects, which give the films an oddly contemporary aesthetic of the kind that clearly appeals to younger viewers, accustomed to the whiz-bang graphics of video games. The films maintain enough of the spirit of the original, however, to suggest that their appeal also has to do with the way they are able to evoke nostalgic visions of a simpler, happier pastoral past, especially for adult audiences. In short, the films look comfortably familiar to young contemporary audiences, while at the same time supplying fantasy fulfillment of desires for something different of which those audiences are probably largely unconscious.

This aspect of the films was obvious enough to warrant prominent discussion in the December 2, 2002, issue of *Time* magazine. Reviewing the film in this issue, Lev Grossman notes that, in our technology-saturated society, science fiction seems to be losing its magic, to be replaced by fantasy, a genre better suited to answer the nostalgic longings of the day. "Fantasy," Grossman argues, "envisions a society modeled loosely on agrarian medieval Europe, though with plenty of Vaseline on the lens. Antitechnology, antiglobalist, it's a misty, watercolored memory of a way we never were. But if the vision is imaginary, the longing for it is very real." In the case of *Lord of the Rings*, Grossman goes on to argue, there is also great appeal in the fact that it is basically the story of a good, clear-cut war in which the forces of good, unambiguously defined as such, win out over the forces of unequivocal evil in straight-up standing battles. The success of the films can thus be taken at least partly as a reaction to the uncertain global situation in a post-9/11 world (*The Fellowship of the Ring* was released only three months after the 9/11 bombings) in which the U.S. war on terrorism is not only directed against nebulous, illusive enemies but also has led the United States to be widely perceived as a global agent of terror in its own right.

The *Lord of the Rings* films thus provide fantasy relief from the difficulties associated with the war on terror, very much in the way the *Star Wars* films answered a need for clear-cut heroism in the difficult post-Vietnam and post-Watergate days of the late 1970s. In this sense, they are also very contemporary, very American works, despite the fact that they were made in New Zealand by a Kiwi director, based on the works of a British novelist from half a century earlier. Thus, it is both the fact that these high-tech, high-budget films broke new ground in their spectacular staging of the events from the novels and the fact that they were perfectly timed that account for their unprecedented success in a film genre that had previously enjoyed lukewarm success at best.

The very Englishness of the *Lord of the Rings* source material (and Tolkien was very open about his desire to create a distinctively English mythology in the books[7]) might be part of its appeal to American audiences, as might its nostalgic appeal to medieval precedents, seemingly so out of step with modern-minded America. After all, these aspects of the books (and, to a lesser extent, the films) contain elements of pastoral tranquility and collective experience that are popular objects of longing for Americans precisely because they are absent from day-to-day American life. Thus, although there might be a great degree of class-based condescension in Tolkien's depiction of the happy, simple-minded Hobbits (read: happy, simple-minded English country folk), the lives of these creatures do contain pastoral elements mostly eradicated from American society by the 1950s. Similarly, the Shire functions as a genuine community (which extends into the collective efforts of the Hobbits, who go forth on the mission to destroy the Ring) of a kind wistfully longed for in American culture, but long gone (if it ever existed) from American reality.

The titanic box office success of the *Lord of the Rings* films has predictably spurred an entire sub-industry dedicated to trawling the library of available fantasy/adventure novels on which to base additional films. Thus, the *Chronicles of Narnia* sequence of children's fantasy novels by Tolkien's friend Lewis is gradually becoming a big-time film sequence as well, beginning with 2005's *The Chronicles of Narnia: The Lion, the Witch, and the Wardrobe*, which grossed $745 million worldwide ($291 million in the United States) on a $180 million production budget. This tidy profit has led to the adaptation of the second *Narnia* book, *Prince Caspian,* into a high-budget film as well, released in May 2008 to only moderate initial box office success in relation to its $200 million production budget. Still, other adaptations from the seven-novel sequence are likely to follow, assuming audiences continue to show up. Indeed, a film adaptation of the third book, *The Voyage of the Dawn Treader*, is already tentatively scheduled for release in 2010.

Lewis was an important scholar of medieval and Renaissance literature, whose work drew in important ways on traditions of medieval romance. Although also a writer of science fiction, he is best remembered today for the *Narnia* series, originally published between 1949 and 1954. This sequence is strongly informed by Christian ideas (which means that it has inevitably offended some Christians). The magical world of Narnia (a sort of parallel universe that four English schoolchildren discover can be entered by passing through a wardrobe in an old English country home) is driven by principles that definitely go beyond the physical laws of our own world but operate in fairly strict accordance with the magical principles of Catholicism, up to and including a hero (Aslan, the talking lion) who is a transparent figure of Christ, with all of the associated powers of magic and morality. No one need ask why the world of Narnia is constructed to differ from our own as it does, because that answer is already supplied: In a very real sense it does not differ at all but merely makes visible the magical elements that already exist (at least according to Christian mythology) in a less visible way in our own world. Moreover, the world of Narnia is viewed through the lens of a group of children who arrive there from our own world, encouraging readers to accept the principles of Narnia (and Christianity) with a childlike innocence (and faith). That kind of faith specifically excludes the sort of critical examination necessary to the process of cognitive estrangement influentially described by Darko Suvin in relation to science fiction, which Suvin saw as politically progressive precisely because of its potential to create such estrangement in its audiences. For Suvin, the best science fiction achieves its power by encouraging readers to think beyond their own experience and to imagine realities different from their own. Suvin, however, famously rejects fantasy because it derives its effects more from emotion than thought and therefore does not create cognitive estrangement in its audiences.

Partly because of the simplicity of its moral structure—and partly because it is presented from the point of view of child protagonists—the original *Narnia* series of novels is very much a work of children's literature, of which it is an acknowledged classic. Moreover, the simple moral structure of the *Narnia* series clearly has an appeal to viewers in search of such verities—and of assurances that there are higher powers looking out for us in our uncertain postmodern world. This is true as much of the recent films (which tone down the overt Christian allegory a bit) as much as the earlier novels. Then again, Philip Pullman's *His Dark Materials* sequence of fantasy novels, which read almost like a rejoinder to Lewis (especially in their anticlerical presentation of the Church as an oppressive, dystopian force in their alternative Victorian world), have also begun to appear on the big screen. The first film in this sequence, *The Golden Compass* (released during the 2007 Christmas season), was only a moderate success at the box office, even though it stripped most of the antichurch material from the original novel (identifying the oppressive force in the parallel world of the film not as the church, but simply as the "Magisterium," although it still carries churchlike undertones). In fact, this film, which relies heavily on expensive computer-generated imagery (CGI) animation, made back only $70 million of its $180 million production budget at the U.S. box office. The film was much more successful abroad (where audiences were perhaps less worried by Pullman's anti-Christian reputation), bringing its worldwide box office gross to over $370 million.

Filmmakers have also begun to tap into the available material in American fantasy literature, but this is clearly an area that continues to be dominated by the British. Efforts such as *The Spiderwick Chronicles* (2008), based on the sequence of children's novels by Tony DiTerlizzi and Holly Black, have enjoyed little critical or commercial success compared with their counterparts based on the much stronger tradition of British fantasy literature. The latter, after all, have a strong built-in following, even though (and by my reading, partly because) the works of authors such as Lewis and Tolkien have a decidedly anticapitalist (and even anti-American) intonation that might be expected to disturb contemporary audiences, especially in the United States.

Robert Zemeckis's *Beowulf* delves even deeper into the historical store of British fantasy literature. Based (rather loosely) on the Old English epic poem of the same title, Zemeckis's film tends more toward the supernatural in its depiction of the hero of the title and his quest to free Denmark of the ravages of the monster Grendel and (ultimately) Grendel's shape-shifting mother. There are some vague interrogations of the concept of heroism, but once again the CGI spectacle is the hallmark of the film, which was released in both a "regular" and a 3-D version. Zemeckis seems to understand that he is producing a spectacle rather than a thoughtful commentary on anything. Indeed, the fundamental technique of the film, which was composed entirely with a digital capture technique similar to that used in the 2004 film *Polar Express*, also directed by Zemeckis, seems to proclaim its self-conscious sense of construction as an exercise in filmmaking technology.

Beowulf was cowritten by Neil Gaiman, whose emergence as an important player in the film industry is further evidence of a recent boom in fantasy film. Gaiman also wrote the screenplay for the low-budget but interesting fantasy *MirrorMask* (2005), while the whimsical big-budget fantasy *Stardust* was based on Gaiman's novel of the same title. Meanwhile, *Coraline*, a film based on a children's fantasy novel by Gaiman, is scheduled for release in early 2009. Gaiman is also reportedly at work on a film project based on his highly successful *Sandman* series of fantasy-horror graphic novels.

Much of Gaiman's work taps into a dark vein in British children's literature, drawing on the works of authors from Lewis Carroll to Roald Dahl. Such writers are very different from Tolkien, and in any case, Gaiman differs dramatically from Tolkien in his ambivalence (rather than antipathy) toward modernity. Meanwhile, this dark vein also provides background to the series of works that topped off the tradition of British children's fantasy literature in the twentieth century, and a series that was itself not necessarily opposed at all to capitalist modernization. Adding in a dash of the old-time Gothic, the *Harry Potter* series of children's novels that appeared in the period from 1997 to 2007 brought children's fantasy to a new peak of popularity and cultural prominence, becoming perhaps the single most important publishing phenomenon in both Britain and the United States during that period, especially in their ability to attract adolescent and preadolescent male readers, a group notorious for its lack of interest in reading conventional fiction. In the seven novels of the *Harry Potter* series—beginning with *Harry Potter and the Philosopher's Stone* (published in the United States and subsequently adapted to film as *Harry Potter and the Sorceror's Stone*) in 1997 and extending through *Harry Potter and the Deathly Hallows* in 2007—author J. K. Rowling creates a convincing alternative world that exists alongside (and sometimes overlaps with) our own contemporary reality, but in which magic and other forms of supernatural occurrences are common, everyday events. Focusing on the education in the ways of magic of the eponymous fledgling sorcerer and his friends, the books present numerous opportunities for fantastic adventures, although these adventures have been criticized as sometimes being too dark and frightening for the children who are presumably the books' intended readers. Whereas the literary merit of the *Harry Potter* books has been widely debated, their popularity is beyond doubt. Translated into numerous languages, the books have sold well over 300 million copies worldwide, attracting a reader-ship of both children and adults. Meanwhile, the film adaptations of the first five novels have made the *Harry Potter* film franchise one of the most lucrative in cinematic history.

Rowling's success (she has reportedly made more money from her writing than any other author in history) obviously asks for comparison with that of Tolkien, although her work is more morally complex and her vision is far different, particularly in that her work, however much it might delve into the supernatural, shows relatively little Christian influence. In fact, extremist Christian groups have been among the most vocal critics of the *Harry Potter* books and films, claiming that their positive portrayal of witchcraft is con-trary to Scripture. In addition, such groups have been bothered by the fact that, despite the prevalence of supernatural forces, the world of the books and films seems devoid of a God figure, while the characters in the books carry on their lives (and their magic) without any appeal to religion.[8] Nevertheless, the *Harry Potter* books do join the works of Tolkien and Lewis as major landmarks in modern British children's fantasy literature, demonstrating what a potent force this literature can be. Moreover, the Potter films share with the *Lord of the Rings* films the characteristic of offering something (magic) not avail-able within the humdrum world of capitalist reality, while offering familiar messages that keep them from being too disturbing or threatening.

The *Potter* films are relatively true to the original books, although they nec-essarily leave out much of the elaborate detail that has seen the books generally increase in length throughout the sequence. The last two books are slightly shorter than *Harry Potter and the Order of the Phoenix*, which was 896 pages in the 2003 hardback edition. The books and films both focus on the title character and on his schoolmates (especially best friends Ron Weasley and Hermione Granger) at Hogwarts School of Witchcraft and Wizardry. They are thus situated in an environment with which young readers can identify. It is also the case that the characters age one year per book, beginning as Harry turns eleven in *Harry Potter and the Philosopher's Stone* and ending with Harry and his friends having reached the age of seventeen in *Harry Potter and the Deathly Hallows*. The fact that the protagonists age as the series proceeds has no doubt helped it to keep a loyal base of young readers, who can watch the characters in the books and films age along with themselves. In addition, this process is highly convenient for the makers of the films, given that the actors playing the key children's roles unavoidably age as the film series proceeds over what will eventually be an eight- or nine-year run. (Daniel Radcliff, who plays Harry, was eleven when the first movie was being filmed and will be roughly twenty-one by the time the last film is released.)

Although the *Harry Potter* sequence of books and films is clearly aimed at young readers, it has attracted a wide following among college students and older adults as well. Still, the fantasy value of the series seems most obvious in relation to its principal audience of children and adolescents. Harry is, after all, a special child, typically surrounded by those who do not understand or appreciate him, thus replicating the default alienated situation of young people in modern capitalist society. He is able to overcome his alienated state in a way that real-world children cannot hope to do, however, largely because he is gifted with special abilities but also because he is able to find a few loyal supporters (e.g., Ron and Hermione, but also adults such as the sage wizard Albus Dumbledore) who do understand his true worth.

Hogwarts School itself carries significant fantasy value as a sort of "good" school that stands in opposition to the schools attended by the readers and viewers of the *Harry Potter* books and films. Granted, Hogwarts is no utopian setting, and Charles Elster is correct when he states that the world of the school "resembles an English boarding school education, with its traditional components of competition and hierarchical relationships" (p. 205). Still, compared with the curricula endured by the various young readers and viewers of the books and films, the subject matter taught at Hogwarts is absolutely exhilarating, partly because of the inherently exciting nature of such subjects as "Defense against the Dark Arts" and partly because the students at Hogwarts are learning (both in the classroom and out) practical skills with identifiable real-world applications. Furthermore, although the faculty at Hogwarts varies in quality and benevolence, there are at least some genuinely devoted, highly skilled teachers, including the headmaster Dumbledore.

What is most striking about Hogwarts and the wizarding world as a whole is how thoroughly they are saturated with ideologies with which even the most benighted of ordinary mortals (or "Muggles," as such people are termed in the *Harry Potter* works) would feel perfectly at home. Indeed, as opposed to the anticapitalist medievalism of the *Lord of the Rings* sequence (at least partly overwritten, as I have noted, by the high-tech aesthetics of the films), the ideology of *Harry Potter* is thoroughly capitalist.[9] For example, as Elster notes, the school promotes an ethos of competition in all sorts of ways, including the central importance of Quidditch matches and events such as the Triwizard Tournament of *Harry Potter and the Goblet of Fire*. It thus is no accident that the very first experience of new "First Years" on arriving at Hogwarts is to be sorted into competing "houses," which immediately sets the tone of competitiveness that will underlie their lives at the school.

The *Harry Potter* series is also shot through with an ethos of consumerism. Indeed, one of its principal fantasy ingredients for young readers involves all of the cool, magical commodities that are acquired by Harry and others in the course of the series.[10] Harry's very first experience of the wizarding world is a shopping trip with the half-giant Hagrid in which he acquires various school supplies, but these are special, exciting school supplies (e.g., a magic wand and various other magical equipment and supplies), not the boring pencils and notebooks of the quotidian world. Moreover, it is during this first spree that Harry learns of the substantial store of wealth being held for him in Gringott's Bank, a discovery that is surely the stuff of which consumerist dreams are made. On this first trip, Harry also admires a sleek Nimbus 2000 flying broom, although he is unable to acquire it at this time, first-year students at Hogwarts being forbidden to have their own brooms. He later does acquire such a broom by special consent when he becomes the youngest ever seeker for his house Quidditch team at Hogwarts, only still later to replace it with a Firebolt broom, the fastest model in the world. Broomsticks are among the most obvious consumer products of the wizarding world, the various makes and models conferring status roughly in the same way automobiles do in the real world of capitalist consumerism.

Harry's success in acquiring such commodities (not to mention such goodies as an Invisibility Cloak and a magical map that can locate anyone in the world) stands in stark contrast to the impoverished life he had lived with his adoptive Muggles family the Dursleys, living in a barren cupboard under the stairs and forced to look on as the bratty Dudley Dursley was lavished with gifts. In short, the magical world of *Harry Potter* supplies a fantasy of escape not from consumerism, but into it. That this should be the case provides one of the best examples in contemporary culture of the close congruence between longings for magic and miracles and longings for material wealth and the goods it can acquire. Then again, Karl Marx observed long ago in his discussion of the "commodity fetish" in the first volume of *Capital*, the mystical properties with which we invest commodities can be understood only by analogy to "the mist-enveloped regions of the religious world" (Marx and Engels, p. 321). The emphasis on consumerism in the *Harry Potter* sequence serves as a sort of literalization of Marx's point, as the fantastic commodities acquired by Harry and others quite literally do have magical properties.

Of course, there is a strong nostalgic element to the phenomenon of the commodity fetish, this mystical reaction to manufactured goods suggesting a yearning for earlier (medieval) times when such goods were handcrafted by individual artisans. Walter Benjamin has famously noted that modern art (especially film), in an age when most works of art are consumed as mechanically reproduced commodities, lacks the quasi-religious "aura" of earlier artworks (such as original paintings), which had been touched by the hands of their godlike artist creator. For Benjamin, writing in 1936 in the shadow of the German Nazis, the shattering of the aura in modern art is primarily a healthy and positive phenomenon that breeds critical populations resistant to manipulations by demagogues such as Hitler, which depend on unthinking reactions of awe and reverence in the face of authority. Thus, whereas Benjamin's conception of the notion of the aura is highly reminiscent of Marx's discussion of the commodity fetish, art for Benjamin is a special sort of phenomenon that resists commodification even as it is prone to fetishization.

Phenomena such as the *Lord of the Rings* and *Harry Potter* books and films (and associated merchandising campaigns) suggest that modern consumer capitalism has been able to commodify art after all, producing products that might lack the sort of aura Benjamin described, but that can still be fetishized, as Marx discussed. This is true whether the work of art itself implicitly endorses consumerism in its content (as in the case of *Harry Potter*) or whether it implicitly rejects consumerism (and capitalism in general) through appeals to the glories of a medieval past (as in the case of *The Lord of the Rings*). The phenomenon might operate differently in the two cases, however. In the case of *Harry Potter*, both the books and the films may receive a special boost in their appeal through their own investment in consumerist desire, which resonates with and reinforces desires that their audiences already feel. Consumerist desire is notoriously unfulfilling, however, so that the alternative is also true: The *Lord of the Rings* books and films might thus have a special attraction for audiences precisely because of their appeals to a medieval nostalgia that resonates with a deep-seated utopian longing for a more authentic form of desire fulfillment than that offered by modern consumer capitalism. The fact that the *Lord of the Rings* books and films by now might have themselves become commodities missing some of their original magic actually could work to make this longing only stronger, because it is fundamentally a longing precisely for something that is perceived to have been lost.

This nostalgic element is especially obvious in the *Lord of the Rings* sequence, which can be read, among other things, as being about the decline of religious faith in the modern world, here decoded as a loss of belief in magic. Meanwhile, if religion is not really a factor in the *Harry Potter* universe, magic certainly is, and the sequence as a whole is informed by fantasy desires for magic and heroism. For example, Harry's adventures constitute a "Chosen One" narrative in which Harry, like the protagonists of so many fantasy and supernatural narratives, finds that he has a special mission in life—and special abilities to carry out that mission. As an infant, Harry is attacked by the evil sorcerer Voldemort, who has just killed Harry's parents. Voldemort, however, finds that his magical powers are not sufficient to kill the baby boy, even though he does leave young Harry with a nasty lightning bolt–shaped scar on his forehead, literally marking him for greatness. Indeed, despite his meager upbringing at the hands of the philistine Dursleys, Harry eventually finds that, in the alternative wizarding world, he is already a famous, near-legendary figure. Part of the success of Harry as a character, of course, comes from the humble and unassuming way that he deals with his newly discovered fame, remaining a likeable, down-to-earth boy despite his growing awareness that he is destined for greatness. Indeed, at several points he saves the entire wizarding world from disaster, usually with Voldemort (whom Harry finally kills in the last book) as his principal foe, although he also at times must overcome the opposition of those who should rightfully be his allies, such as the bureaucratic Ministry of Magic in *The Order of the Phoenix*. Still, Harry does have staunch allies (such as Dumbledore, but especially including his friends Hermione and Ron) on whose help he greatly depends, much in the mode of Buffy and her gang of Scoobies.

Of course, *Harry Potter* nods to fantasy tradition in a variety of ways, not the least of which is its depiction of the wizarding world as somewhat antiquated (although in this case more Victorian than medieval), older than the "normal" world, conceding that magic has an inherently old-fashioned air to it in this day and age. In its endorsement of consumerist desire and in its various other ratifications of capitalist ideologies (even its seemingly "political" gestures are usually critiques of authoritarianism, racism, and so forth, in modes that would be considered quite politically correct and orthodox within American culture), the *Potter* series is uniquely capable of having it both ways, providing fantasy escape from consumer capitalism while at the same time assuring viewers and readers that it is okay to hang out at the mall and to lust for that latest pair of designer jeans. The second of these, of course, is available in any number of works of American culture, but the Britishness of the Potter series gives it access to nostalgic alternatives that are hard to come by in an American context. Little wonder, then, that the most successful American fantasy adventures, such as the *Pirates of the Caribbean* and *Shrek* sequences, have abandoned these alternatives altogether in favor of a sleek postmodern hipness that regards the past as a rich source of (possibly naïve) material that the culture of the present is free to use to its own ends, thanks to our much more sophisticated contemporary perspective on things.

COOL MAGIC: THE AMERICAN POSTMODERN EPIC FANTASY

American fantasy films of the decades before *Lord of the Rings* were less successful partly because they were less aesthetically impressive (owing to the unavailability of sufficient special effects technology and budgets) and partly because they failed to answer the basic fantasy needs to which both *Lord of the Rings* and *Harry Potter* respond so well. Actually, before the special effects revolution ushered in by films such as *Star Wars* at the end of the 1970s, there were few fantasy films at all, with *The Wizard of Oz* continuing to loom as the major example of the genre in American film. Fantasy films appeared in bulk in the 1980s, no doubt partly because advances in special effects technology made them possible, but also surely as an escapist response to the cynical materialism that pervaded American society in the Reagan era, perhaps best captured in Oliver Stone's film *Wall Street* (1987). Fantasy films such as *The Neverending Story* (1984) tended to be simplified efforts directed at children, although some, such as Jim Henson's *Labyrinth* (1986), clearly sought to appeal to adult viewers as well. This film cast rock star David Bowie in a key role as the ruler of a mystical alternative world of magic that lies beyond the reach (and perception) of most people in our world. Ron Howard's ambitious *Willow* (1988), produced by *Star Wars* creator George Lucas, took the genre in a more adult direction as well, although Rob Reiner's *The Princess Bride* (1987), going for a more fairy tale–like atmosphere that might have been at home in a Disney animated film of the 1940s or 1950s, might have been ultimately the most successful of the fantasy films of the 1980s.

Of the more action-oriented fantasy films (sometimes designated as "heroic" "fantasy," or "sword-and-sorcery" films) of the 1980s, John Milius's *Conan the Barbarian* (1982) stands out as a particular box-office success—and as the film that gave bodybuilder Arnold Schwarzenegger his big break in show business. *Conan*, loosely based on the character created by Robert E. Howard in the 1930s, was followed by a more child-oriented sequel, *Conan the Destroyer* (1984), as well as the spinoff film *Red Sonja* (1985), both of which also starred Schwarzenegger. All of these films are full of action but are also presented with a tongue-in-cheek campiness that recognizes their over-the-top nature, while inviting audiences in on the joke. American filmmakers, it would seem, have a great deal of trouble taking fantasy adventure entirely seriously.

The action fantasy *Highlander* (1986), directed by Australian music-video pioneer Russell Mulcahy, takes itself a bit more seriously but still includes campy elements, such as the outrageously campy performance of screen legend Sean Connery as a foppish but deadly "Immortal." These Immortals are members of a mysterious race who have long lived among humans and who (for some unexplained reason) are fated to do battle with one another until at last only one of them is left standing, endowed with the collective power of them all and thus mighty enough to rule the world, for good or ill. This film was a standout among the fantasy films of the 1980s, largely because of its inventive mythology. For example, because Immortals can be killed only by decapitation, they tend to battle one another mostly with swords, which opens the way for considerable swashbuckling action. Although not a box office hit, *Highlander* gained something of a cult following, triggering the production of a whole series of sequels, as well as *Highlander: The Series*, which represented one of the first and most successful forays of the fantasy genre into television, lasting for six seasons in syndication from 1992 to 1998 and garnering a loyal and dedicated, if relatively small, audience. *Highlander: The Series* was thus a forerunner of both *Hercules: The Legendary Journeys* (1995–1999) and its spinoff *Xena: Warrior Princess* (1995–2001), probably the best known fantasy series of 1990s television. The *Highlander* series differs from most fantasy, however, in that it is set primarily in our own modern world (rather than a mythical past or alternative world), although the long lives of the Immortals allow for numerous flashbacks to earlier times.

Action fantasies such as *Conan* and *Highlander* can be seen as the forerunners of more recent films such as *Beowulf* or *300* (2006), although the latter probably owe more to the post-9/11 fantasy craze than to their 1980s predecessors. This is especially the case with *300*, which is built around a "savage war" plot that seems to suggest support for the U.S. war on terror, the U.S. invasion in Iraq, and (in advance) support for a potential U.S. conflict with Iran. Then again, *300* is an example of film as pure spectacle, and its substantial box office success (which turned a $65 million production budget into a take of over $450 million worldwide) probably owes as much to its cutting-edge CGI of bloody battle than to any specific political message. Directed by Zack Snyder and based on the graphic novel written by Frank Miller, *300* is an historical epic dealing with the Battle of Thermopylae in 480 B.C. It is also a militarist cliché-fest, soaked in blood and testosterone, glorifying violence and sacrificial death for one's "country," even though countries as we know them did not exist at the time of the events depicted in the film. Like Mel Gibson's *Braveheart* (1995), this is a film that does not want to be confused with the facts—and is not interested in historical accuracy. What it is interested in is the presentation of spectacularly bloody battle sequences as hordes of near-naked men impale one another on various sharp objects, demonstrating sadomasochistic tendencies that are actually more reminiscent of Gibson's *The Passion of the Christ* (2004) than of *Braveheart*. What makes *300* even more problematic is that its subject matter (involving an historical battle in which 300 Spartan warriors led a contingent of roughly 7,000 Greek soldiers against an invading Persian army of roughly 1 million) offers ample opportunities for commentary on the present-day military and political situation in the Middle East. Unfortunately, the film (following the graphic novel) goes all out in its historically inaccurate presentation of the Spartans as paragons of Western reason and democracy, whereas the Persians are presented as cruel, vicious, and entirely depraved Oriental religious fanatics.

The box office success of *300*, despite widespread outcries about its reprehensible Orientalist politics, illustrates that the fantasy appeal of such films need not necessarily be nostalgic but can respond to quite contemporary concerns, even if the film (as in this case) happens to be set in the historical past. In a related way, the hugely successful *Pirates of the Caribbean* films, although set in a vaguely defined past (and a vague sense of the past is typical of such postmodern works) are driven by an extremely contemporary sensibility. The films themselves (as with the *Lord of the Rings* films) are intensely modern special effects extravaganzas, the products of state-of-the-art filmmaking technologies. In addition, these films do not even have novelistic originals to point back to but are based on rides in the Disneyland and Disney World theme parks, so that their "originals" are already highly mediated and fictionalized versions of the real historical phenomenon of Caribbean piracy. Interestingly, the *Pirates of the Caribbean* films are often explicitly critical of capitalist modernization and of its tendency to reduce life to a profit-oriented routine lacking the magic and adventure that the films associate with the more free-wheeling world of Caribbean piracy. Nevertheless, piracy itself is a sort of metaphor for capitalism, and the *Pirates of the Caribbean* films can be as focused as the *Harry Potter* works on the importance of festishized objects, even if these objects usually must be acquired by more adventurous means than a simple purchase. The films, in fact, are essentially a series of quest narratives in which the principles seek to retrieve (amid a great deal of tongue-in-cheek postmodern self-consciousness) these objects.

Although the *Pirates* films clearly draw on a nostalgic longing for adventure of a kind that is associated with the lost days of Caribbean piracy, there is also a very American (and postmodern) self-consciousness about this nostalgia that sets it apart from the more traditional (and self-serious) British nostalgia that informs the *Lord of the Rings* novels and (although to a lesser extent) films. The spirit of the *Pirates* films (all directed by Gore Verbinski) is perhaps best represented in the bravura performance of Johnny Depp as pirate captain Jack Sparrow, the central character in the sequence. Depp's performance is brilliantly self-parodic as he overplays the rascally (but ultimately loveable and courageous) Sparrow in a manner that perhaps no other contemporary actor could get away with. Swaggering (and staggering) through the films with a liquor-slurred British accent, Depp gives his character just the right amount of silliness to make him seem harmless and unthreatening, allowing audiences to identify with his position, even though he is an opponent of the law and order that Americans supposedly so revere.

Pirates of the Caribbean: The Curse of the Black Pearl (2003) seemed something of a gamble with its $140 million production budget at a time when pirate films were decidedly out of fashion. It proved to be money in the bank, however, with a worldwide gross of more than $650 million, thanks largely to Depp's brilliant performance, solidly backed by the winning personae of the younger stars, Keira Knightley and Orlando Bloom—the latter of whom had risen to prominence as the dashing elf warrior Legolas in the *Lord of the Rings* films, thus providing a link between the two franchises. Knightley plays Elizabeth Swann, the daughter of the governor of British colonial Jamaica; Bloom plays blacksmith Will Turner, the son of a pirate. Despite their different class origins (and the film, in good American fashion, suggests that such differences can easily be overcome), both characters are respectable and generally law-abiding members of society, although they end up finding themselves aligned with the amusingly dishonest Sparrow, whose criminal behavior is at least consistent and reliable, against the hypocrisy of the forces of authority in the film. Of note, in this and the subsequent films, the historical adventure plots are effectively supplemented by strong supernatural elements (the central, eponymous artifact of the film is the *Black Pearl*, a ghost ship), the filmmakers having rightly sensed that a pirate-based adventure narrative and a supernatural adventure would work well together, being built on similar desires for escape from the mundane. It also helped, of course, that pirate lore had long involved a strong element of the supernatural, which provided ready-made entry points into supernatural material for the film.

The huge success of this first film ensured that a sequel would be made. Thus, 2006 saw the appearance of *Pirates of the Caribbean: Dead Man's Chest* (2006), a film whose colossal production budget of $225 million was repaid with a worldwide gross of over $1 billion. This film introduces the efforts of Lord Cutler Beckett (Tom Hollander) and the East India Trading Company to tame the Caribbean and to make the region safe for the conduct of modern business. It thus becomes a displaced version of the traditional "taming of the West" frontier narrative, including the usual message that this taming removes valued mystery and magic from life in the area. Although carrying an aristocratic title, Beckett serves as an emblem of capitalist modernity, dedicated to the pursuit of profit. Here he is perfectly willing to resort to mystical means in pursuit of that end. In particular (in this series the more far-fetched the plot the better), Beckett seeks to use Jack Sparrow's magical compass to retrieve the heart of the mythical (but here, real) Davy Jones, possession of which will allow him to control Jones himself and thus exert supernatural power over the world's oceans (and burgeoning international commerce).

Pirates of the Caribbean: At World's End (2007), with a production budget of $300 million, nearly reached the billion-dollar mark as well, taking in a worldwide gross of $960 million. Although some critics thought the series was growing a bit tired at this point (while the plots were growing increasingly complicated to the point of incomprehensibility, especially for young audiences), this third film is in many ways the most interesting of the series. It treats in a particularly effective way the continuous thread that runs through all the *Pirates* films involving the sense that growing capitalist rationalization is making the world increasingly inhospitable to rollicking pirates such as Sparrow and his crew, whose world of adventure is rapidly giving way to a world of business and commerce, epitomized by the operations of the British East India Trading Company. By the time of the third film, in fact, there are hints that Sparrow might soon be the last pirate left on the face of the earth, where magic is quickly being replaced by money as a source of seemingly supernatural power. As the officious Beckett tells the supernatural Davy Jones (Bill Nighy), early in the film, "This is no longer your world, Jones. The immaterial has become … immaterial." As fellow pirate captain Hector Barbossa (Geoffrey Rush) tells Sparrow later in the film, "The world used to be a bigger place." "The world's still the same," responds Sparrow. "There's just less in it."

The film builds toward a final, near-apocalyptic sea battle between Beckett (and the forces of law and order) and Sparrow (and the forces of rule-breaking piracy), in which audiences are clearly expected to side with the pirates. Beckett makes his position clear as he prepares (he thinks) to destroy Sparrow once and for all: "It's nothing personal, Jack. It's just good business." Of course, Sparrow is not so easy to destroy, and the outnumbered and outgunned forces of the pirates manage to hold their own through the intervention of magic and the aid of the voodoo priestess Tia Dalma (Naomie Harris), an incarnation of the goddess Calypso.

In some ways, then, this final battle pits traditional Godlike magic against modern technology and financial resources. In short, it is an almost exact replication of the battle between "old" gods and "new" gods that lies at the center of Gaiman's *American Gods*. There is a sense, however, in which all of the characters in *Pirates of the Caribbean*, even the supernatural ones, are really just Disneyfied stock figures from popular culture, even if Depp's performance gives the figure of the pirate captain a new twist, whereas Knightley's Elizabeth Swann turns out to have resources and abilities that go far beyond those of the conventional damsel in distress, the stock figure from which she is derived. Indeed, the *Pirates of the Caribbean* films are quite overtly (and gleefully) constructed of bits and pieces of residue from the cultural past, giving them a far more postmodern feel than either *Lord of the Rings* or *Harry Potter*. If these films suggest a belief in magic, it is not really the magic of witches, goddesses, or Davy Jones, but the magic of the movies and of popular culture in general, especially as reflected in the Disney theme parks, which center, after all, on an area known as the Magic Kingdom.

Pop cultural magic is also at the center of another American fantasy sequence, which just happens to be the most commercially successful animated series of all time, although it is not, interestingly enough, a Disney product. This is the sequence *Shrek* (2001), *Shrek 2* (2004), and *Shrek the Third* (2007), all of which were produced by DreamWorks Animation, the principal competitor of Disney/Pixar in both animated film and children's films. The *Shrek* films feature a title character and protagonist who is a large green ogre (voiced by Michael Myers). In short, their hero is a stock villain from the fairy tale tradition that provides the basic material of the films, except that the *Shrek* films give this material an added postmodern twist by turning most of the tropes from the tradition (many of which are best known through Disney films) on their heads. Thus, not only is the hero an ogre, but the usual rescuer of damsels in distress, Prince Charming (voiced by Rupert Everett), is a pompous, preening villain, while the damsel in distress herself, Princess Fiona (voiced by Cameron Diaz), might be a legitimate princess, but she is ultimately also an ogre—who gleefully shares with Shrek (whom she eventually marries) ogre pleasures such as farting in a bath of mud. Rather than Beauty and the Beast, we thus get Beast and the Beast, although these are charming and benevolent beasts indeed. Shrek gets the girl and lives happily ever after, not only reversing the usual fate of ogres in fairy tales but also becoming the ironic inversion of his predecessors among movie monsters, such as King Kong. Imagine if *King Kong* had been a musical comedy in which the touch of Kong transforms Ann Darrow into a giant gorilla in her own right, whereupon the two fall in love and rule Skull Island together, raising lots of little giant apes in contented domesticity and possibly visiting New York from time to time to take in some shows.

The first *Shrek* film, which made $484 million globally and $268 million at the U.S. box office, actually ushered in the twenty-first-century fantasy craze, opening (in the United States) seven months before the first *Harry Potter* film and eight months before the first *Lord of the Rings* film. Meanwhile, *Shrek 2*, with $441 million in domestic box office revenue (third highest of all time), outdrew any of the *Potter*, *Rings*, or *Pirates* films in the United States, although its $920 million worldwide box office total was outstripped by the two top films from each of these other franchises. As in the *Pirates of the Caribbean* sequence, all of the magic here is tongue in cheek; indeed, the *Shrek* franchise is even more avowedly self-parodic than the *Pirates* franchise; it is a sort of postmodern pastiche of fantasy that pokes fun at the whole genre, while meanwhile adopting a self-consciously anachronistic hipness through the dialogue of its very contemporary wise-cracking characters and (perhaps even more obviously) through its cool, pop music soundtracks, so different from the dreamily nostalgic soundtracks of earlier Disney films. Indeed, much of the self-conscious hipness of the *Shrek* films is achieved at the expense of its Disney source material, the classic Disney films thus being identified, in comparison, as decidedly old fashioned and unhip.[11]

Even a cursory look at the *Pirates* and *Shrek* franchises shows that the most successful American fantasy films simply do not take magic as seriously as do their British counterparts. For one thing, American history, beginning afresh as it were with the onset of the colonization of what was quite seriously considered to be the "New World," self-consciously lacks a medieval past, medieval elements having been rejected from the national narrative as informed by ignorance, superstition, and aristocratic oppression. For another, such appeals to magic are simply out of step with the national identity of the United States as an ultramodern, high-tech, cutting-edge enterprise, dedicated to the propagation of Enlightenment rationalism and the eradication of medieval stupidity. I would argue, however, that this very lack of a medieval past (and of the magical elements so frequently associated with it) creates a sense of loss and a fervent desire for the magical, which results not only in the popularity of such book and film franchises as *The Lord of the Rings* and *Harry Potter* but also in the production of more properly American fantasy adventures such as the *Pirates of the Caribbean* and *Shrek* sequences. In the process, Captain Jack Sparrow and Shrek become the quintessential American heroes: larger than life, able to access magical powers beyond the ken of ordinary mortals, and staunchly being who they are, no matter what the neighbors might think. Indeed, the particular conception of heroism that informs U.S. cultural history can tell us a great deal about the longings that American culture attempts to fulfill, as I discuss in the next chapter.

Two

HEROISM IN AMERICA: THE LONGING FOR HEROES IN AMERICAN HISTORY AND AMERICAN CULTURE

In Bertolt Brecht's *Life of Galileo* (1947), the title character proclaims, "Unhappy is the land that needs a hero." Brecht's point is an anti-individualist one, of course, just as the fact that American culture has so long been fascinated with heroes (making it an unhappy land, indeed, per Brecht's Galileo, himself a hero of science) can be taken as a reflection of American individualism. Per the official American vision, we all supposedly have the potential to become heroes, although this very idea itself means that truly extraordinary heroes of the kind American culture seems to want to worship must somehow be set apart from the ordinary heroism achievable by anyone. Little wonder, then, that the heroes celebrated in American popular culture have tended to be superhuman, and perhaps even supernatural.

Heroes with superhuman abilities certainly appear in other world cultures, and, as Richard Reynolds has noted, superhero narratives tend to have mythic dimensions that resonate with several cultural traditions. Superheroes are uniquely prominent in American culture, especially in the modern era, and the mythic structure of their narratives is often distinctly American. Tracing the mythic significance of superhero figures in American culture, John Shelton Lawrence and Robert Jewett argue that superheroes are figures of the "American monomyth," largely because "the supersaviors in pop culture function as replacements for the Christ figure, whose credibility was eroded by scientific rationalism. But their superhuman abilities reflect a hope for divine, redemptive powers that science has never eradicated from the popular mind" (pp. 6–7). Peter Coogan agrees, arguing that "most superhero stories, especially the more formulaic tales, precisely fit the American monomyth structure" (p. 123). Among other things, superheroes are distinctly American cultural icons because of their close family resemblance to the quintessentially American figure of the frontier hero.

AMERICAN HEROES AND ANTIHEROES: KINGS OF THE WILD FRONTIER

Jewett and Lawrence are no doubt largely correct in their argument that the prominence of superheroes in American culture is centrally related to the importance of religion in American history and that American superheroes tend to be Christlike figures with missions of salvation. Other aspects of American history have exercised an important shaping influence on American views of heroism as well, including the existence of a frontier that presented obstacles that could seemingly be overcome only by superhuman courage, strength, and determination. The frontier hero is one of the central icons of American culture, as can be seen in the early prominence of such literary figures as James Fenimore Cooper's Natty Bumppo. There is also a long tradition of larger-than-life American frontier heroes arising from a mythic tall-tale tradition of folk heroes. Sometimes, even real-world frontier heroes became folk heroes surrounded by their own tall-tale traditions, including such figures as Davy Crockett and Daniel Boone, made more mythic by the fact that their exploits occurred on a then-distant and still quasi-mythic frontier that made it easy to promote them as superhuman figures. It is also telling, however, that such promotions were often a matter more of branding and marketing than of myth. Thus, although Crockett had long been a semi-mythic hero (thanks partly to the circumstances of his death at the Battle of the Alamo in 1836), he did not receive full-bore mythic status until he became the central figure in a brief Disney-produced television series based on his life in the 1950s, starring Fess Parker in the title role. Parker also starred in two associated Disney films of the period, *Davy Crockett, King of the Wild Frontier* (1955) and *Davy Crockett and the River Pirates* (1956), the popularity of which helped to spur one of the first successful co-marketing campaigns in U.S. history, as American children flocked to stores to buy coonskin caps, powder horns, toy muskets, and other items associated with the Crockett legend. In America, heroism sells, and American heroes, however superhuman or even supernatural, are often reduced to the status of marketing icons.

Other American folk heroes have also been associated with the frontier, as in the case of Johnny Appleseed, an environmentally friendly (and religiously inspired) folk hero who traveled the West planting apple trees because he believed that his guardian angel told him to. The legend of Appleseed was based on John Chapman (1774–1847), a pioneer nurseryman who introduced apple trees to large parts of Ohio, Indiana, and Illinois. Other frontier folk heroes include such figures as the giant lumberjack Paul Bunyan (a legend initiated by a newspaper reporter in 1906) and John Henry, a mighty steel-driving African American (possibly based on a real railway worker from the 1870s). Both Bunyan and Henry are associated with phenomena that were central to the conquest of the frontier, although both also stand as emblems of old-fashioned human hard work and muscle power, fighting rear-guard actions against technological modernization but ultimately displaced by the growth of automation and the superior power of machines. Particularly important in this category of hero (because he is so directly related to the narrative of the taming of the West), is Pecos Bill, a giant cowboy (in the "big man" tradition of Bunyan and Henry) who famously "tamed the wild west." A fictional character introduced in short stories by Edward O'Reilly in 1923, Pecos Bill was lost as an infant and raised by coyotes. As an adult, he had superhuman strength and stamina, as well as an unmatched knowledge of the natural environment of the Wild West. Pecos Bill is a classic example of the "invented" folk hero, that is, one who was imagined by a single creator rather than evolving more organically through folk culture. Such invented heroes are again especially prominent in American culture, no doubt because the United States emerged as a nation during the High Enlightenment, declaring itself modern from the very beginning and specifically disavowing the feudal past of Europe. The United States was thus an invented nation, founded according to certain specific principles rather than growing organically out of long cultural traditions. As a result, as Gaiman dramatizes in *American Gods*, the United States has no genuine myths in the sense that myths typically arise in this organic way.

The invented nature of the typical American folk hero helps to explain the fact that so many real-world figures have emerged as quasi-mythic heroes whose real-world exploits provide a starting point for subsequent exaggeration and fictionalization. Thus, the most important predecessor of Pecos Bill was not a fictional folk hero such as Bunyan, but the real-world figure of Buffalo Bill Cody, a man who helped greatly to invent his own folk hero status. Cody parlayed a real-world career as a soldier, scout, buffalo hunter, and Indian fighter into one of America's first great media marketing phenomena. Many of his exploits were real, and he received the Medal of Honor in 1872 for "gallantry in action" for his services as a scout for the Third Cavalry Regiment of the U.S. Army, in which he had first enlisted in 1863 at the age of seventeen. Having already gained considerable media attention for his exploits on the frontier (largely through a series of dime novels authored by Ned Buntline), Cody turned to show business, forming a touring company that eventually evolved (in 1883) into "Buffalo Bill's Wild West," an elaborate extravaganza that placed Cody very much in the same league as his contemporary P. T. Barnum as a great American showman.

Cody's show featured a variety of acts and guest performers (including the famous Sioux chief Sitting Bull), but it centered on Cody's own re-enactments of frontier exploits by himself and others. His most successful routine was probably a re-enactment of the Battle of the Little Bighorn, with Cody playing the role of General George Armstrong Custer. The 1876 killing of Custer (an early media star even before his death) became one of the great American media events of the nineteenth century, providing a frisson of fear that made frontier adventure all the more exciting. Custer's death also led to stepped-up military actions that quickly led to the collapse of Indian resistance to westward U.S. expansion and thus to the end of such adventures, just as Cody and Barnum were on the rise as showmen.[1] Indeed, that the eras of the closing of the frontier and of the rise of showmanship should coincide is probably no accident; such spectacles as Barnum's circus and Cody's Wild West show were no doubt intended to provide the American public with some relief from the thirst for adventure that was becoming harder and harder to quench with reports of adventures on the actual frontier. In any case, the combination of Cody's showmanship and of its basis in his own frontier exploits made Buffalo Bill a virtual emblem of the American national identity. He also became quite wealthy and was one of the most famous men in the world, sometimes taking his show to Europe, where it was greeted by enthusiastic audiences, although it would be hard to gauge just how much of this enthusiasm arose from condescending visions of the United States as an exotic and savage land, lacking the refinements of European civilization.

Slotkin ("Buffalo Bill's 'Wild West'") notes Cody's great success as a showman and argues that Cody became an emblem not just of the past taming of the American frontier but of the beginnings of American imperial expansion abroad. Cody can also be taken as one of the founders of modern American media culture, and his legend would ultimately be extended through his appearances as a character in any number of later films and other works of popular culture, a situation foreseen by Cody's own appearances (playing himself) in two films during his own lifetime. By the time he died in 1917, however, World War I was well under way, and the innocent age of American adventurelust was largely over. More mythic successors such as Pecos Bill enjoyed only limited success, and by the Depression decade of the 1930s, the great age of American folk heroes appeared to have passed.

Cody's career helped to demonstrate the marketability of heroism. Marketable products, however, must be in step with the times, and therefore the terms of American heroism have changed as American culture itself has changed. The popular culture of the 1930s, dominated by film, would continue to produce hero figures. This was, after all, the decade in which Errol Flynn rose to prominence in such swashbuckling adventures as *Captain Blood* (1935) and *The Adventures of Robin Hood* (1938). The protagonists of these films (both played by Flynn) are, respectively, a pirate and an outlaw, signaling the extent to which so many of the heroes of American popular culture during the 1930s were actually antiheroes. For example, the heroes of the Westerns that came into prominence during this period were quite often antiheroes as well. Whereas we are now accustomed to the antiheroic heroes of the revisionist Westerns of the 1960s—such as Clint Eastwood's laconic spaghetti-Western cowboy or the lovable rogues of films such as George Roy Hill's *Butch Cassidy and the Sundance Kid* (1969)—we sometimes forget that the estimable John Wayne (who became an icon of right-wing American jingoism during the 1960s) rose to stardom playing an outlaw (however virtuous) in his turn as the Ringo Kid in *Stagecoach* (1939) and went on the play dark figures such as the brutal Thomas Dunson in Howard Hawks's *Red River* (1948).

Some of the most memorable "heroes" of the films of the 1930s were the monsters from such films as James Whale's *Frankenstein* (1931) and Merion C. Cooper and Ernest B. Schoedsack's *King Kong* (1933), the first of whom stands (among other things) as an emblem of the dangers of runaway modernity (science run amok), whereas the second (among many possible allegorical readings) serves as a sentimental marker of a traditional past for whom there is no longer a place in the modern world. Frankenstein's monster and the giant ape King Kong are remarkable as film characters partly because of the way they come off as so much more human than the humans who torment them. Indeed, the heroes of the 1930s were to a great extent humanized, stripped of their former superhuman status, and made much more ordinary, although they often still performed deeds of extraordinary heroism. As Bradford Wright notes, Depression-era popular culture tended to celebrate the common man, enacting the idea that "virtue resided within regular, unassuming Americans" (p. 10). For Wright, a key example of this phenomenon is the gangster film, which he argues "usurped the Victorian myth of the self-made man and perverted it into a gloriously self-destructive revenge narrative" (p. 10).

Closely related to the gangster film is the phenomenon of hard-boiled detective fiction, which rose to prominence at about the same time. In some ways, the most representative antihero figures of the 1930s were the hard-boiled detectives in the novels of such writers as Dashiell Hammett and

Raymond Chandler. Operating on the margins of the law and not necessarily following all of the official rules, detectives such as Hammett's Sam Spade and Chandler's Philip Marlowe were essentially modern-day outlaw figures, righting the wrongs that they could but always with the understanding that there were bigger and more systematic wrongs that were far beyond their power to correct. As such, they were quintessentially American individualist heroes, although they often showed a world-weary skepticism about the possibility of ultimate victory that can be taken as a key marker of a growing skepticism about the role of heroes in the modern world.

Such characters, along with the seriously flawed Everyman protagonists from the novels of such writers as James M. Cain, would go on to establish themselves even more firmly within American popular culture by their appearances in the noir films of the 1940s and 1950s, although their roots in the troubled decade of the 1930s always remained visible. Indeed, if the protagonists of Hammett and Chandler still carried resonances that reminded some observers of the protagonists of the chivalric romance, Cain's protagonists had no such mythic undertones. It might thus be significant that figures such as the fallen insurance salesman Walter Huff in Cain's *Double Indemnity* (1943)—renamed Walter Neff in Billy Wilder's 1944 film adaptation—would become far more representative film noir protagonists than would the rough-edged but ultimately virtuous detectives of Hammett and Chandler. Wilder's film version is one of the defining works of the film noir. All the elements of that genre are on full display in the film: Shadowy lighting and extreme camera angles reinforce the brooding atmosphere, and a tough, cynical antihero (who nevertheless has a soft spot) seeks ill-gotten gain while working both with and against a slinky femme fatale. The film is also notable for its snappy, rapid-fire dialogue, cowritten by Chandler and director Wilder. James Agee, in an early review, noted that the film is "soaked in and shot through with money and the coolly intricate amorality of money" (p. 119). In *Double Indemnity*, as in film noir as a whole, corruption and violence reside in every aspect of American life, whereas the general tone of the film suggests the anxiety that pervaded American society at the time. The myth narrative of the savage war, interrupted by the realities of World War II, was under serious strain.

The phenomenon of film noir itself certainly indicates a gritty turn in the American mindset during and after World War II, in what I have termed elsewhere the beginnings of a "post-utopian imagination," in which the products of American culture of the period seemed to find it increasingly difficult to imagine anything genuinely better than the soul-destroying routine that informs the daily grind of corporate capitalism.[2] There remains, however, a strain within the American popular imagination that continues to long for something greater and more meaningful than the commodification of everything that is the texture of daily life under late capitalism. If the difficulty of imagining heroes in a classic vein drove much of American culture in dark antiheroic directions beginning in the 1930s, it was also the case that the same decade saw the rise (history is always dialectical!) of an opposed tendency toward heroes who were even more heroic—and even more virtuous—than the classic heroes of the past.

It is not contradictory but virtually predictable that the 1930s would also see the introduction of the modern superhero. It is certainly no historical accident that genuine superheroes in the modern vein were first introduced in the 1930s, or that Superman, the first of the great superheroes, remains the most mythic and iconic American superhero in the early years of the twenty-first century. Created by Canadian-born artist Joe Shuster and American writer Jerry Siegel in 1932 (when both were still teenagers in Cleveland, Ohio), Superman did not actually appear in print until June 1938, in the first issue of *Action Comics*. From that point, the Man of Steel was unstoppable, becoming the centerpiece not only of a wide range of cultural products (comic books, comic strips, radio serials, live-action and animated television series, video games, and films), but of an entire American mythology.

It should be noted, incidentally, that Superman initially had fewer powers than he would eventually have—for example, he could not fly in his first comic book appearances but could simply jump really high. He also had a very different personality that placed him more in line with the tough and cynical hardboiled heroes of the 1930s than with the self-serious defender of conventional virtue that he would eventually become. Moreover, throughout his various incarnations, he has also maintained his alternative identity as Clark Kent, a figure very much in line with the Everyman heroes of the 1930s. Meanwhile, Superman's initial wise guy persona was distinctively American and very much in line with other American cultural heroes of the time. Indeed, however much he changed over time, he was from the very beginning an avowedly American hero, from his primarily red-white-and-blue costume to his clearly pro-American ideology, embodied in his eventual famed declaration that his mission on earth was to serve as the defender of "truth, justice, and the American way."

Certainly, the character of Superman has mythic dimensions that potentially transcend the American context. He is quite clearly a figure of both Christ and Moses; however, these religious dimensions might themselves be distinctively American, as Jewett and Lawrence extensively argue. The extensive mythology surrounding Superman's powers and background has grown and varied over the years, creating numerous complications and contradictions in his portrayal, although the central elements of his story are reasonably consistent. They also constitute one of the best-known fictional creations in American cultural history. In the most common version of this story, Superman was born Kal-El on the distant planet Krypton, then sent to earth on an escape rocket by his father, the scientist Jor-El, on the eve of the destruction of his home planet. The small boy arrives on earth, where the weaker gravity and the radiation of the yellow sun give him extraordinary powers, including flight, super strength, virtual indestructibility, and a variety of visual abilities (such as x-ray vision). Taken in by Jonathan and Martha Kent, a kindly childless couple in Smallville, Kansas, Superman is raised as a human child (named Clark Kent), only gradually discovering and developing his considerable powers. As a young adult he moves to the giant city of Metropolis (originally modeled by Shuster on his native Toronto, but later commonly seen as a stand-in for New York City). There, he maintains his secret identity as Clark Kent, working as a bespectacled, mild-mannered reporter for *The Daily Planet*, the city's leading newspaper. Meanwhile, Superman becomes a public figure, battling evil in his signature caped costume.

Superman became even more clearly a national emblem of the United States during World War II when, joined by the even more overtly patriotic Captain America, he carried the fight against Germany and Japan into the pages of America's comic books. Superheroes in general proliferated rapidly after the initial success of Superman, although some of these—Batman is the classic example—had a much darker tone and drew on other currents (e.g., film noir and hard-boiled detective fiction) in their vision of the hero. Meanwhile, even as youth culture became a larger force within the American culture industry in the 1950s, superhero comics declined dramatically in popularity in the years following World War II. This decline was partly because comics themselves were under assault by critics such as psychiatrist Fredric Wertham, who, in works such as *Seduction of the Innocent* (1954), saw comic books as a serious threat to the moral fiber of America's youth—although Wertham focused mostly on the crime and horror comics (e.g., EC's *Tales from the Crypt*) that had already superseded superhero comics in popularity.[3]

Superman himself remained popular through it all, partly because he also became a key icon of 1950s American television, the rise of which also contributed to the crisis in comics in the 1950s. Meanwhile, as the 1950s became the 1960s, a general skepticism toward most of the older and more established superhero figures opened the way for the newer, hipper, and younger superheroes of the resurrected Marvel comics. The antiauthoritarianism that marked the attitudes of so many young Americans during the 1960s, however, did lead to a greater recognition of the conservative, even fascistic implications of superheroes, and even heroes in general, somewhat in the spirit of the warning from Brecht's *Galileo* decades earlier. Conversely, these new-style, more human superheroes also had numerous precedents in American culture, echoing, among other things, the outcast common-man status of the protagonists of film noir. Moreover, as Bradford Wright notes, the superheroes of the 1960s drew in many ways (especially in their tendency to defend society while remaining aloof from it) on the archetype of the Western frontier hero (p. 205), making them classic figures of American culture.

Such heroes, in the gleefully hucksterish hands of chief editor Stan Lee, took the once failing Marvel to the top of the heap in the comic-book indus-try, and the very extent to which they were self-consciously hawked to young readers as consumer products only served to make them all the more Amer-ican. It is also telling that Marvel heroes such as the Hulk and Spider-Man seemed to have a special appeal to members of the 1960s counterculture, who saw the marginal social status of such heroes as similar to their own, despite the fact that Marvel never really endorsed the counterculture in the pages of their comics, while becoming a virtual embodiment of single-minded capi-talist profit-seeking in their business practices. As Wright notes, such Marvel superheroes were often viewed in the same company as countercultural heroes such as Bob Dylan and Ernesto "Che" Guevara, a situation that would seem to provide support to Thomas Frank's arguments noted previously, about the complicity between 1960s consumer capitalism and the counterculture. Af-ter Marvel, superheroes were the ultimate example of the commodification of heroism, manufactured to sell comic books—not to mention the eventually lucrative aftermarket in action figures, T-shirts, and other paraphernalia.

The more human (and sometimes less virtuous) superheroes of Marvel Comics were very much in tune with other developments in American culture in the 1960s and 1970s. For example, by the beginning of the 1970s the heroes of Western films were figures such as the charming rogues Butch Cassidy and the Sundance Kid or the even more unheroic John McCabe from Robert Alt-man's *McCabe and Mrs. Miller* (1971). The heroes of war films were transmo-grified into the antimilitarist figures of "Hawkeye" Pierce and "Trapper John" McIntyre in Altman's hugely successful and influential *MASH* (1970), which spawned what would eventually become one of the most beloved television series in American history, running on CBS from 1972 to 1983.

Perhaps the classic (debunking) treatment of heroism in the American pop-ular culture of the 1970s was also directed by Altman, whose superb but little-appreciated film *Buffalo Bill and the Indians, or Sitting Bull's History Lesson* (1976) figures Buffalo Bill Cody (played here by megastar Paul Newman in a performance that brilliantly lampoons his own stardom)[4] as a self-promoting forerunner of the manufactured heroes of modern American media culture. Released in July 1976 in the midst of the American Bicentennial celebrations, *Buffalo Bill and the Indians* is one of the most radical assaults on the mythology of America in all of American film. Focusing on the show "Buffalo Bill's Wild West," an extravagant staging of the mythology of the American West that was one of America's most successful show-business phenomena before the advent of the film industry, the film demonstrates the element of theater and spectacle that was central to the mythologization not only of the West, but of America as a whole. Buffalo Bill is presented in the film as pompous, preening, and self-absorbed, so obsessed with his own image that he is beginning to lose the ability to distinguish between reality and his own intentionally fabricated images. Bill, played at just the right pitch by Newman, is a drunk who has only one drink a day (in a huge schooner) and a womanizer who consorts only with opera singers, thus enhancing the air of theatricality that already surrounds him. Even Bill's famous long hair is fake, as is, one suspects, much of the patriotic rhetoric with which he seeks to present himself as the quintessential American hero—as a sort of allegorical representative of the American national identity. Given his allegorical status, the implications of Bill's fabricated image are huge. As one of his admirers suggests with unintentionally ominous irony, "It's a man like that made this country what it is today."

Set in 1885, when Buffalo Bill's Wild West show was just hitting its stride, the film devotes a great deal of its time to scenes from the show, which is rousing entertainment but also represents an extremely staged and stylized version of the West, despite its claims to historical authenticity. As the film begins, the famous Sioux chief, Sitting Bull (Frank Kaquitts), is about to join the show, as he actually did for a period during 1885 and 1886. Much of the film is structured around an opposition between Buffalo Bill, as charlatan and simulacrum, and Sitting Bull, a genuine hero, whose quiet dignity stands in sharp contrast to the superficial showmanship of Buffalo Bill. By extension, the traditional culture of the Sioux is suggested as an authentic alternative to the fabricated and commodified culture of modern America. Sitting Bull, as it turns out, has joined the show not in quest of wealth or fame but as an attempt to help his people, of whom only a little more than 100 remain after recent massacres at the hands of the American military. He hopes to use his income from the show to provide blankets and other needed supplies to his people and to parlay his participation in the show into an audience with U.S. President Grover Cleveland (Pat McCormick), to whom he hopes to plead the case of his people.

Not surprisingly, tensions immediately flare between Bill and Sitting Bull, who objects to the show's falsification of history and in particular to Bill's plan to restage the massacre of General Custer and his men at the Little Bighorn as a case of cowardly betrayal on the part of the Sioux. Instead, Sitting Bull suggests an authentic restaging of a massacre of the inhabitants of a peaceful Sioux village by the U.S. Cavalry. Moreover, as if Bill did not have enough problems, writer Ned Buntline (Burt Lancaster), whose dime novels were largely responsible for creating the myth of Buffalo Bill in the first place, shows up at the camp and refuses to leave when Bill, not wishing to be reminded of the origins of his myth, tries to get rid of him. Buntline plays a marginal but crucial role in the film, providing commentary that indicates the manufactured nature of Bill's celebrity and, by extension, American celebrity as whole. As he tells Bill when he finally agrees to leave, late in the film, "It was the thrill of my life to have invented you."

Finally, Bill agrees to let Sitting Bull participate in the show by simply riding his pony alone about the arena, assuming that such a no-frills performance will lead audiences to jeer and humiliate the proud chief. Instead, Sitting Bull's regal presence wins the day, and the crowd cheers him wildly, confounding Bill, who looks on. Sitting Bull then turns out to be prescient as well, as President Cleveland, in the midst of his wedding trip, arrives with his new bride and asks for a command performance of the show. The president is a pompous buffoon, however, with a tendency to spout empty platitudes of the kind favored by Buffalo Bill. Cleveland refuses even to hear Sitting Bull's request, declaring it impossible to fulfill even without knowing what it is.

Soon afterward, word comes that Sitting Bull has been found dead. (In reality, Sitting Bull was assassinated in 1890, several years after leaving the show.) That night, Bill sees a vision of the chief and tries to explain and justify himself to the apparition; clearly, there is a level at which Bill understands the complete inauthenticity of his image and everything it represents. Nevertheless, the show goes on; the next day, Bill adds a new routine in which he easily defeats Sitting Bull, now played by his former interpreter, William Halsey (Will Sampson), in hand-to-hand combat. The crowd cheers wildly at this allegorization of genocide, and the film ends with a close-up of Bill/Newman, with blue eyes shining and perfect teeth gleaming, a perfect vision of the hero as celebrity and the star as con man.

Buffalo Bill and the Indians was largely shunned by audiences and bashed by critics. Daniel O'Brien described the film as "a dull disappointment, a failed attempt to add a note of subversion to the patriotic celebrations of America's Bicentennial year" being a typical critical judgment (pp. 69–70). This negative reaction, however, was probably because of the way in which the film set itself so declaredly against the patriotic grain of the Bicentennial year, when Americans, reeling from the defeat in Vietnam and the revelations of

Watergate, were almost desperate for a remythologization of America and its past, a mood that was in direct contrast to the film's further demythologization.

This climate gave rise to several works of popular culture that responded precisely to this renewed longing for myth. Thus, the largely shunned *Buffalo Bill and the Indians* was therefore quickly followed in American film by such hugely successful mythic counterstrokes as *Star Wars* (1977) and *Superman: The Movie* (1978). These two films remain, respectively, the most mythic of all American science fiction and superhero films. They were also colossal box office hits, appealing greatly to the sensibilities of a late-1970s America that was hungry for a rousing, old-fashioned adventure in which good triumphed over evil—preferably with the aid of superhuman forces, whether they be the "Force" of *Star Wars* or Superman's solar-powered super abilities.

Both good and evil in these films are also defined in conventionally American ways. In both films, the emphasis is on the success of righteous and capable people in battling against evils that either arise from or are ineffectively resisted by institutional authority. *Star Wars* draws on numerous sources, from Joseph Campbell's writings on myth to the science fiction serials of the 1930s. Near-legendary for its groundbreaking special effects yet successful largely because of its ability to appeal to older, nostalgic longings in its audience, *Star Wars* represents the perfect all-American combination of science and magic, modernity and nostalgia. Of course, such combinations give rise to complexities of interpretation, and *Star Wars* can be seen as anything from a subversive celebration of rebellion against authority, to a fascistic declaration of the superiority of the elitist Jedi knights to the contaminated, inhuman (and part machine) forces of the Empire. Thus, seeing *Star Wars* as a key example of the dark side of the American fascination with mythic heroes, Jewett and Lawrence announce their view that the film "exemplifies the American monomyth's images of the innocent peaceful community that is corrupted by aggressive outsiders with appetites for pleasure and power. It also betrays a yearning for a time past, when life was simpler and politics was less important than issues of public well-being" (p. 274).

Much has been made of the mythic dimensions of *Star Wars*, although its simple good-versus-evil plot derives as much from classic Hollywood film as it does from any source in myth. This is not to say that the classic Hollywood film does not itself derive much of its energy from its ability to tap into the same sort of basic, archetypal images and motifs as myth. It does, however, emphasize the fact that *Star Wars* is an unabashed work of popular culture and that much of the film's success can be attributed to its unpretentious celebration of the kind of simple, straightforward oppositions that had given the pulp science fiction of the 1930s its innocent appeal. After the trying times of Vietnam and Watergate, American audiences were quite ready for a return to this innocence in their popular culture, eager for the kind of reassurance provided by simple verities and uncomplicated expressions of the ultimate power of good to defeat evil.

This same hunger on the part of American audiences led fairly soon after the release of *Star Wars* to the election of Ronald Reagan to the U.S. presidency. The Reagan message—with its call for a return to traditional values, its presentation of international politics as a simple opposition between good and evil, and its belief in the fundamental value of free enterprise—appealed to the same sort of desires as did *Star Wars*. The success of *Star Wars* announced a new desire for an optimistic message about the possibility of a better future, a message also delivered by the Reagan campaign and, later, the Reagan presidency. Indeed, the very language of the Reagan administration often closely echoed that of the film, as in the famous characterization of the Soviet Union as an "evil empire." Little wonder then that the most important attempt on the part of the Reagan administration to expand the technological capabilities of the United States to fight "evil" involved a proposal to develop a science fiction–like network of laser-based orbiting space weapons that came to be known as the "Star Wars" program. This label (first derisively attached to the program by Senator Edward Kennedy but later embraced by the Reagan administration) is no mere coincidence in terminology: There is evidence that Reagan's vision of the system (and most other things) was strongly influenced by Hollywood films, including *Star Wars* itself, but also going back to the 1940 film *Murder in the Air*, in which Reagan himself played a Secret Service agent who prevents a foreign spy from stealing the plans for a powerful new defensive weapon that could stop and destroy any attacking vehicle or missile.

The element of mysticism that underlies *Star Wars* also recalls the religiosity of the Reagan administration, although this connection is complicated by the fact that the religious and philosophical resonances of the Force that lies behind the Jedi Knights (more reminiscent of Japanese samurai than European medieval knights) are much more Buddhist and Taoist than Christian. It would, however, be a serious mistake to see *Star Wars* as a simple celebration of Eastern mysticism as opposed to Western materialism. Luke Skywalker, as the young prince coming of age and assuming his full capabilities and responsibilities, is a stock figure from Western fairy tales, just as Princess Leia (eventually revealed in *The Return of the Jedi* to be his sister) is essentially the stereotypical damsel in distress, although one with considerable resources of her own. Finally, Han Solo is a stock figure from American film, especially Westerns, in which individualist loners (usually played by actors such as John Wayne or Clint Eastwood) frequently become reluctant heroes when confronted by evil.

To a large extent, the opposition in *Star Wars* is couched not in terms of East versus West, but of human (the rebels) versus inhuman (the Empire). Emperor Palpatine, looking somewhat like the grim reaper with his darkly hooded cadaverous visage, seems anything but human. Darth Vader, the most prominent villain in the original three *Star Wars* films, has lost his humanity: As announced by the signature whooshing of his mechanical respirator, he is more machine than living being, most of his body having been replaced by mechanical parts. Even all those legions of Imperial Stormtroopers, who are presumably human, seem inhuman because of the armor they wear, making it more acceptable to have them serve in the film largely as cannon fodder.

This human-versus-inhuman structure represents an us-versus-them mentality that reinforces the good-versus-evil polarity of the film. It also makes the seemingly clear moral message of the film somewhat problematic, however, in that it tends to send an almost subliminal suggestion that those who are like us are good, whereas those who are unlike us are evil. For example, the Imperial Stormtroopers (who are slaughtered en masse in the film) seem to be human, but the film intentionally dehumanizes them in ways that seem to invite us to ignore the humanity of those whom we have identified as enemies. This same kind of thinking can also be seen in the representation of aliens in the film. As the famous cantina scene makes clear, the faraway galaxy in which *Star Wars* is set is populated by several intelligent alien species; however, these aliens appear to play a very marginal role in galactic politics, where humans (or former humans) remain the only major players. The very fact that the film's most memorable portrayal of aliens occurs in the cantina scene (where most of the alien patrons seem to be criminals or outcasts of one kind or another) could be very telling. Other aliens depicted in the film and its sequels (Jabba the Hut, the Sand People, the Jawas) tend to be criminals or outlaws as well. Whenever aliens are portrayed sympathetically (Chewbacca or the Ewoks of *Return of the Jedi*), it is with a substantial amount of condescension (they tend to resemble cuddly pets) that clearly marks them as subsidiary to humans.

Superman: The Movie (and its immediate 1980 sequel *Superman II*) were the first major superhero films, but they might also be considered part of the science fiction film boom ushered in by *Star Wars*. In his overt attempt to endow *Superman* with an epic feel (battling against the desire of producers Alexander and Ilya Salkind to cut the budget and to give the film a more comic, campy tone), director Richard Donner borrowed a great deal quite directly from *Star Wars*. At the same time, Donner was building on the long mythic legacy already established in American culture by the Superman character himself. As

I have noted elsewhere, there are numerous points of similarity between *Superman* and *Star Wars*, partly because the grand music of John Williams is used to enhance the epic feel of both films and because John Barry served as the production designer for both films.[5]

The idealized nature of the Superman character made him a virtual personification of the kind of dependable moral rectitude that American audiences longed for in the late 1970s, while his virtually unlimited power reminded audiences that nice guys need not finish last. Meanwhile, as with Luke Skywalker, Superman is very much a figure of the Chosen One, destined for greatness and fated to serve as a champion of good against evil, essentially as an accident of birth. There is, then, something profoundly conservative in these films. Jewett and Lawrence have noted the conservatism of superhero figures as whole, seeing them as secularized personifications of a hope for redemption through the intervention of supernatural agencies. Noting the essential Americanness of superheroes, they conclude that "only in a culture preoccupied for centuries with the question of salvation is the appearance of redemption through superheroes comprehensible" (p. 44).

The mythic resonances that inform the *Star Wars* film sequence have never quite been matched in American science fiction, although the *Star Trek* sequence of films and television series comes close, with its more secularized vision of a future world of better living through technology. Perhaps the closest we have to the texture of *Star Wars* is Andy and Larry Wachowski's sequence of *Matrix* films, including *The Matrix* (1999), *The Matrix Reloaded* (2003), and *The Matrix Revolutions* (2003). Here, the relatively conventional science fiction dystopian theme of a future world in which humans are enslaved by machines is supplemented by high-tech martial arts sequences and a mythic structure that presents its hero, Neo (Keanu Reaves), as an almost Christlike Chosen One, resurrected to bring salvation to a downtrodden humanity.

Similarly, although superhero films have become a huge box office phenomenon (and marvels of computer-generated film technology), none of them have quite achieved the mythic vibe that inhabits the first (and, to some extent, the second) *Superman* film. After the first two *Superman* films, that franchise itself descended into camp with *Superman III* (1983) and *Superman IV: The Quest for Peace* (1987), as if the cynical decade of the 1980s could simply no longer keep a straight face when confronted with a genuinely epic hero. Meanwhile, the next successful superhero films after the first two *Superman* films were Tim Burton's *Batman* (1989) and *Batman Returns* (1992). Batman, of course, had long served in American culture as a kind of counterpart to Superman. Not only is Batman more human (although bearing most of the accoutrements of the superhero, he in fact has no superpowers, strictly speaking), but he is also darker and more morally conflicted than the Man of Steel. Burton's films, set in a dark, dystopian Gotham City, create a noirish atmosphere that nicely captures Batman's personal darkness, while including enough campy elements to be good fun, winking at audiences in acknowledgment of the pulp sources of the films—a tendency that would unfortunately lead the next two *Batman* sequels down the road to campy silliness. Still, the two Burton-directed *Batman* films are striking in their ability to capture in visual style the dark side of a superhero who had already gained the appellation "the Dark Knight" in the comics. This designation was made especially prominent with Frank Miller's decidedly dark graphic novel *Batman: The Dark Knight Returns* (1986), which features an aging, cynical, and particularly vicious caped crusader. Miller's work was a clear influence on the original *Batman* film, as was Alan Moore's *Batman: The Killing Joke* (1988), especially in its impact on the depiction of the Joker in the film. These two works also exerted an imported influence on Christopher Nolan's stylish *The Dark Knight* (2008), now the highest-grossing superhero film of all time.

Such works as *The Dark Knight Returns* signaled a turn toward darker, grimmer, and more adult subject matter in the superhero comics of the following years. Indeed, comics themselves took a dark turn during this period, as evidenced by Miller's *Sin City* sequence of graphic novels, the protagonists of which often have superhuman abilities, accompanied by moral flaws that would disqualify them from being designated as superheroes in any normal sense. This turn in the comics world, and the darkness of the first two *Batman* films (and the silliness of the third and fourth films), can be taken as a marker of growing skepticism toward the idealized superhero figure like Superman. This skepticism can also be taken as growing doubt about the role of the United States as a force for good in the world. It might be telling that in the most commercially successful Superman narrative of the 1990s, television's *Lois & Clark: The New Adventures of Superman* (which ran for four seasons on the ABC network, beginning in 1993), Superman is both more humanized (owing to the emphasis on Clark Kent's personal relationship with Lois Lane) and less an allegorical figure of American virtue. This change is signaled by the fact that he now identifies his mission as the defense of "truth and justice," dropping the traditional third term, "the American way."

Still, the success of the first two *Batman* films, along with rapid increases in computer animation technologies, opened the way for a whole new wave of superhero films by the end of the twentieth century, with the *Spider-Man* sequence leading the way in terms of box-office success. It is important that Spider-Man is a much more human figure than Superman. For one thing, he is human rather than an alien from another planet. Furthermore, not only are his powers far more limited than those of Superman, but they were acquired by sheer accident rather than fated by birth. He is also younger and less mature than the classic Superman character, simultaneously dealing with the responsibilities of having superpowers and the normal problems of adolescence. If Batman has more in common with the antiheroes of hard-boiled detective fiction and film noir than with the mythic and Christlike Superman, Spider-Man (however heroic he might be) is a decidedly democratized figure. Far from standing apart from humanity as a conventional Chosen One, in many ways he has less in common with Superman than with the youthful audiences who have flocked to see the three films based on his character, released over the period from 2002 to 2007.[6]

Superheroes of the 1990s were often even antiheroes, or at least far more complex than the morally unambiguous Superman, for example, such comic book (and later film) heroes as Mike Mignola's Hellboy or the X-Men's Wolverine. The 1990s, however prosperous they might have been, saw a great deal of redefinition of the American hero. Figures such as the nerd (now turned dynamic Internet entrepreneur) became a new sort of hero: In addition, conventional hero figures were harder and harder to find in the real world. Warfare became more and more high tech and remote controlled during this era. The 1991 Gulf War (the biggest American military conflict of the decade) was thus a war essentially without heroes—unless one counts figures such as General Norman Schwartzkopf, who gained a certain media-generated fame for his efficient management of the war but came nowhere near actual combat. Indeed, the real "heroes" of the Gulf War were media figures such as CNN's Peter Arnett, who became stars amid a round-the-clock media blitz that turned the war into a live television miniseries. It is also probably crucial that Bill Clinton served as the American President during most of this decade. Although a "poor boy made good" and thus ripe material for Capraesque heroization as a man of the people (and arguably one of the most effective presidents of the twentieth century), Clinton never achieved the kind of respect commanded by most previous presidents. Instead, he became known more for his minor (and somewhat adolescent) sexual dalliances than for balancing the budget or overseeing one of the greatest periods of economic prosperity in American history. Far from being a godlike (or even fatherly) figure, Clinton was dubbed the first rock 'n' roll President,[7] even starring in his own VH-1 documentary of that title.

Of course, just as the demise of conventional idealized heroism in the 1930s led to the opposed rise of superheroes, the diminished aura of the American Presidency in the 1990s led to several popular representations of idealized figures who might be termed "superpresidents." Whereas many representations of the presidency in popular culture reflected the new down-to-earth status of the office (Ivan Reitman's 1993 comedy *Dave* is a typical example), other representations produced idealized presidents, from the Kennedyesque Josiah Bartlet of television's *The West Wing* (NBC, 1999–2006), to the action-hero presidents of such films as Roland Emmerich's *Independence Day* (1996) and Wolfgang Petersen's *Air Force One* (1997).

Independence Day is particularly interesting for my purposes because it is a film that in fact rehearses an entire range of modern hero roles, as various protagonists mobilize to defend the earth from the threat of an invasion by aliens bent on the destruction of the human race. For example, Jeff Goldblum plays electronics wizard David Levinson, a version of the new-style computer-geek-as-hero; Will Smith plays a key role as fighter pilot Steven Hiller, a more conventional action-style hero; and First Lady Marilyn Whitmore (Mary McDonnell) even gets to have her heroic moments. That these three hero figures are, respectively, Jewish, African American, and female is surely no accident, but part of an intentional strategy. The most heroic role of all is reserved for a middle-class white male, American president Thomas J. Whitmore (Bill Pullman). Unlike the draft-avoiding Clinton (and later George W. Bush), Whitmore is a former war hero who had served as a fighter pilot in the Gulf War—a fact that itself represents the fantasy that there *were* prominent heroes in that war. Especially in the latter part of the film, President Whitmore's rhetoric of defiance strongly anticipates the "bring-it-on" rhetoric of the second Bush administration's "war" on terrorism. Moreover, the film essentially endorses this rhetoric (justified by the evil and nonhuman nature of the foes against whom it is aimed), depicting Whitmore's turn from compromising politician to staunch military commander as a decidedly positive development that makes Whitmore the kind of strong leader that many Americans want. Whitmore—a young, handsome, charismatic former war hero—is a President much more in the mold of John Kennedy than of either Clinton or Bush. In terms of the film's function as reinscription of the old national narrative of the United States as a staunch defender of right in a savage war against evil foes, one might also consider Whitmore a kind of fantasy President. Not only does he provide strong and dramatic leadership in a terrible national crisis, but he is also depicted (in contrast to the popular perception of politicians in the 1990s) as a figure of absolute virtue, a dedicated family man who is, we are reminded at least twice in the film, virtually incapable of telling a lie. From this point of view, it is even possible to see his initial tendency toward political compromise as a virtue, his shift to a more hawkish attitude in the wake of the alien attacks simply indicating how he is able to change his leadership style to match the situation at hand.

Whitmore, it should be noted, is able to provide strong leadership not only for the United States but for the world. After he gives the go-ahead for Levinson's far-fetched (but ultimately successful, of course) plan to lower the alien shields by means of a computer virus, Whitmore has no trouble at all in eliciting the complete cooperation of military forces around the globe, even with the global communications system on the fritz. In fact, he seems able to give instructions directly to troops in the field, even without going through their governments. The American government is, in fact, the only one that we see in the film, making it the de facto government of the world. Much of the value of this film as an Americanist fantasy therefore comes from its vision of the United States as the unquestioned leader of the entire world, able to make policies that all other nations will follow without question or resentment. Rightly so, because—in this film at least—American leadership saves the day, thanks to the all-American combination of Levinson's geeky intellect, Hiller's smart-aleck valiance, and Whitmore's noble decisiveness.

The immediate response of military forces around the world to Whitmore's call to action is not very realistic even in such a crisis, but then *Independence Day* is not a film that is much concerned with realism. This is a film designed to entertain with spectacular action and touching moments of human emotional contact; as such, it is not designed to stand up to much thoughtful scrutiny. Nevertheless, there is one fascinating element of the film that should be closely analyzed, and that is the contradictory nature of its self-conscious effort to serve as an American national allegory. The Americans of the film are completely outgunned, faced with a foe far superior to them in firepower and technological know-how. As such, the film is perfectly in keeping with what is widely regarded as a typical American tendency to root for the underdog—despite the fact that, in the real world of geopolitics, the United States is not an underdog but the most powerful nation on the planet. Little wonder then that to produce its idealized fantasy visions, *Independence Day* has to go outside the real world and introduce evil foes from outer space—just as the search for pop cultural heroes in the 1990s often pointed toward superheroes, rather than conventional human heroes, even if the superheroes of the decade tended to become darker, grittier, and more fallible than prototypical superheroes such as Superman.

HARD-BOILED MAGIC: THE VAMPIRE DETECTIVE

The hard-boiled detectives of novelists such as Dashiell Hammett and Raymond Chandler and (to a lesser extent) the troubled and tortured protagonists of the novels of James M. Cain and Jim Thompson (and of film noir) are in many ways the signature heroes of modern American culture. Sometimes tough, sometimes achingly vulnerable, they are always fundamentally alone and aloof from society (whether by choice or not), yet they often devote themselves to defending that society from internal and external threats and to upholding a code of honor, even if their own particular codes (and definitions of right and wrong) are not always well aligned with the mainstream values of the society they are defending. As a result of this misalignment, they are often rejected, even despised, by those they defend and protect, driving them even further into isolation: Their good deeds, far from winning them an entry into the bosom of society, make them more outsiders than ever.

There is, of course, something fundamentally modern, even fundamentally capitalist about this sort of alienated individualist hero (or antihero), who serves as a sort of allegorical stand-in for the typical modern capitalist subject, or at least the modern *masculine* capitalist subject, given that they are almost always male and that women typical serve more as obstacles and threats to their heroic projects than as heroes, or even sidekicks. There is also something typically American about this sort of hero, and in a way that predates the emergence of the United States as the paradigm of capitalist modernization in the early twentieth century. In particular, they have much in common with the frontier heroes of nineteenth-century America, both in the loneliness with which they pursue their tasks and in the way their struggles seem almost designed to separate them from society rather than to make them a part of it.

Hard-boiled protagonists such as Sam Spade and Philip Marlowe also have much in common with vampires. It is certainly clear that hard-boiled detective fiction, film noir, and much horror occupy atmospherically similar worlds. For example, both hard-boiled detectives and vampires inhabit a world mostly of night, living on the margins of a society that does not understand or accept their eccentric natures. Both tend doggedly to pursue their own particular projects, however much those projects might estrange them from the mainstream. Indeed, "good" vampires have a great deal in common with hard-boiled detectives as alienated figures operating on the margins of society, so the phenomenon of the vampire detective is a natural fit, especially given the tendency toward postmodern genre mixing in recent American culture. Meanwhile, as Foster Hirsch notes, "fragments of noir have always appeared in the horror film" (*Detours*, p. 307). It seems inevitable, therefore, that vampires and noir characters would occasionally encounter each other in the same film, as they do in Robert Rodriguez's *From Dusk Till Dawn* (1996), scripted by Quentin Tarantino. Here, runaway criminals wind up in a vampire bar in Mexico, with spectacularly bloody results. There are other films in which detectives track supernatural or satanic criminals, as in Alan Parker's *Angel Heart* (1987) and Gregory Hoblit's *Fallen* (1998).

It is one thing to have detectives or criminals battle against vampires. It is quite another to make the vampires themselves the protagonists who fight against evil, especially as, with the figure of Bram Stoker's Dracula looming over the genre of vampire fiction, vampires had, through most of the twentieth century, functioned principally as figures of pure malice (often in league with Satan), bereft of the sympathy granted such pop cultural icons as Frankenstein's monster or King Kong. To make matters worse, vampires are smart; they know very well what they are doing and therefore cannot claim the innocence of King Kong or the monster from the Frankenstein movies, nor can they claim the mindlessness of the zombie, which would, by the end of the twentieth century, join the vampire as paired icons of capitalist monstrosity.[8]

This very status, as the most rejected and despised of all sentient monsters, would seem to make the vampire an almost inevitable candidate for outsider heroism. After all, what if one were somehow a "good" vampire, yet remained despised because of society's racial (if you will) prejudice against vampires in general? It should come as no surprise, then, that by the late twentieth century, vampires came more and more to be represented in American popular culture as at least partly sympathetic figures. The extremely popular "Vampire Chronicles" of Anne Rice—which began with *Interview with the Vampire* (1976)—are perhaps the central marker in this trend toward more complex characterization of vampires.[9] This novel was later adapted reasonably successfully to film by Neil Jordan in 1994; however, *Queen of the Damned* (2002), a film adaptation of the second and third novels in Rice's ten-novel sequence, was not well received. Indeed, sympathetic vampires have not generally fared well on the big screen: The most successful has probably been the protagonist of the *Blade* films, but he is half human and spends most of his time battling—in action-hero mode—against vampires (and the vampire side of his own nature).

Rice's lonely Lestat, despite his sophistication and French origins, is described as speaking English in a mode reminiscent of Sam Spade, although he is not, strictly speaking, a detective. The first full-blown representation of a vampire detective in popular culture was probably the 1989 CBS television movie *Nick Knight*, starring Rick Springfield as a vampire police detective. This one-shot film then provided the inspiration for a German-Canadian-American follow-up series entitled *Forever Knight*, which features Nicholas de Brabant (Geraint Wyn Davies) as an 800-year-old vampire who lives in modern-day Toronto, where he works as a police detective (under the name Nicholas Knight) as an attempt to make up for the sins of his early vampire days, when he killed and fed on humans. He is also engaged in a project, aided by police medical examiner Dr. Natalie Lambert (Catherine Disher), to restore himself to the humanity he lost when he "crossed over" to become a vampire back in the year 1228. This sense of vampirism as an affliction that its sufferers hope to overcome is quite typical of the vampire narratives of the 1990s, which tend (in keeping with the popular anxieties of the day, especially concerning AIDS) to treat vampirism as a sort of disease. Conversely, if "good" vampires are figures of the radical alienation felt by people in the era of late capitalism, then the loss of humanity suffered by vampires becomes a marker of the dehumanization suffered by people as a result of the psychic consequences of life within the unstable context of late capitalism.

Knight, it turns out, was sired (i.e., turned into a vampire) by vampire master Lucien de Lacroix (Nigel Bennett), with whom he still carries on an ongoing battle in the present day, a battle that mirrors his own interior struggles between his human and vampire sides. These struggles are also central to the competing attractions he feels for Natalie and for seductive vampire Janette du Charme (Deborah du Chêne), also sired by Lacroix back in the thirteenth century. Indeed, much of the energy of the show comes from its ability to capitalize on the note of sexuality that has often informed vampire myths, in this case including even hints of a sort of homoerotic attraction between Knight and Lacroix.

For the most part, *Forever Knight* takes its mythology seriously, including supplying a long and complex historical background for the characters, going all the way back to the Roman Empire. There are, however, moments of comic relief, especially those provided in the first two seasons by Knight's partner in the Toronto police, Detective Donald Schanke (John Kapelos). Schanke (pronounced "Skanky") is a crude and obnoxious (but oddly lovable) boor, constantly confused and surprised by Knight's seemingly strange behavior, never catching on to the fact that his partner is a vampire. Typical of his role in the show is a first-season sequence in which he takes Knight's seemingly abandoned 1962 Cadillac Coupe de Ville convertible out for a spin, reliving adolescent experiences in such a car but not realizing that Knight is hiding out in the trunk, which he habitually uses as a refuge from sunlight (which, in this series, as in most vampire narratives, is deadly to vampires). To make matters worse, a murderous villain has cut the brake line, causing Schanke to crash Knight's beloved car.

Forever Knight never garnered a large audience, running mostly in marginal venues such as CBS's *Crimetime after Primetime* late-night lineup, where it ran for a summer before going into syndication. It has also been rerun on the Sci Fi channel and is currently available on DVD, maintaining an ongoing presence to the delight of its small but loyal fan base, which has helped to turn the series into a cult hit. The motifs at work in *Forever Knight* have also maintained a presence in American popular culture, most directly in the recent Canadian-produced series *Blood Ties*, which began running in the United States on the Lifetime cable channel in March 2007. The twist here, however, is that the detective protagonist is a woman, Victoria Nelson (Christina Cox), a former police detective who left the force because of her failing eyesight but somehow still manages to function quite nicely as a private eye. Nelson (also the protagonist of the sequence of novels by Tanya Huff on which *Blood Ties* is based) is herself a highly interesting character, a tough, strong, independent woman who joins the list of female heroes appearing in American popular culture in the past two decades. The series owes much of its character, however, to the fact that Nelson is aided in her work (which typically involves thwarting supernatural criminals) by vampire Henry Fitzroy (Kyle Schmid), the son, no less, of England's notorious King Henry VIII. Fitzroy is a typical misunderstood vampire protagonist, lurking on the edges of polite society and doing what he can to keep a low profile and to help Nelson fight evil, meanwhile working as a graphic novelist and thus simultaneously exercising his twin passions for art and literature.

Of the various television series featuring vampire detectives, easily the most successful (both commercially and aesthetically) so far has been the *Buffy* spinoff, *Angel*. This series features a title character (played by David Boreanaz) who is a vampire but who (as a result of a gypsy curse) has a soul and is able to feel guilt for the horrible crimes of his vampire past. As an eighteenth-century vampire called Angelus, he had been among the most brutal and bloodthirsty of all vampires. Now, driven by painful memories of his various victims, he seeks to fight evil (and to "help the helpless") wherever he can, although he knows that he cannot possibly do enough good deeds to make up for his bad ones. He thus remains a tormented soul—and must in fact remain that way thanks to the curse. To add still another twist to Angel's existential angst, the curse stipulates that if he ever experiences even a moment of complete happiness, he will revert to his former evil self. This is something that happened to him during the second season of *Buffy*, after he experienced a moment of sexual bliss with Buffy herself—although he managed to be resurrected as a "good" vampire in Season Three. Angel eventually leaves Sunnydale for Los Angeles to seek redemption—and (for the safety of all concerned) to get away from Buffy, for whom he still feels a powerful attraction.

Airing for five seasons on the WB (from October 1999 to May 2004), *Angel* in its original run overlapped *Buffy*, which ran from 1997 until May 2003. At times, *Angel* drew larger audiences than its parent series, although it also tended to attract slightly older audiences, owing to its darker tone and more mature characters and subject matter.[10] Nevertheless, the family resemblance between *Buffy* and *Angel* remains strong: The two series employed much the same creative team, producing the same mixture of supernatural darkness and hip, postmodern humor, sprinkled liberally with references to contemporary popular culture. Angel himself, however, as an eighteenth-century man, is decidedly unhip, and the series gets considerable comic mileage out of his inability to dress fashionably, dance the latest dances, talk the latest lingo, or generally be cool—which, by the late 1990s, was of course itself a version of *being* cool, especially if one is also tall, handsome, and heroic.

In addition to Angel himself, Cordelia Chase and Wesley Wyndam-Pryce (Alexis Denisof), both characters from *Buffy*, are major characters in *Angel*, working for the private detective agency that the vampire establishes in Los Angeles. *Angel* also features occasional (and sometimes extended) visits from several other *Buffy* characters, including two appearances by Buffy herself (although only one with Sarah Michelle Gellar in the role). The vampire Spike (who eventually succeeded Angel as Buffy's vampire lover) becomes a major presence in the latter part of *Angel*, although Willow, the troubled slayer Faith, and the vampires Drusilla and (especially) Darla are important characters as well. Among other things, the extensive intertextual links between *Buffy* and *Angel* add a sort of substance to both series, making the imaginary worlds in which they take place seem more real, while enhancing audience identification with the characters. As with *Buffy*, the characters and their interrelationships are the key to the success of *Angel*, which in fact goes beyond its parent series in presenting genuinely poignant, sometimes tragic human drama—even though its central character is not, strictly speaking, human. In the early first-season episode "I Will Remember You" (November 23, 1999), for example, Buffy comes to Los Angeles to visit Angel, triggering a series of events that find the vampire restored to full humanity and thus able to experience true happiness with his beloved Buffy. Realizing, however, that the loss of his superhuman vampire powers will render him unable to protect Buffy and others from evil, Angel elects to become a vampire again, although this sacrifice means that he must forgo happiness forever.

Angel also establishes extensive intertextual links with film noir (in both its look and content) and the hard-boiled detective tradition, echoing many familiar motifs in its portrayal of Angel as a private detective. In the early episodes of the first season, Angel establishes his detective agency and hires as his staff Cordelia Chase and Allen Francis Doyle (Glenn Quinn), an Irish human-demon hybrid, who experiences visions sent to him by the supernatural entities known as the Powers That Be. These visions, although sometimes quite cryptic, signal to Angel where his help is needed. In the episode "Hero" (November 30, 1999), Doyle, who has lived a checkered life as a con man and lovable rogue, eventually heroically sacrifices himself to save Angel and help defeat a gang of racist, Nazi-like demons bent on the destruction of all human-demon hybrids.. Before dying, however, Doyle passes his powers on to Cordelia, who subsequently experiences the visions that instigate many of Angel's cases.

The first season is largely episodic, with Angel saving a different helpless soul each week and the primary continuity provided by the growth of the characters and their relationships. For example, the formerly spoiled and self-centered Cordelia grows stronger and braver now that she is on her own, becoming a more and more useful member of Angel's team. After the death of Doyle, this team is joined by Wyndam-Pryce, who, having been fired as a Watcher, has now declared himself a "rogue demon hunter." The bumbling Wyndam-Pryce is initially used largely for comic relief, although he occasionally shows himself capable of genuine heroism. He too gradually gains strength and confidence (and ultimately develops a dark side), although he and Cordelia (who had enjoyed a brief romantic link in *Buffy*) continue to snipe at and be jealous of one another. Angel also develops a somewhat strained relationship with LAPD detective Kate Lockley (Elisabeth Röhm), echoing the traditionally strained relations between hard-boiled private detectives and the police, although here with hints of a potential romantic attachment (which never quite pans out) as well.

The second season turns to a more continuous plot, much of which centers around Darla, who had been Angel's sire (the vampire who initially turned him into a vampire) back in the eighteenth century, subsequently becoming his lover and partner in a program of mayhem and murder that lasted for the next century and a half, until the curse transformed Angelus into Angel. Meanwhile, the ongoing battle between Angel Investigations and the evil law firm of Wolfram and Hart (which specializes in supernatural matters—and presents the series with the opportunity for an unending stream of lawyer jokes) becomes much more central to the series in this season. Indeed, the law firm resurrects Darla as part of their complex plot to conscript Angel for use in their own dark purposes, which might include triggering the Apocalypse. The Angel-Darla plot line adds resonance to the depiction of Angel as a tragic hero, while the series itself gains extra dimensions through the addition to the Angel Investigations team of Charles Gunn (J. August Richards), a young black man who has devoted himself to defending the denizens of the mean streets of Los Angeles from vampires and other supernatural threats.

The episode "Epiphany" (February 27, 2001) brings the Angel-Darla relationship to a climax (literally), while addressing the question of religious faith in a particularly direct way. In this episode, Angel has had a sexual encounter with Darla but has emerged with his soul intact, the experience having been empty and meaningless. He then has an epiphany and concludes that life as a whole is, in fact, meaningless. Near the end of the episode, he shares his new existentialist view of life with Kate: "In the greater scheme, or the big picture, nothing we do matters. There's no grand plan, no big win. If there's no great, glorious end to all this, if nothing we do matters, then all that matters is what we do. 'Cause that's all there is. What we do now. Today." For Angel, however, the very meaninglessness of life makes it all the more important to continue his fight to help the helpless and right the wrongs of the world. As he tells Kate, "I want to help because I don't think people should suffer as they do. Because if there is no bigger meaning, then even the smallest act of kindness is the greatest thing in the world."

Conversely, Kate seems to have experienced an (opposite) epiphany of her own, triggered by a brush with death caused by an apparent suicide attempt. Angel saves her from this, bursting into her apartment in the nick of time. As a vampire, Angel is supposedly unable to enter the dwelling of any human unless is invited to do so, and he had never been invited to enter Kate's apartment. The fact that he could enter anyway, narrowly averting her death, has caused her to conclude that a higher power was at work. "I have faith," she tells Angel. "I think maybe we're not alone in this."

The last several episodes of the second season veer off in a new direction, in a multiepisode plot arc in which Cordelia is spirited away into the demon dimension of Pylea, and the rest of the team goes there to try to rescue her. The solidarity shown by the team in the rescue attempt caps off what is the hallmark of the second season—the evolving personal relationships among the various characters. These last few episodes also bring new prominence to an additional character, Lorne (Andy Hallett), a benevolent demon nightclub owner who often assists the team. Lorne (full name Krevlornswath of the Deathwok Clan) is a native of Pylea and thus particularly helpful in the rescue. Cordelia is indeed safely returned to our dimension, along with Winifred "Fred" Burkle (Amy Acker), a beautiful young human physicist who had also been trapped in Pylea for five years.

In Season Three, Fred becomes a member of the Angel Investigations team, which evolves more and more into an unconventional sort of family, held together by bonds of genuine caring that provide the heart and soul of the series. Meanwhile, the family motif becomes even more direct in the middle of the season, with Darla giving birth to Angel's child (nobly sacrificing her own life so that the child can live), despite the fact that vampires are not supposed to be able to reproduce. Angel becomes a doting father to the baby boy, whom he names Connor and who seems fully human. Unfortunately, a vengeful time-traveling vampire hunter (whose family Angelus had killed back in the eighteenth century) kidnaps Connor, aided by Wesley, who thinks he is helping the boy. Connor is then whisked away into the hellish demon dimension of Quor-Toth, unreachable by any magic Angel is able to summon. Connor returns after only a few weeks of our time, now a teenager with formidable fighting abilities and superhuman strength, agility, and toughness. He is also determined to kill Angel, whom he has been taught to hate while in Quor-Toth. Connor ends the season by imprisoning Angel in a steel coffin and dropping him to the bottom of the ocean, where he presumably will live in eternal torment. At the same time, Cordelia has impressed the Powers That Be so much that they help her to ascend to a higher plane of existence, leaving the material realm altogether.

Not surprisingly, both Angel and Cordelia quickly return at the beginning of Season Four, while Wesley, cast out for helping to kidnap Connor, gradually rejoins the group as well. The series does evolve in important new directions in this season, however, moving well away from its initial focus on Angel himself as a sort of revamped film noir hero and moving into much bigger and more supernatural themes. In particular, it puts more and more emphasis on the possibility of an impending Apocalypse (even as *Buffy*, then in its seventh and last season, was simultaneously moving in a similar direction). The plot of *Angel* in the fourth season is particularly complex but also more continuous than in previous seasons, as numerous events (at first seemingly unrelated) gradually combine to build toward the birth of a mighty superhuman entity, known as Jasmine (Gina Torres), who uses her godlike powers to mesmerize the entire population of Los Angeles (and gradually beyond), leaving only Angel, Fred, Wesley, Gunn, and Lorne to try to mount a resistance to her all-encompassing power. All other potential enemies of Jasmine (including the Los Angeles branch of Wolfram and Hart) are destroyed. Cordelia, who had given birth to Jasmine so that she could take human form, lies ill in bed. Connor, the father of Jasmine's human manifestation, becomes one of Jasmine's most important henchmen. Jasmine uses her power to establish a tranquil, seemingly utopian society, the downside of which is that her subjects have sacrificed much of their free will to live in peace and prosperity—and the fact that Jasmine must maintain herself by literally devouring several humans a day.

Eventually, Angel is able to break Jasmine's spell over the general population, and Jasmine is killed by Connor. Human society returns to normal, although Cordelia lies in a coma. Connor, realizing that his "miraculous" birth and all of the other subsequent events of his life had been brought about simply as part of the plan to give Jasmine power over humanity, feels particularly cursed, lost, and confused. As a reward for stopping Jasmine's reign of peace on earth, the Senior Partners of Wolfram and Hart want to make Angel the head of their now-restored Los Angeles office and give him its full resources (which are considerable) to do with as he will.

Angel and the others, who initially spurn this offer as a Faustian deal, find that they are ultimately unable to refuse the chance to gain such resources to use in their battle to fight evil and help the helpless. This development sends the series into a whole new direction in the fifth season, although it also raises an important question. Are Angel and his team ostensibly being rewarded for striking a blow in favor of evil by destroying Jasmine and thus restoring humanity to its former state of corruption, violence, and poverty? Did they really do the right thing? This question is complicated still further in the fifth season, as the various characters come to grips with their lives as officials of Wolfram and Hart, trying to use the resources of the evil firm to do good but finding that they now live in a much more complex world that requires finesse, strategy, and compromise, as opposed to their relatively simple former life of finding and fighting evil. Actually, most of the characters adjust to their new positions rather well, including Gunn, who undergoes a procedure to make him a sort of super-lawyer, with unmatched knowledge of both human and demon law. Fred becomes the head of the well-equipped research department of the newly constituted firm, while Lorne becomes head of the Entertainment Division. Wesley becomes the firm's official expert on occult matters, taking advantage of their incredible database of information. Only Angel feels completely out of place as CEO of the new firm, a situation not aided by the fact that the untrustworthy vampire Harmony (Mercedes McNab), another character from *Buffy*, resurfaces as Angel's secretary (although she prefers to be called a personal assistant, of course).

The cast of characters is further augmented during this season when none other than Spike (James Marsters), apparently obliterated at the end of *Buffy*'s final episode the previous season, shows up at Wolfram and Hart. Initially, however, he is only an incorporeal spirit. Much of the action of the early episodes centers on the (ultimately successful) attempts of Fred and her scientific team to make Spike corporeal again before he fades away forever. Spike is a lively addition to the series, although he never quite achieves the poignancy of his appearance in *Buffy*, in which his gradual evolution into a "good" vampire was both difficult and complex, made more so by the continuing suspicion with which he was viewed by Buffy and the Scoobies. Perhaps the most poignant moments of the fifth season of *Angel* have to do with the death of

Fred when her body is occupied by an ancient demon known as Illyria; Fred's death is then followed by that of Wesley—with Illyria, changing her form into a simulacrum of Wesley's beloved Fred, at his side.

The darkness of Season Five is alleviated by occasional comic moments, however. Indeed, the punctuation of dark events with moments of comedy (and the insertion of wacky dialogue into even the darkest and most serious of conversations) remains a hallmark of the series. The largely comic episode "Harm's Way" (April 28, 2004) begins with a hilarious corporate promotional video in which a cheerful narrator extols the virtues of the new Wolfram and Hart. Among other things, we are told, the Los Angeles firm has "put down roots in this glamorous city that grow deep, and branches that reach right into the heart of every major corporation, including Yoyodyne, Weyland-Yutani, and Newscorp." *Yoyodyne* is the name of a fictional defense contractor introduced in Thomas Pynchon's novel *V.* (1963), as well the name of an evil corporation in the spoofy science fiction film *The Adventures of Buckaroo Banzai across the Eighth Dimension* (1984). Weyland-Yutani, of course, is the evil corporation featured in the first three films in the *Alien* franchise, though it is missing from the fourth film because (we learn in the extended director's cut of that film) it has been taken over by Wal-Mart. This satirical slap at the Wal-Mart corporation (which is apparently even more ruthless and voracious than Weyland-Yutani, a suggestion that fits Wal-Mart's real-world reputation), is very much in the same spirit as *Angel's* inclusion of the famously right-wing real-world media conglomerate Newscorp in the list of corporations under the influence of Wolfram and Hart.

Angel reaches its conclusion in "Not Fade Away" (May 19, 2004), an episode rife with double meanings as Angel and his team prepare for one last battle, living the day leading to it as if it will be their last. Having discovered that a group known as the Circle of the Black Thorn represents the Senior Partners on this level of reality, Angel conceives a plan to kill every member of the Circle in one last flourish, just to send the message that, although it might not be possible to defeat the Senior Partners, it is still possible to resist their power. Angel wants to demonstrate that humans (and a few vampires and demons) will never give in, no matter how hopeless the battle against evil. He thus hopes to win a sort of poetic victory, even though he expects to be killed with his entire team. As the episode ends, the Circle has been destroyed, but all of the humans on Angel's team have been killed or mortally wounded, whereas Angel, Spike, and Illyria begin what seems a hopeless battle against an army of demons and dragons sent for them by the Senior Partners, enraged by Angel's defiance of them. The Apocalypse, apparently, has begun at last—although it is actually only the series, not the world, that ends as the last episode blinks out *in medias res*—just as the series itself was cancelled by the WB even as Joss Whedon and his creative team thought that it was still going strong.

What makes us human, this finale seems to say, is the ongoing fight against evil in all its forms. If this message is taken metaphorically, it can be seen as a progressive political statement about the importance of the ongoing fight for social and economic justice, despite the seeming difficulty in surmounting all of the injustices in the world. Angel himself, figured throughout the series as a champion whose curse makes him a sort of Chosen One, becomes seemingly even more heroic in his willingness to undertake the battle, despite the fact that it will almost certainly lead to his death. Conversely, there is something troubling and unsatisfying about the implication in this last episode that evil can never be defeated and that those who try will always be destroyed—an implication that goes along rather too nicely with the message conveyed so carefully in so much contemporary popular culture that capitalism can never be defeated, so that it is foolhardy to try.

Other more recent television series have also explored the motif of the vampire detective, although so far with only limited success. *Moonlight* (which began airing in the fall 2007 season on CBS) is the latest entry in this subgenre. Created by Trevor Munson and *Beauty and the Beast* creator Ron Koslow, *Moonlight* initially had a direct link to *Angel*, in that *Angel* co-creator David Greenwalt was slated to be the showrunner of the new series. However, Greenwalt withdrew from the project for personal and health reasons before the pilot was shot, and Chip Johannessen took over as show runner. *Moonlight* resembles *Angel* in many ways, primarily in that its central character, Mick St. John (Alex O'Loughlin) is a Los Angeles detective who uses his superhuman abilities as a "good" vampire to help those in need. The character of St. John is otherwise very different from that of Angel, however. Although certainly troubled by his vampire status—which he acquired when his new wife Coraline (Shannyn Sossamon), whom he had not known as a vampire, bit him on their wedding night—St. John is nevertheless much less tormented than is Angel. Sophisticated and suave, St. John is also much more hip and in touch with the times than the hunky-but-nerdy Angel, dressing well and living in an ultrachic apartment. He works largely alone rather than heading a team as does Angel, although he does have at least one close vampire friend and mentor in Josef Konstantin (Jason Dohring), a roguish but likable centuries-old vampire who lacks St. John's determination not to use his powers to harm humans.

As is usually the case in vampire lore, the vampires of *Moonlight* are essentially immortal, although they must drink blood to sustain themselves. St. John seldom feeds on humans (and then only in emergencies or other special circumstances), preferring to feed on blood acquired from sources such as the morgue and blood banks. He and the other vampires of this series find sunlight extremely unpleasant and uncomfortable but can go out in it for limited amounts of time without suffering serious damage. In another change from typical vampire mythology, a stake to the heart only paralyzes the vampires of *Moonlight*, who can be killed only by fire. The vampires of the series are driven by biology and not by any sort of supernatural evil, although many turn to crime because of their need for blood and because of their marginal status within human society. Others, however, maintain seemingly normal lives as respectable professionals, meanwhile living in an extensive secret subculture within the human culture of Los Angeles.

Moonlight treats vampire mythology almost entirely seriously, and the series lacks the campy and humorous touches that helped to make *Buffy* and *Angel* successful. Instead, it depends on the normal action and suspense of a crime drama, with St. John battling primarily against human criminals. As a result, much of the action and suspense of the series has very little to do with the fact that St. John is a vampire, although he does occasionally cross swords with rogue vampires or other superhuman foes. Following the precedent set by *The X-Files* (among others), *Moonlight* also seeks to generate interest through the sexual/romantic tension that exists between St. John and journalist Beth Turner (Sophia Myles), a reporter for an Internet television news site. Turner, who is romantically linked with Los Angeles assistant district attorney Josh Lindsey (Jordan Belfi), discovers very early on in the series that St. John is a vampire but agrees to keep his secret, despite her professional urge to get the scoop on the hidden vampire culture of Los Angeles. In the fourth episode, "Fever" (October 20, 2007), Turner even insists that St. John feed on her blood (sucked from her wrist, not her neck), so that he can recover his strength after nearly being destroyed by a walk through the desert sun in an effort to save a young pregnant woman from gangsters. This feeding establishes an important bond between St. John and Turner, just as a similar feeding connected Victoria Nelson and Henry Fitzroy in the first episode of *Blood Ties*, which aired seven months earlier.[11] Indeed, the sexual chemistry between St. John and Turner runs high, although her relationship with Lindsey initially keeps them apart, establishing an ongoing tension in some ways reminiscent of that in the popular 1980s television (detective) series *Moonlighting*. Indeed, the title *Moonlight* is so similar to that of *Moonlighting* that one suspects an intentional reference, despite the otherwise vast differences between the series.

In the episode "Love Lasts Forever" (January 11, 2008), Lindsey is kidnapped by drug dealers, then shot as St. John attempts to rescue him. The prosecutor then dies in Turner's arms after St. John (himself now heavily involved in an effort to restore his own humanity) refuses to turn Lindsey into a vampire to allow him to continue life in that mode. This refusal causes considerable tension between St. John and Turner, although of course it opens the way for them to be together, a situation complicated by the reappearance of Coraline in St. John's life. Coraline's reemergence also brings with it fresh information about vampire lore. Coraline had been a member of the inner circle of King Louis XVI of France, and the king was himself a vampire. The French Revolution therefore was largely an attempt to rid France of vampire rule, and the frequent beheadings of the Reign of Terror occurred because that was one of the few methods to kill a vampire.

Coraline also seems to have discovered a "cure" for vampirism, information that eventually leads to the success of St. John's long effort to regain his humanity as well. Following directly in the footsteps of Angel, however, he intentionally resumes his vampire status to regain his superhuman abilities, which enables him to rescue Turner from other vampires. Turner then subsequently gives up her job as a reporter for fear that her connections there will lead to the revelation of St. John's status as a vampire, and their relationship has a general green light as the first season closes.

The first season of *Moonlight* was cut short by the fall 2007 writers' strike, and the series was not renewed for a second season on CBS. In the meantime, there are currently rumors of the possible return to the Sci Fi channel of the previously canceled supernatural detective series *The Dresden Files*. This series, based on a series of novels by Jim Butcher, is an interesting variation on the theme of supernatural detective. In this series (which aired on the Sci Fi channel for a single twelve-episode season in early 2007), protagonist Harry Dresden (Paul Blackthorne) is a wizard who uses his magical powers to solve crimes and fight evil in his role as a private detective in Chicago. Thanks to the preexistence of the novels, *The Dresden Files* comes equipped with a well-developed mythology, despite its short run on television. Chicago, in this series, is inhabited by an array of supernatural creatures, many of whom know about and interact with each other, although the general populace is largely ignorant of the forces that exist in their midst. Many of these creatures (which include stock figures such as vampires, werewolves, and ghosts) are evil, which leaves plenty of work for Dresden to do in his attempt to protect the general populace. Given that few people in the world of the series believe in the supernatural, Dresden has trouble attracting clients and seems rather impoverished, living in his shabby storefront office—along with his sidekick Hrothbert "Bob" Bainbridge (Terrence Mann), an ancient spirit with extensive knowledge and expertise in magic.

Dresden's rather seedy lifestyle is a key element of the series, helping to create an atmosphere reminiscent of the hard-boiled detective fiction of the 1930s. In addition to the Butcher novels, *The Dresden Files* shows the clear influence of predecessors such as *Forever Knight* and *Angel*, although it goes farther than either of those series in attempting to recreate the look and feel of hard-boiled detective and film noir traditions. These themes are once again given a defamiliarizing twist by the supernatural elements that are so important to the series. For example, in the mode of most hard-boiled detective fiction, the private eye Dresden has an uneasy relationship with the police. Dresden's most important contact among mere mortals is beautiful policewoman Connie Murphy (Valerie Cruz). A skeptic who is never quite able to believe in magic despite her experiences with Dresden, Murphy nevertheless quite often employs the wizard as a consultant to help to solve particularly enigmatic cases that seem to involve supernatural elements. There is also considerable romantic tension between Murphy and Dresden, although this tension does not develop into an actual romantic relationship during the first-season run of the series.

The ongoing appearance of so many television series that explore the intersection between the vampire genre (and other supernatural genres) and the detective genre suggests the perceived promise of this generic mix. The relative lack of success among supernatural detective programs, however, suggests that it is difficult to come up with a compelling formula for such programs. Formula is the key word, because one of the biggest weaknesses of the vampire detective genre thus far is the tendency toward formulaic structures. No doubt part of this problem occurs because vampire lore is itself well developed and comes to the programs with a mature mythology that they can effectively modify only to a limited extent. This situation is then exacerbated by the fact that commercial television programming tends toward the formulaic in general. If, as I have maintained throughout this book, the appeal of such supernatural programming has to do with a longing for something beyond the rationalized day-to-day world of capitalism, then this tendency toward formula (a sort of rationalization of the supernatural) is a severe shortcoming.

One of the most consistent formulas in the supernatural detective genre involves the fact that it seems to have become obligatory for vampire detectives to have a passionate (but problematic) relationship with a human partner. This is true partly because of the prevalence of sexuality as a traditional part of the lure of vampires and partly because television executives seem enthralled with such relationships. Mulder and Scully of *The X-Files* loom as important prototypes, but difficult romantic relationships between vampire men and human women are central to most vampire detective fictions, including most centrally the relationship between Buffy and Angel, but there are also the relationships between Buffy and Spike, Angel and Kate Lockley, and Angel and Cordelia, as well as Nicholas Knight and Natalie Lambert in *Forever Knight*, Nelson and Fitzroy in *Blood Ties*, St. John and Turner in *Moonlight*, and Dresden and Murphy in *The Dresden Files*. Meanwhile, that all of these vampire/supernatural detectives are male suggests (among other things) the possible ongoing presence in American culture of anxieties about female sexuality that would make a female vampire protagonist harder for audiences to accept than a male one, even in an era when strong female protagonists have become something of the norm. Could *Buffy the Vampire* have been as successful as *Buffy the Vampire Slayer?*[12]

Although Buffy might be aligned with humans and against vampires, she is not herself fully human. Moreover, she represents an important movement in the culture of supernatural television, in which superhuman female protagonists have so often been of a softer and more nurturing variety. Before Buffy, the most prominent female supernatural television protagonist was probably Samantha Stephens (Elizabeth Montgomery), a pretty housewife and mother who also happened to be a powerful witch in the sitcom *Bewitched* (ABC, 1964–1972). Even after *Buffy*, women with supernatural power have tended to be of the softer sort of protagonist, such as Allison DuBois (Patricia Arquette) in NBC's *Medium* (2005–) or Melinda Gordon (Jennifer Love Hewitt) in *The Ghost Whisperer* (CBS, 2005–). Meanwhile, both DuBois and Gordon are married, and DuBois has three children. In all respects, they lead much more ordinary lives than does Buffy, who is herself very much an outsider: not just a woman with unusual gifts, but a heroine who is not quite human.

GIRLS KICK BUTT: THE FEMALE ACTION HERO

Buffy is still a key figure in the emergence in the 1990s of an unprecedented number of extremely popular female heroes and superheroes—although ultimately this phenomenon can be traced back to Sigourney Weaver's roles as Ripley in the *Alien* films, beginning in 1979. Linda Hamilton's turn as the hard-muscled Sarah Connor in *Terminator 2: Judgment Day* (1991) can be taken as a crucial landmark as well, especially given her evolution from the softer and rather conventionally girly Sarah Connor of the original *Terminator* (1984). The emergence of these newer, tougher female heroes was initially in the realm of science fiction, in which such women have seemed less surprising than in more realistic genres. Although Ripley evolves as a multidimensional character as the *Alien* sequence proceeds through its four films, she is fighting primarily for her own survival, whereas Connor, even in *Terminator 2*, is primarily a mother fighting to protect her child, even if saving the human race from destruction by its own machines is an expected by-product of her son's survival.

Ripley and Connor are heroes, but not superheroes—although the line between the two categories has increasingly blurred in recent years. As the 1990s moved forward, a new style of female superhero would emerge, as opposed to the older, more scantily clad female heroes, of which Wonder Woman is the classic case and Sheena of the Jungle is perhaps the most sexist case. Particularly in the 1984 film version (starring television sex symbol and *Playboy* cover girl Tanya Roberts), Sheena's main superpower seems to be looking really good naked.[13] Female comic-book superheroes had already begun to evolve in the 1970s and 1980s, but the first prominent mass-market appearance by one of these new-style female superheroes occurred in the original film version of *Buffy the Vampire Slayer* (1992). Scripted by the then little-known Joss Whedon, *Buffy* relates the efforts of its eponymous protagonist (played by an athletic, blonde, and pretty Kristy Swanson), who is a seemingly typical California high-school girl. Buffy must handle the discovery that she is the Chosen One, gifted with superpowers and fated to defend humanity against the threat of vampires. In the film, Buffy never quite settles into her fated role (or evolves beyond her original stereotypical mall-loving, cheerleader-type persona), though the film has some good moments, most of them involving the comic turn of Paul Reubens (better known for his earlier role as Pee-wee Herman) as an over-the-top vampire. Meanwhile, the premise had clear potential as a rejoinder to the horror film cliché of the pretty blonde girl as helpless victim, a promise that would ultimately come to fruition in Whedon's later television adaptation of the same concept, which aired for seven seasons from 1997 to 2003 and became one of the landmark programs in television history.

In the meantime, the syndicated television series *Xena: Warrior Princess* had gone on the air in 1995, featuring the statuesque Lucy Lawless in the title role of a bad-girl-turned-good, battling evil wherever she finds it in an attempt to make amends for her own former misdeeds. Although still scantily clad (in the Wonder Woman tradition), Xena was tough, violent, and tenacious—and fairly clearly (though not ostentatiously) lesbian. These characteristics certainly set her apart from her predecessors among female heroes, but the campy undertones of the show tended to undermine any attempt to read the series as a strong feminist statement.

In France, Luc Besson's *Nikita* (1990) ushered in the 1990s with its tale of a tough, street-hardened woman who, given the proper training, becomes an effective espionage agent and assassin. This portrayal was clearly in tune with trends in American culture in the early 1990s, and it is no surprise that the film was quickly remade in an Americanized version in 1993 in the form of John Badham's *Point of No Return*, with Bridgette Fonda giving the central character (now known as Maggie Hayward) an only slightly softer and more feminine edge. By the beginning of 1997, the same concept was the basis for a television series (premiering two months before the TV *Buffy*) that would air for five seasons on the USA cable network. This series, entitled *La Femme Nikita*, in many ways returned more to the spirit of the original French film. To make it more palatable for American television audiences, the pre-training Nikita (now played by Peta Wilson) was actually innocent of the most serious street crimes of which she had been guilty in the original.

La Femme Nikita enjoyed considerable critical success and a reasonable amount of commercial success. It was also the direct forebear (though the German film *Lola rennt* was an important stylistic predecessor as well) of the much more commercially successful *Alias* (which ran on ABC, 2001–2006), which featured Jennifer Garner as Sydney Bristow, a somewhat softer and more feminine (but still decidedly capable and even deadly) female secret agent. Bristow was the first such figure to be featured in an ongoing series on a major network, and *Alias* drew significant attention from the press (if only a moderate viewership), largely because of its strong female protagonist. In-deed, the role of Bristow propelled Garner into superhero film roles as Elektra Natchios in the comic-book adaptations *Daredevil* (2003), in which she played a secondary role, and *Elektra* (2005), in which she was the central character.

Of course, female secret agents in recent popular culture can all look to Mrs. Emma Peel (Diana Rigg) of the 1960s British series *The Avengers* as a crucial predecessor. It is no surprise that the 1990s also saw an American film adaptation (this time with rather disastrous results) of *The Avengers* (1998), with Uma Thurman in the title role. Meanwhile, Mrs. Peel's propensity for form-fitting leather outfits made her a sartorial model for all sorts of ass-kicking female heroes in the 1990s and beyond. Michelle Pfeiffer's form-fitting Catwoman costume in *Batman Returns* (1992) was a relatively inde-pendent influence, leading to a similar costume for Halle Berry in title role of the *Catwoman* film (2004), a role for which Berry (who won a Best Actress Oscar in 2002 for her role in *Monster's Ball*) had prepared by playing the superpowered mutant Storm in *X-Men* (2000) and *X2* (2003). Form-fitting black was also the order of the day for the genetically engineered protagonist of the *Dark Angel* television series (Fox, 2000–2002), launching star Jessica Alba into a major movie career that has included a role as Susan Storm in the two *Fantastic Four* superhero films (2005 and 2007).

Flexible, skin-tight black costuming also worked well for the martial arts antics of Carrie-Anne Moss as Trinity in *The Matrix* (1999), a film that drew heavily on the fight choreography of Hong Kong martial arts films, which were also a major influence on Quentin Tarantino's two *Kill Bill* films (2003 and 2004). Here Uma Thurman dropped the stylish costuming and glamorous look for her turn as The Bride/Beatrix Kiddo in two films that made her perhaps the deadliest film heroine yet, while also recalling a strong tradition of female action heroes in Hong Kong martial arts films, beginning with Pei-Pei Cheng and Angela Mao in the 1960s and 1970s. Such actresses would remain virtually unknown in the United States until Ang Lee's *Crouching Tiger, Hidden Dragon* became a sensation in America after its Christmas 2000 release, propelling Michelle Yeoh to stardom.

By the early years of the twenty-first century, glamorous Hollywood starlets—including Kate Beckinsale in the two *Underworld* films (2003, 2006) and Charlize Theron in *Æon Flux* (2005)—were lining up to play action hero roles, although generally maintaining a glamorous look (and usually in skin-tight black costumes). One exception is the three *Resident Evil* films (2002–2007), which propelled Milla Jovovich into action stardom in her role as a butt-kicking superpowered zombie killer. Jovovich is mostly sans the glamorous look and clothing in this film, although we see enough skin to realize that Jovovich has been spending a lot of time at the gym. Jovovich's Alice is probably the toughest and grimiest of all the female action heroes to date, although she nevertheless manages to be one of the sexiest as well. This is no doubt partly due to the fact that audiences have by this time seen enough female action heroes to be able to look past the dirt and bruises, partly because the films carefully introduce a few scenes that give us views of a sexy, cleaned-up, and scantily clad Jovovich, and partly because even Alice's tough-girl costuming usually allows hints of what's underneath. An example of this is when she unaccountably struts through the postapocalyptic world of *Resident Evil: Extinction* (2007) with bare thighs and garters, amid her otherwise functional costume. Jovovich's considerable physical charms are on more conventional display in the somewhat unfortunate *Ultraviolet* (2006); here, while looking more glamorous, she remains courageous and deadly—fighting this time mainly on the vampire side against sinister vampire-hating humans.

Amid all these powerful women heroes (many of them quite imposing in stature), it would be the television Buffy, played by the diminutive and decidedly cute Sarah Michelle Gellar, who would emerge as the most important female superhero in turn-of-the-century American popular culture.[14] In addition to being petite and frail looking, Gellar's Buffy was also quite young (she was sixteen at the beginning of the first season but appropriately aged one year for each year that the program was on the air). Buffy is a genuine super-hero, however, gifted not only with superhuman strength and preternatural toughness but also endowed with a strong sense of mission and dedicated to defending humanity from evil (although reluctantly at times and much to the detriment of her own personal life).

In fact, much of the attraction of *Buffy* for its many unusually devoted fans involves the title character's struggles to be a normal teenage girl (and later young woman) despite the fact that she is "the one girl in all the world" who has been fated to defend humanity against vampires and other sources of demonic evil. These struggles have also helped to make Buffy a highly contro-versial figure with some reviewers. Critics have seen her ill-fated desire to be a "normal" girl with nice clothes and an attentive boyfriend as a sign that she and the show have not escaped the gravitational pull of either consumerism or patriarchy. Part of Buffy's remarkable evolution as a character over the seven seasons of the series, however, is her gradual realization that her dreams of normality can never be achieved, a realization that gives her character a decid-edly dark edge but does not prevent her from continuing to fight to protect "normal" people from the evil forces that threaten them.

In many ways, the emergence of such figures as Xena, Nikita, Bristow, and Buffy is no doubt a positive development with strong feminist implications, but it is not unequivocally so. For one thing, these new ass-kicking female heroes operate very much in a masculine vein, solving problems with physical violence and generally finding it impossible to sustain viable intimate relation-ships because of their roles as heroes. Aiming her critique at *Xena* and *Nikita*, as well as *Buffy*, Mary Magoulick notes that these female figures continue to operate "in the tradition of male action heroes," while deriving much of their strength from the male figures who train them, advise them, and autho-rize their actions—such as Buffy's "Watcher," Rupert Giles (p. 731). Further, Magoulick notes that these women, because of their strength, are constantly in danger and under assault, sometimes even from those closest to them. She goes on to add that, "in addition to suffering violence, torment, and hatred even from loved ones, these women are humiliated by men fairly routinely" (p. 741). Finally, she notes that these powerful women must use all of their resources simply to survive, leaving little time or energy for building a new utopian space in which they need not suffer from such difficulties.

One might add that the rise of such female hero figures in the 1990s, as the stature of heroes in general was rapidly diminishing in American culture, is a bit problematic, suggesting that women can be heroes only when heroes have lost much of their aura of greatness. Even Magoulick has acknowledged that the preponderance of critical reaction to such series, in both the popular press and academic studies, has been positive, even among feminist commentators. This positive response has been especially strong with *Buffy*, the critical commentary on which is laced with self-consciously gushing "confessions" of fanhood by serious feminist scholars and critics, who seem very much to identify with Buffy and her struggles. Anne Billson begins her monograph on *Buffy* (published by the redoubtable British Film Institute, no less) by noting her long and intense engagement with television in general and suggesting that Buffy finally provided her with the strong female role model for which she had unconsciously been searching in a lifetime of television viewing. Similarly, Roz Kaveney notes her "obsession" with *Buffy*," noting that the show had "just about everything I wanted" (*Reading* pp. 1, 2). *Buffy* scholar Rhonda Wilcox has devoted an entire book-length study (*Why* Buffy *Matters*) to the unabashed praise of the aesthetic qualities of the series, presenting an extended argument for why it should be considered "art, and art of the highest order" (p. 1).

Buffy is singled out specifically as the Chosen One, fated to fight vampires as her main mission in life, and much of the emotional power of the series comes from her struggles with the alienation and loneliness that come from being different from those around her. Of course, these struggles make her a much more human figure with whom viewers (who have all experienced such struggles at one time or another) can identify. This could be especially true of female viewers, but one could also argue that Buffy is a problematic feminist heroine precisely because she is labeled as unique and different from other women. The ability to perform the feats that she does arises from a mental and physical strength that no other woman can hope to achieve. Buffy's sidekick Willow (Alyson Hannigan) is a talented witch who, in the last two seasons of the show at least, achieves superhuman powers that go well beyond those of Buffy. Willow's ascent to virtual omnipotence, however, is a highly problematic motif that nearly leads to her moral destruction (absolute power corrupts absolutely), while maintaining the suggestion that her girl power depends on superhuman abilities unavailable to ordinary women.

The rise of Willow as a sort of co-power to Buffy indicates the way in which the series addresses the desire for community: One could argue that what makes Buffy stand out among superheroes is that she depends on her friends and allies (even when they themselves are not super) to a far greater extent than had any superhero before her. Buffy and her "Scooby Gang" of supporters might be called the first real collective protagonist in the superhero genre in this sense. Granted, superhero "teams" (e.g., the Justice League of America and the X-Men) had long been popular in the comics and in television cartoons, but these teams are distinguished by the fact that each member tends to have unique powers, making them function more as a group of individual persons than as a genuine collective. The Scoobies tend to have special abilities as well (i.e., Willow's witchcraft, Giles's arcane knowledge of the occult), but they are a tightly knit group that relies largely on teamwork to succeed, especially when Buffy is not available. Moreover, Buffy is special in the extent to which she relies on help from allies who are not themselves superheroes— as in several key moments when Xander Harris (Nicholas Brendan), the most human of them all, saves the day.

In this sense, *Buffy* provides an important twist to the Chosen One motif that was so prevalent in the depiction of American pop cultural heroes in the late twentieth century. Although the series places great emphasis on Buffy's unique status, she still gets by only with a little help from her friends, even if she can never quite be as close to them as they are to each other. The series even provides plot twists that allow other slayers, especially the troubled Faith, to appear and interact with Buffy. The series ends on a spectacular note as a small army of young women is able to attain Slayer powers (with the help of a magic spell from Willow) and thus fight off one last apocalyptic assault on the human world by the demons of Sunnydale. Buffy is thus an unusually democratic version of the Chosen One. Although she has special powers and a special mission that set her apart from others, Buffy remains emotionally vulnerable and in many ways all too human. Ultimately, she becomes a sort of tragic figure (at one point plucked back from bliss in heaven to continue the fights against evil on earth), whose mission precludes any chance of the normal life she so craves.

This version of the Chosen One narrative seemed to resonate with something in the popular consciousness and no doubt partly accounts for the great appeal of the series, making Buffy a Chosen One with whom audiences can identify while still admiring her heroic exploits. The same might be said for the Harry Potter phenomenon, which was almost exactly contemporaneous with *Buffy* (the first Potter novel appeared a few months after the debut of *Buffy* in 1997). Wilcox, noting the numerous parallels between the stories of Buffy and Harry, has suggested that their mutual Chosen One status is the most important similarity between them (pp. 66–78).

One could argue that both *Buffy the Vampire Slayer* and the *Harry Potter* sequence of books and films subvert the Chosen One narrative altogether by making their protagonists so dependent on the help of others. They do, however, maintain the special status of their protagonists, who must finally bear the central burden in the fight against evil. For a real contrast to the Christian Chosen One, one would have to turn to China Miéville's British children's fantasy novel *Un Lun Dun* (2007). Set in a magical parallel London (*Un Lun*

Dun = UnLondon) somewhat in the tradition of the simultaneous parallel worlds of Lewis or Rowling, *Un Lun Dun* features two adolescent English girls who become involved in a cataclysmic crisis in the magical world. One of them, Zanna, is identified by prophecy as the Chosen One but ultimately has essentially nothing to do with the outcome of the crisis. Her friend Deeba, the "Unchosen," comes to the fore and saves the day—not because she was fated to do so but because she has the courage, strength, and determination to take the right action at the right time. Miéville's Marxist message (running very much against the current of American popular culture) is clear: Human beings, not gods or abstract plans and fates, are the agents of history.

BUFFY KEEPS IT COOL

If Buffy is important because of her gender, she is also important because of her young age. Indeed, a general turn toward younger (often teenage) protagonists has been one of the hallmarks of supernaturally themed television and film from the 1990s onward—fueled at least in part by the desires of producers to appeal to the coveted youth demographic. This turn is not surprising and strongly supports the basic premise of this volume, that the fascination with the superhuman and the supernatural in American culture is closely related to the ethos of consumerism. After all, the rising trend toward marketing for the youth demographic is one of the key movements in consumerism of the past half century, so it makes sense that superhuman and supernatural narratives would slant more and more toward that market if these narratives are the consumerist phenomena that I claim them to be.

One of many phenomena of the 1950s that made the decade a particularly crucial one in American cultural history was the growing prominence of youthful (young adult, adolescent, and even younger) consumers as a target market for capitalist enterprises of various sorts, including those associated with the culture industry. Although observers, such as Jon Savage, have documented a long history of youth culture as a special category that extends well back into the nineteenth century, it is certainly the case that the 1950s (or at least the "long" 1950s, i.e., the postwar period from 1946 to 1964) is the period in which "teenagers" were identified as (and molded into) a marketing demographic, especially in the United States. Thus, whichever fears might have been at large in the anxiety-ridden decade of the 1950s about youthful rebellion and juvenile delinquency, the fact is that this decade saw the beginning of a process (completed in the supposedly subversive 1960s) in which teenagers became central to the marketing plans of major Western corporations.

Among the first pop cultural genres to steer in the direction of teenage audiences was the horror film, a natural fit given the tendency of teenagers to think of themselves as misfits in the mode of alienated monsters such as Frankenstein and King Kong. Thus, amid a general resurgence in the horror movie (thanks largely to youthful audiences), the 1950s saw the creation of a whole new genre of monster films aimed specifically at teenage viewers. Titles such as *I Was a Teenage Frankenstein* (1957), *I Was a Teenage Werewolf* (1957), and *I Was a Teenage Mummy* (1962) are indicative of the phenomenon, whereas films such as *Teenagers from Outer Space* (1959) linked the horror and science fiction genres—as well as the "juvenile delinquent" genre of such films as *Blackboard Jungle* (1955) and *High School Confidential* (1958). Among all these teenage monsters and alien invaders were also several films—the central example here is probably *The Blob* (1958)—in which teenagers (propelled by a youthful inventiveness and vigor that their more mature elders lacked) played a central role in defeating monstrous enemies.

With all of this emphasis on teenagers within supernatural contexts, it was only natural that teenage superheroes would soon follow. After all, such characters are natural fantasy figures, fulfilling the desires of adolescent audiences to be able to dream of being someone truly special, while providing fantasies of power to youthful consumers who were frustrated by their own lack of clout in modern American society. Actually, teenage characters had long been featured in superhero comics as a way of attracting adolescent readers, although these characters (Batman's Robin is the leading example) were typically merely the sidekicks of more adult heroes. Even young Billy Batson, the alter ego of Captain Marvel, seemed to be transformed into an adult whenever he summoned his magically endowed superpowers. The introduction of Spider-Man in Marvel Comics' *Amazing Fantasy* in August 1962, however, announced the arrival of a genuine teenage superhero. Spider-Man was not only the alter ego of teenager Peter Parker but also remained a teenager (with a full array of adolescent problems) even when in superhero mode. Given spider-like superpowers as a result of the bite of a radioactive spider, the geeky teenager Parker thus became an ideal fantasy figure for millions of teenage readers. The character was an immediate hit, soon receiving his own comic imprint, *The Amazing Spider-Man*, which began publication in 1963 and went on to become Marvel's best-selling series. Many other comic-book teen superheroes followed, including the prominent role played by teenage characters in Marvel's *X-Men* series of comics, which began in 1963.

Given Marvel's success with teenage superheroes, it should come as no surprise that DC Comics, long the dominant publisher in the comics industry but fast losing market share to the upstart Marvel, soon responded with teenage superheroes of their own. A particularly overt foray into teen marketing was the introduction of DC Comics' Teen Titans, beginning in 1964. This group of youthful superheroes did not actually become a major success until they were reintroduced as the slightly older New Teen Titans in 1980, partly in response to the late-1970s success of *The X-Men* (which also featured older characters than the original 1960s comics). The Teen Titans (featuring Robin, now *sans* Batman, as well as many other youthful heroes) then reached their greatest audience in the *Teen Titans* anime-style animated series that ran from 2003 to 2006 on the Cartoon Network, featuring substantially younger versions of the heroes—and attracting younger audiences.

Again, the move to teenage superheroes is a fairly predictable one, given the importance of the teenage demographic to box office success. In a similar way, horror movies of the 1990s and beyond, following in the footsteps of their 1950s predecessors, have increasingly catered to younger audiences, typically featuring groups of teenage and college-age protagonists threatened by some sort of evil, supernatural or otherwise. Particularly notable here are the three *Scream* films (1996, 1997, 2000), all of which were directed by horror maven Wes Craven, but all of which are designed to inject a new note of postmodern hip generic self-consciousness that appeals to sophisticated contemporary teen audiences who have seen and heard it all before. The first film grossed $170 million, with a production budget of only $14 million, and the two sequels grossed roughly the same, although production costs had escalated to $40 million by the third film. They were successful enough to become an important film franchise in their own right, meanwhile reenergizing the teen horror genre and triggering a spate of imitators, the most notable of which is probably *I Know What You Did Last Summer* (1997).

Of course, Freddy, Jason, and other established icons of the horror film had long shown a suspicious preference for victims in the coveted teen-and-college-age demographic, so that such films are really tapping into a well-established slasher film tradition. That they self-consciously announce themselves as something "new" and "cool" thus represents a success that is at least as much a matter of marketing savvy as of any sort of aesthetic innovation. The very congruence between consumerist desire and the longing for supernatural thrills, however, makes the horror film such an ideal candidate for this sort of targeted marketing. Discussing the disturbing focus of so much recent capitalist marketing on teenagers, Alissa Quart notes that marketing research shows that even today's jaded teens tend to be more idealistic than their elders, more given to "utopian" longings for something beyond the humdrum world of everyday life under capitalism. Marketers, notes Quart, then attempt to take advantage of this fact by "ensuring that the idealists in the teen crowd are hooked up with teen television shows such as *Buffy the Vampire Slayer,* *Charmed,* and *Dark Angel*—all of which, the marketers say, speak to teens' needs for 'religion and spirituality'" (p. 192).

It is not clear whether *Dark Angel* quite belongs on this list, although it certainly features a superhuman teenage protagonist. The other two series (*Charmed* features a group of young sisters who happen to be powerful witches engaged in an ongoing battle against supernatural evil) certainly speak to supernatural longings, however. Meanwhile, Quart's observation calls attention to the fact that, however important teenagers might be as a target audience for the film industry, it is the world of television that really dominates culture-based marketing to teenagers or anybody else. It was no accident, of course, that *Buffy* premiered a mere three months after the release of *Scream* (*Charmed* debuted a year and a half later), tapping as it does into many of the same cultural energies. It is also interesting that *Buffy* star Sarah Michelle Gellar is a featured performer in the second *Scream* film, as well as in *I Know What You Did Last Summer.*

In any case, the most important figure in the 1990s move to younger superheroes was clearly Buffy Summers, a figure who herself was much influenced by such comic-book characters as Kitty Pryde. *Buffy* creator Joss Whedon is himself a devotee (and writer) of comic books, the world of which has exerted a powerful influence on his distinctive vision, which is displayed most centrally in *Buffy the Vampire Slayer.* Thus, if one of the hallmarks of that series is its tendency to challenge the conventions of commercial television, surely one reason for that is that the series draws so much upon alternative traditions, especially the comics. The series also challenges the overall conventions of the various genres in which it participates, whatever the medium.

Much has been made of the opening scene of the first episode of *Buffy,* in which a young man and woman break into a local high school in search of vaguely transgressive fun. The woman is young, blonde, and pretty, if perhaps slightly too old for high school. The man looks like a typical bad boy, and given that we already know that this is a vampire story, the scene has been set for a vampire attack. By generic horror film convention, we know that either the two will start to have sex and then be attacked by a vampire, or the man himself will turn out to be a vampire and attack the woman. This is *Buffy the Vampire Slayer,* however, and neither of these expectations is realized. Instead, it is the woman who morphs into a vampire—assuming the bumpy vamp-face that would become a trademark of the series— and then attacks the man.

Numerous commentators have pointed out that this first scene already announces the way in which *Buffy* would delight in challenging generic conventions throughout its seven-year run. This opening scene, in which the pretty blonde turns out unexpectedly to be not the victim but the vampire directly rhymes with the central conceit of the entire program. The pretty, petite, blonde Buffy turns out not to be a helpless victim of vampires and other demons but a formidable fighter who can not only defend herself very well, thank you, but also who often takes the offensive in her battle to defend her friends and family, her hometown of Sunnydale, California, and—by extension—the world from such monsters. Such reversals of generic expectations are very much at the center of *Buffy*'s project, although genre boundaries are crossed in other ways as well, most notably through the liberal intermixing of different genres (horror, fantasy, science fiction, teen soap, and so on) and modes (as when a tone of hip comedy intermixes with dark threats to the existence of the world as we know it).

Such mixing of modes and genres is, of course, one of the reasons why *Buffy* is so frequently described as a key example of postmodern television. Whereas the series is first and foremost an entry in the tradition of vampire horror tales, it contains (at least in the beginning) an almost equal admixture of the teen soap opera. The various protagonists must struggle with the normal problems of adolescence, meanwhile handling the implications of the fact that their local high school happens to sit directly over a Hellmouth, a sort of gateway to hell through which evil energies (and various monsters) seep into Sunnydale. The presence of this Hellmouth thus gives Sunnydale itself a hellish quality that brings the series into the realm of the "strange enclave" subgenre. As it often does, the presence of this quality potentially becomes a critical commentary on idyllic visions of the American small town as a locus of wholesome traditional values.

This mixing of modes and genres in *Buffy* is surely one of the reasons why the program was able to stay fresh and compelling through seven seasons, even as the characters grew older and moved beyond the high school setting that had originally been so crucial to the success of the series. The series maintains a hip engagement with contemporary popular culture throughout, which no doubt increases its appeal to younger audience members, who thereby feel that it is an integral part of the culture they call their own. Not only do Buffy and the Scoobies frequently allude to popular culture in their dialogue, but pop culture is woven into the very fabric of the series, as when it often features live performances from cool bands in The Bronze, the teenage night club frequented by many of the characters. One of the distinctive features of *Buffy* is the way its characters age and mature, essentially in real time, becoming one year older for each season, as announced by an annual episode that features Buffy's latest birthday. By the end of the seventh season, Buffy is approaching 23 (and Sarah Michelle Gellar had just turned 26), and the program is no longer, strictly speaking, teen centered. The series remains self-consciously fresh and hip in its later seasons, even as it becomes darker and more serious in tone, however. It even introduces, strangely and suddenly, a new teenage character in the person of Buffy's magically produced younger sister Dawn (Michelle Trachtenberg) at the beginning of Season Five, surely at least partly in response to the perceived need to have at least one Scooby be still a teenager, helping the show to maintain its youthful point of view.

Buffy retains this youthfulness partly because of its skepticism toward authority, which typically reads as a "don't-trust-anyone-over-twenty-five" skepticism toward the older generation. Far from the conventional bildungsroman, in which youthful rebels learn to respect and accept authority as they grow and mature, *Buffy* features central characters who only accumulate more and more reasons *not* to trust authority as they grow older. Granted, Giles (Anthony Stewart Head) is a consistently positive figure, although (like almost everyone in the series) he has his dark moments. Giles definitely stands apart from the other Scoobies because of his age, serving as a mentor figure whose status as a sort of magic nerd removes any question that he might turn out to be unexpectedly hip, although we do learn that he had experienced a wild period in his youth. Buffy's mother Joyce (Kristine Sutherland) has her positive moments as well, but she is also a bit clueless, taking years to figure out that Buffy is a vampire slayer, despite all the evidence that is right in front of her. In general, the older generation in *Buffy* is either irrelevant to the lives of the main characters, a decided nuisance to the main characters (as with Principal Snyder—played by *Star Trek: Deep Space Nine*'s Armin Shimerman), or downright evil—as in the case of Mayor Richard Wilkins III (Harry Groener), who is the main villain of Season Three. Wilkins eventually emerges (during the ceremony at which most of the Scoobies are graduating from Sunnydale High) as a giant snake demon that destroys the high school but at least provides the service of devouring Snyder.

Snyder's horrific demise has a special comic charge for youthful viewers who perhaps would like their own principals to meet a similar fate. As with everything else in *Buffy*, the generation-gap motif is treated with considerable humor throughout, and usually, however, at the expense of the older generation. The best example here is the third-season episode "Band Candy" (November 10, 1998), in which candy bars sold to raise money for the Sunnydale High Band turn out to have magical ingredients that make adults who eat them mentally and emotionally revert to being teenagers—with hilarious subsequent results. Giles's reversion to his teen punk days as "Ripper," is particularly amusing, although the adults in general appear ridiculous. Granted, the immature and irresponsible behavior of these adults-turned-teenagers could potentially be read as a criticism of teenagers and as a reminder that adults actually do know (and behave) better, even if young viewers are probably more likely to see these reverted adults as inauthentic teenagers. Their ridiculousness is mostly because they are attempting (unsuccessfully) to mimic genuine teenagers. It is precisely because the older generation is not cool that their efforts to be cool turn out so badly.

This reading is reinforced by the fact that all of the comic shenanigans in this episode are set against the simultaneous evil machinations of Wilkins, the town's central figure of adult authority. Moreover, the negative depiction of the demonic Wilkins, the highest political authority in Sunnydale, is indicative of the way in which most authority is treated with great skepticism in *Buffy*. In the fourth season, when Buffy and Willow go to college (but remain in Sunnydale, attending the local university so Buffy can be around to fight vampires and demons as they emerge from the Hellmouth), the most important adult authority figure they encounter is their psychology professor Maggie Walsh (Lindsay Crouse). Walsh is the head of a top-secret government organization known as The Initiative, which has a large subterranean headquarters and research facility hidden beneath the university. All of the vampire and demon activity in Sunnydale has finally gotten the attention of the federal authorities, and The Initiative is charged with finding a way to combat the threats emerging from the Hellmouth. To prevent panic, they keep their operations top secret, giving the entire operation a conspiratorial (and villainous) air. When their research efforts turn to the capture of various demons and vampires—including the evil-but-oddly-lovable Spike (James Marsters)—so that they can subject them to a variety of gruesome experiments, our sympathies for once are with the vampires, who are the lesser of two evils when compared with the secret forces of the U.S. government. Indeed, The Initiative's capture of Spike (and subsequent planting of a chip in his brain that makes him incapable of violence against humans) is the beginning of the process of rehabilitation that ultimately makes him one of the series' most compelling heroes.

Predictably, the efforts of The Initiative to fight monsters lead them to create a monster of their own, a superpowered Frankensteinian cyborg named Adam (George Hertzberg). Adam (predictably) turns on his makers and begins to build his own cyborg army, becoming the main apocalyptic threat to humanity in this season. Naturally he is defeated by Buffy, although his powers significantly exceed her own and she can overcome him only through a sort of mind meld that allows the other Scoobies to merge with her and add their collective power to her own.

This depiction of the U.S. government as involved in a secret conspiracy that ultimately threatens the existence of the human race may be the closest *Buffy* comes to an openly subversive political statement. Of course, viewers had seen it all before (and treated it more seriously) in *The X-Files*. The general suspicion toward authority (even the Watchers' Council, the main authority overseeing humanity's fight against vampires, turns out to be more of a threat than an aid to Buffy) gives the series a vaguely transgressive air that no doubt helps it to appeal to younger viewers, pleased for once to see authority held up in a critical light on commercial television. The antiauthoritarianism of *Buffy* is vague enough to leave significant room for variant interpretations of the actual politics of the series, many of which are summarized by Jeffrey Pasley, who ultimately concludes that the series is liberal and progressive. Pasley is with the majority of observers, but Neal King comes to almost the opposite conclusion, arguing that *Buffy* is "merrily racist" in its cavalier acceptance of the mass slaughter of vampires (p. 199). King finds something vaguely fascist about the series in its depiction of Buffy and the Scoobies as an elitist group of superior citizens who stand apart from the masses.

Much of the disagreement about the politics of *Buffy* probably comes from the fact that the series is so careful to wear its politics lightly. *Buffy* either keeps potentially controversial political statements so subtle that they are hardly noticeable or simply makes these statements with a consistent self-deprecating humor that prevents the series from becoming preachy, which would, of course, not be cool. For example, the episode "Anne" (September 29, 1998), which begins the third season, potentially makes some of the series' strongest statements about the exploitation of workers under capitalism. Upset by her killing of Angel at the end of Season Two (and unaware that, like Arnold Schwarzenegger, he'll be back), Buffy has left Sunnydale to get a break from her life as a Slayer. She gets away from the Hellmouth only to run afoul of a demonic conspiracy that takes advantage of displaced young people like herself by conscripting them to work as slave laborers in a hellish subterranean work camp. The potential allegorical connections to capitalism are pretty clear here, just as the subsequent Buffy-led rebellion smacks of the proletarian revolution envisioned by Marx. Indeed, Buffy even battles her demon captors with (of all weapons) a hammer and sickle, the implements that made up the official insignia of the Soviet Union.

Few of the series' core viewers, however, would probably even think of this episode as a commentary on capitalism, and fewer still would pick up the hammer-and-sickle allusion. Indeed, the more obvious "message" of the series is simply the rather banal one that one cannot escape one's troubles by running away from them—or even that running away from home is an especially bad idea for teenage girls. Similarly, few would be likely to see a condemnation of capitalism as a system in the other direct engagements with capitalist exploitation of workers in the series. One example of this is when the Master, a particularly insidious vampire, sets up a Fordist assembly line for the mass extraction of human blood in "The Wish" (December 8, 1998).[15] Another such engagement occurs during Buffy's turn as a fast-food worker at the Double-meat Palace in Season Six. Buffy suspects that this fast-food restaurant literally turns its workers into commodities, chopping them up and serving human meat as the secret ingredient that adds extra zing to their burgers (although that ingredient actually turns out to be processed vegetables). This would seem to make it the perfect metaphor for capitalism, but teenage viewers, many of whom have probably worked in fast-food restaurants themselves, would be more likely to see this motif simply as an extension of the high-school-as-hell metaphor that was so central to the first three seasons. The fact that fast-food jobs are hell, however, is more likely to be seen as a local commentary on the lousy jobs available to teenagers rather than as a global commentary on capitalism.

Buffy also critiques the consumerist mentalities of some of the characters, especially in its early depiction of popular rich girl Cordelia Chase (Charisma Carpenter), whose shopping mania is a key element of her shallow, selfish, and narcissistic persona. The series never really questions the fact that Buffy herself, however, feels a typical teenage gravitational pull toward the local mall, nor is it really critical of Giles when he eventually becomes a small-scale capitalist in his own right, opening a magic shop in Sunnydale. The magical items made available in this store often lead to near-disastrous results (making magical implements easily available in Sunnydale is probably not a good idea), and Giles's employee, the former vengeance demon Anya (Emma Caulfield) satirizes capitalist greed in her comic obsession with profit-making through the shop. Anya's greed is so comical as to lack satirical force and seems related more to her demonic background than to any coherent critique of capitalism.

Vampires have sometimes been seen as emblems of capitalism, as when Marx declares in the first volume of *Capital* that capital itself is merely "dead labor that, vampire-like, only lives by sucking living labor, and lives the more, the more labor it sucks" (pp. 362–63). Successful superheroes require compelling supervillains, and the success of *Buffy the Vampire Slayer* no doubt derived at least in part from the growing interest in vampires that marked American culture in the 1990s. This interest came about partly because the mechanism of vampirism, (which requires an exchange of bodily fluids) resonated with the AIDS scare that was central to the public consciousness of the 1990s.[16] Again, however, the series does not really emphasize the possible parallels between capitalism and vampirism, except perhaps in the Master's blood factory in "The Wish." Throughout much of Seasons Four through Seven, vampires fade into the background as villains, replaced by an array of demons, an evil goddess, the machinations of The Initiative, and (in Season Six) the somewhat bumbling villainy of a group of frustrated nerds.

Vampires do return with a vengeance, however, as the series builds toward its climax, when a vampire army threatens to overrun Sunnydale once and for all. The final episodes build toward a dramatic confrontation in which Buffy and the Scoobies (now augmented by Faith, Spike, and a bevy of neophyte slayers) must face the most serious apocalyptic threat yet seen in the series. They succeed, of course, apparently closing the Hellmouth once and for all, although Sunnydale itself is destroyed in the process. Not to fear, though; there is still work to be done. In the wake of all this destruction, Giles reminds Buffy and the other survivors that there is still another Hellmouth in Cleveland, and thus still more evil to be opposed.

This jokelike response to the cataclysmic events that have just occurred (including the deaths of Anya and Spike) is typical of the series. It is also typical of the series that the final battle against the First Evil and his army of vampires is won with the aid of a magic scythe that Buffy luckily acquires just in time, and a magic amulet that Spike heroically uses to create a massive energy burst that destroys the Hellmouth and Spike along with it (although he is later resurrected to become a major character in *Angel*). These magical objects are pure cliché, as is Spike's heroic sacrifice. Whedon and the other creative forces behind *Buffy* were never afraid to descend into cliché, gleefully plundering motifs from other works of popular culture to create a series filled with postmodern pastiche of its predecessors, never so proud as to be above even the hokiest of motifs if it helped to move the plot along and tell the story.

This refusal to take itself too seriously or to regard itself as too artistically sophisticated to descend into cliché is surely one of the reasons why *Buffy* was able to evade the danger of being "square" for all those years. Crucial here is the treatment of religion, that most vexed of all topics (except perhaps sex, which is actually closely related) in American culture. Despite the presence of so much supernatural material (with a special emphasis on vampires, witches, and demons, all of which have a long association with Christianity), the "Buffy universe" is essentially free of a God figure. The closest we ever see to such a figure is probably the "Powers That Be" of the *Angel* spinoff series, and the very existence of this pantheon of godlike figures serves as a direct rejection of Christian and other monotheistic cosmologies. *Buffy* certainly avoids the pitfall of endorsing Christian cosmology or promoting "goody-goody" Christian values, which made supernatural programs such as *Touched by an Angel* and *Joan of Arcadia* so ultimately boring. Granted, traditional Christian symbols such as crosses and holy water are still somewhat effective against vampires in *Buffy*, but this effectiveness is fairly limited and does not seem related to any particular holiness of such items. As one vampire quips in the episode "Doppelgangland" (February 23, 1999), when faced with a vial of holy water and a cross, "Whatever."

Buffy knows better than anyone that there are supernatural powers in the *Buffy* universe, but God does not seem to be one of these powers. Furthermore, Buffy has particularly little use for organized religion as a means of coping with the supernatural, because it seems not to offer significant support in her battle against evil, a battle so difficult that Buffy has little time for anything that will not help her in the fight. Buffy does not campaign against religion; it is just that she is too busy for what she clearly regards as irrelevant. In "The Freshman" (October 5, 1999), when Buffy is confronted by a campus proselytizer who asks her if she has found Jesus Christ as her personal savior, she simply blows him off, saying, "You know, I meant to, and then I just got really busy."

Whedon and the other creative forces behind *Buffy* seem to recognize the power of the American longing to explore the supernatural. They also recognized that this longing comes more from a desire to fill a psychic void in contemporary reality than from a genuine belief in God, which they carefully avoid, even addressing as part of their effort to sidestep various pitfalls that might make the series too predictable and formulaic. Of course, the biggest danger faced by *Buffy* in its efforts to escape routine was simple repetition. How many vampires could Buffy vanquish, however vigorous and full of martial arts flourishes the fight scenes might be, before it simply became routine? To make matters worse, many of the vampires Buffy encounters in the early seasons are former classmates at Sunnydale High, making them seem significantly less exotic. To counter this tendency, Season Five of *Buffy* opens with "Buffy vs. Dracula" (September 26, 2000), in which the famed East European vampire comes to Sunnydale specifically in search of Buffy, whose reputation in the global vampire community has apparently grown. The suave and sophisticated Dracula seems determined to seduce Buffy just to prove that his powers are great enough to do it, thus making him the insufferable male boor who thinks he is God's gift to women. Dracula is nonetheless genuinely different from the run-of-the-mill Sunnydale vampire, including possessing powers (e.g., mind control and instant teleportation) that go well beyond those of ordinary vampires. Even Dracula, however, is ultimately reduced to vampire cliché. Not only does Buffy resist his charms (and eventually dispatch him with the usual stake through the heart), but she is there waiting for him when he rematerializes from being vanquished, something we have seen no other vampire do in *Buffy*. Buffy, however, has seen it before and is there waiting for him. In a delicious moment of self-referentiality that completely confuses the boundary between truth and fiction, Buffy asks, "Don't you think I watch your movies?" With more than a hint of boredom at Dracula's predictability, she stakes him again; he again turns to dust, then once again starts to rematerialize. Buffy just looks at him in exasperation. "I'm standing right here," she says impatiently, whereupon he apparently gives up and heads back to Transylvania, or wherever he usually resides.

Buffy avoids a descent into routine in several ways, including the introduction of complex and different vampire figures such as Angel and Spike, both of whom differ substantially from the vampire norm—and both of whom ultimately have sexual relationships with Buffy that add a new dimension to her relations with vampires. As Patricia Pender notes, "*Buffy* is a television series that delights in deliberately and self-consciously baffling the binary; the juxtaposition of mundane reality and surreal fantasy in the lives of the Slayer and her friends evokes a world in which the sententious morality of black-and-white distinctions is itself demonized as an unnatural threat from an ancient past" (p. 35).

Ultimately what *Buffy the Vampire Slayer* manages to be, above all else, is "cool," with all the vaguely countercultural flair that this designation implies in contemporary American culture. From this point of view, it makes perfect sense that the series would be vaguely critical of both capitalism and organized religion, without really taking a stand against either. Neither of these institutions, after all, is regarded as cool in American culture, yet staunch opposition to either is uncool as well. As Joseph Heath and Andrew Potter have convincingly argued (extending the earlier arguments of Thomas Frank, focusing on the 1960s), however, the whole idea of counterculture is perfectly consistent with and supportive of consumer capitalism. Furthermore, Heath and Potter note that coolness is a crucial aspect of most conceptions of counterculture, which for them means that cool is a thoroughly consumerist notion, with the nonconformist emphasis of coolness simply meaning that, to be cool, one must attempt to do "whatever other people are *not* doing." In modern consumer society, this translates into staying just ahead of the curve by purchasing the newest and most innovative products.

Heath and Potter differ from those who would see the promotion of coolness simply as a Madison Avenue marketing strategy that manipulates the population into incessant consuming in the never-ending quest to be cool. For them, cool is "the central status hierarchy in contemporary urban society," essentially playing the role in late capitalism that class had played in capitalism's earlier classic phase (p. 191). Furthermore, they note that "cool" operates according to a strictly binary logic: Either something (or someone) is cool, or it (or they) isn't/aren't. Thus, "the rise of cool as the central status system of the counterculture represents nothing short of the society-wide triumph of the logic of high school" (p. 192). This last comment returns us to the matter of *Buffy*, even as it suggests that the sweeping discussion of Heath and Potter seemingly ignores the fact that "cool" as a status category still has more purchase among the young, and among those (i.e., humanities professors, television writers, and advertising copywriters) whose job it is to stay in touch with the mental processes of the young.

The avowed coolness of *Buffy* thus explains much of its attraction both to youthful audiences and to academic critics, who have made "Buffy studies" a thriving field of serious critical study. This phenomenon also represents a significant colonization by the cool of a new cultural area, superhero narratives having previously been mostly the preserve of alienated, uncool, even nerdy youths. *Buffy* is thus part of the rise of the nerd hero as discussed previously, and self-consciously so, as the series seeks to define a new combination of coolness and nerdiness that moves beyond (and rejects) more conventional notions of the cool (as embodied by Cordelia and her clique of "popular" girls in the early seasons) and of the nerd (as embodied by Warren, Andrew, and Jonathan, the nerdy trio of villains from Season Six). In this sense (and many others), *Buffy* was very much in step with the times, as indicated by the fact that, during its run, new superhero films had made Spider-Man and the X-Men cool as well.

TEENAGERS FROM OUTER SPACE: TEEN ANGST AND THE SUPERHERO NARRATIVE

Buffy is a most unusual superhero figure but is also a typical figure of her contemporary culture, which self-consciously sought to take the superhero narrative in new (and more marketable) directions. It was inevitable therefore that Buffy would quickly be followed by other teenage superheroes on television, featuring protagonists who struggle with the pressure to be cool while simultaneously growing into adulthood and into the full realization of their superpowers. The quintessential example of the teen superhero television series is no doubt *Smallville*, which began broadcasting on the WB network in 2001 and has as of this writing just completed its seventh season, now on the CW network. *Smallville* is decidedly less cool than *Buffy*, but it nevertheless attempts to inject a strong dose of coolness into the narrative of the most traditional and uncool of all superheroes: Superman. The series tells the story of Clark Kent's teenage years in Smallville, Kansas, as he gradually discovers the superpowers that will one day make him Superman. *Smallville* is respectful of the rich heritage of Superman lore from comics, television, and film, and it draws on this heritage quite liberally. It also updates the Superman mythology substantially in an effort to appeal to contemporary audiences. For example, in this series, a toddler Kal-El lands on earth in the late 1980s, making him approximately the right age for the events of the show to be contemporaneous with the broadcasts. Moreover, whereas traditional Superman stories had clearly portrayed Superman as the character's primary identity and the Clark Kent persona as an assumed disguise, *Smallville* makes the Clark Kent identity the character's real one. In fact, in this series he has yet to assume the role of Superman at all.

Clark's identity is very much at the center of *Smallville*, as the character (played by Tom Welling) struggles like any teenager to discover the kind of adult that he is going to be. In his case, however, the past is also a mystery, and many episodes are devoted to Clark's attempts to discover his origins and to understand the source of the superhuman powers he gradually acquires as he grows older. Meanwhile, the more he learns about his superpowers and his extraterrestrial origins, the more separated he becomes from the other teenagers at Smallville High. Not only does he realize that he is different from normal teenagers, but he also understands—at the urging of his adopted human parents, Jonathan and Martha Kent (John Schneider and Annette O'Toole)—the importance of keeping his special nature a secret from anyone outside his immediate family, lest it draw the attention of those who might seek to harm him or at least to harness his powers for their own ends.

This necessary secrecy adds a substantial complication to the life of Clark, who in most ways seems to be an unusually mature and well-adjusted teenager, thanks presumably to the wholesome upbringing and solid (all-American) values that his adopted parents have provided. In fact, Clark himself is never cool in the series, which must accordingly derive its coolness from that of the cast of supporting characters. Clark does, however, have a dark side (which, among other things, can be activated by exposure to red kryptonite); one of the ways in which the series departs from most previous Superman stories is in its suggestion that Clark's father, Jor-El (never seen, but voiced by Terence Stamp) might have been an evil megalomaniac and might have sent Kal-El to earth for purposes of conquest and domination. Although destroyed with the planet Krypton, Jor-El literally lives on in spirit, infesting by seemingly mystical means various objects on earth and frequently attempting to exert a negative influence on his biological son.

Stamp had played the evil General Zod in *Superman II* (1980), so his casting as Jor-El places the latter within the tradition of Superman villains. *Smallville* employs several examples of this kind of allusive casting, including the casting of O'Toole, who had played a grown-up Lana Lang (who had been

Clark Kent's childhood sweetheart) in *Superman III* (1983). Perhaps the most striking example of this kind of casting in *Smallville* was the appearance of a quadriplegic Christopher Reeve in a small recurring role as Dr. Virgil Swann, a scientist mentor who helps Clark to understand his past. Of course, Reeve had been a large part of that past through his role as Superman/Clark Kent in all of the first four *Superman* movies. To further this connection, Margot Kidder (who had played Superman's adult love interest Lois Lane in the films) later appears as Bridgette Crosby, an associate of Dr. Swann.

Examples of intentionally allusive casting in *Smallville* extend even beyond the Superman world. In the episode "Exposed" (November 3, 2005), Tom Wopat makes a guest appearance as a politician who happens to be an old friend of Jonathan Kent—thus reminding viewers of Schneider and Wopat as Bo and Luke Duke in *The Dukes of Hazzard* (1979–1985), a television series that was roughly contemporaneous with the original run of *Superman* movies. Wopat even makes his first appearance in the episode by careening into the Kent farmyard driving a souped-up Dodge Charger, a car clearly designed to resemble the General Lee, which played such a major role in *The Dukes of Hazzard*. In another episode, Schneider, again as Jonathan Kent, amusingly listens to the theme music from *The Dukes of Hazzard* on his pickup truck's radio.

This kind of engagement with other works of American popular culture is one of the many ways in which *Smallville* resembles *Buffy the Vampire Slayer*, although it never quite achieves the hipness of the latter series in this sense. Of course, the most important popular text with which *Smallville* engages in dialogue is the whole Superman legacy. As the series proceeds, it employs an increasing amount of material from other parts of the DC Comics universe, particularly in its clever use of young versions of other superheroes. These superheroes are generally like Superman, members of the Justice League of America (JLA). In the episode "Run" (October 20, 2004), Bart Allen (Kyle Gallner) appears, a superfast runner able to outrace even Clark—and who is, of course, an early version of the alter ego of The Flash. In the Season Five episode "Aqua" (October 20, 2005), Clark encounters a young man, Arthur Curry (Alan Ritchson), who surprisingly can swim even faster than Clark himself. Curry has come to Smallville as part of an attempt to stop a project that Lex Luthor is developing for the U.S. military that could have devastating effects on marine life. Comic book fans, however, also know that "Arthur Curry" is the alter ego of the superhero Aquaman, a member of the JLA—although in this episode he is humorously identified as a member of the *Junior Lifeguards* of America. Soon afterward, the DC Comics character Victor Stone (the alter ego of Cyborg, a member of the Teen Titans) appears in *Smallville* in the episode "Cyborg" (February 16, 2006) as a human-machine hybrid created through still another of Luthor Corp's sinister research projects. In the sixth season, Jason Hartley appears as Oliver Queen (aka Green Arrow) in several episodes, beginning with "Sneeze" (October 5, 2006). Queen then reappears in "Justice" (January 18, 2007), leading a superhero group that includes Bart Allen, Arthur Curry, and Victor Stone—obviously an early version of the JLA.

Smallville also nods toward *Buffy the Vampire Slayer* by casting James Marsters, so memorable as Spike in *Buffy*, as recurring character (beginning in the fifth season) Professor Milton Fine (the alter ego of traditional Superman antagonist Brainiac). In fact, *Smallville* resembles *Buffy* in several ways, just as it also shows the clear influence of *The X-Files*. The basic scenario of *Smallville* involves a teen protagonist with superhuman powers, who struggles to come to grips with those powers while also attempting to pursue a normal life among the other teenagers of his small town, which seems plagued by an amazing number of weird happenings that challenge Clark to the limit of his growing abilities. In short, *Smallville* has the same basic scenario as that of *Buffy*. Thus, the "Scooby Gang" of *Buffy* is here replaced by Clark's circle of high-school friends, including Lana Lang (Kristin Kreuk)—whom Clark has loved since childhood—and buddies Chloe Sullivan (Allison Mack) and Pete Ross (Sam Jones III). Jones, however, left the show after the end of the third season, and (in a deviation from canonical Superman mythology) the fourth season sees the arrival of Lois Lane (Erica Durance), Chloe's cousin from Metropolis. In another deviation from the canon, Metropolis is within easy driving distance of Smallville; Lois comes to Smallville and gradually becomes an increasingly important member of Clark's circle of friends and supporters. She might also be the coolest of the major characters, which among other things leads her to regard Clark as a sort of bumpkin, although there is clear sexual tension between the two.

Perhaps the most interesting member of Clark's circle is the young Lex Luthor (Michael Rosenbaum), who had long served as Superman's most important human enemy in the world of the comics but who here starts out as a troubled but well-meaning young man who is gradually corrupted, largely by the influence of his nefarious father, billionaire industrialist Lionel Luther (John Glover). Lex and Clark strike up a close but complicated friendship after Clark uses his super strength to save Lex from death in an auto accident. Lex also spends a great deal of time attempting to learn the secret of Clark's powers, whereas Clark expends considerable energy trying to hide his powers from Lex. Lex's gradual transformation into the villain that he will one day become mirrors Clark's growth into the figure of Superman and provides one of the most important continuous plot arcs of the series.

Just as the Hellmouth makes Sunnydale a special site for supernatural happenings in *Buffy*, Smallville represents a concentrated locus of weirdness (and thus is a strange enclave), largely because of the aftereffects of the meteor shower from the explosion of Krypton, which accompanied the original landing of Kal-El's spaceship in the town. Among other things, this shower was responsible for making the young Lex lose his hair, giving him the totally bald appearance that he had long had in the comics. The shower, which consists primarily of various forms of kryptonite, also causes considerable problems for Clark, leaving the town liberally seeded with the one substance that can rob him of his powers and make him vulnerable. This kryptonite also exercises numerous strange effects on the human inhabitants of Smallville, many of whom are transformed into "meteor freaks," superhuman villains (actually more reminiscent of the monsters of the week of *The X-Files* than the vampires and demons of *Buffy*), whom Clark must battle, using his own evolving superpowers. Despite occasional detours into the mystical and into such territory as Native American myth, there is very little of the genuinely supernatural in *Smallville*; the powers of both Clark and his antagonists have "scientific" explanations that have to do with Clark's extraterrestrial origins and the effects of kryptonite on some humans.

In the midst of all this, Clark must also struggle with the problems of a typical teenager, which are in his case exacerbated by his lack of coolness, although that is surely less of a disadvantage in Smallville than it would be in, say, Metropolis. Teenage superhero dramas such as *Buffy* and *Smallville* get a great deal of mileage out of the ways their unique protagonists allegorize the alienation that is universal under late capitalism but that is particularly acute among teenagers. *Roswell* (which ran for two seasons from 1999 to 2001 on the WB, then for another season on UPN) makes this connection even more direct, in that its teenage protagonists are extraterrestrials. Based on the *Roswell High* series of young adult novels by Laura J. Burns and Melinda Metz, the series builds on the extensive unidentified flying object (UFO) mythology that surrounds the city of Roswell, New Mexico. In particular, the series is based on the long-established rumors that an alien spacecraft crashed in the desert near Roswell in 1947. In the series, this spacecraft carried a group of young humanoid aliens, who survived the crash in the suspension pods that held them aboard the craft. Decades later, they emerge from the pods, lost and confused, and wander through the desert, looking exactly like young human children (because, we eventually learn, they are actually alien-human hybrids, created especially to enable them to live on earth). Two of them, Max and Isabel, are found together and are subsequently adopted and raised by the wholesome, affluent Evans family. A third, Michael, wanders alone and is eventually placed in a foster home with the abusive alcoholic Hank Guerin, who lives in a trailer park. The three eventually meet and realize that they have a common origin, although at first they know very little about their past. Thus, unlike Clark Kent or Buffy Summers, they at least have others of their own kind to rely on. Raised as brother and sister, Max and Isabel especially provide support for each other, while also having loving adoptive parents. Without this kind of family support, Michael remains an outsider among outsiders.

Much of the plot of *Roswell* has to do with the efforts of the three aliens (who are teenagers as the series begins) to discover the secrets of their past while keeping those secrets from the humans around them (including Max and Isabel's loving adoptive parents). Meanwhile, they develop romantic relationships with local humans, giving the series an added element that sometimes approximates teenage soap opera. This aspect of the series continues throughout its run, though the later seasons tended to put more emphasis on science fiction elements and less on relationships in comparison to the first season. The most important of these humans is Liz Parker (Shiri Appleby), who, in the very first episode, is fatally shot by a robber in the Crashdown Café, her father's diner, where she works as a waitress. Max (Jason Behr), who has long had a crush on Liz, is unable to resist using his powers of molecular manipulation (which Michael and Isabel share, although they are unable to use them to heal humans) to save Liz and heal her wound—even though he knows that by doing so he risks revealing the closely guarded secret that he shares with Isabel (Katherine Heigl) and Michael (Brendan Fehr). Liz and Max subsequently develop an on-again/off-again relationship, complicated, of course, by his extraterrestrial origins. We also learn that Liz's healing by Max has transformed her, giving her alien powers as well. Michael develops an even rockier relationship with Liz's friend Maria DeLuca (Majandra Delfino), complicated both by his alien origins and his earthly alienation, which makes it difficult for him to trust or relate to anyone.

As *Roswell* proceeds, we gradually learn that the three extraterrestrial protagonists are from the planet Antar, where Max was created as the clone of the overthrown king (modified with human DNA). He was meant eventually to return to the planet and reclaim the throne. The suggestion that Max is fated to lead and rule contributes to the construction of an almost Arthurian mythology surrounding the political situation on Antar and the involvement of the Roswell aliens in that situation. Michael turns out to be the clone of Max's right-hand man and commander of his armies, although there is a faction on Antar that believes Michael should in fact be king. Isabel (who has the power to enter and observe the thoughts and dreams of others), is indeed

Max's sister—or at least the clone of the sister of the king of Antar. She is fated, supposedly, to be Michael's wife, although (independent minded as she is), she rejects this concept and, in the third season, marries earthling Jesse Ramirez (Adam Rodriguez).

Being different often places the Roswell aliens in considerable jeopardy, both from earthly forces that would seek to harness and use their abilities and from their enemies on Antar, who wish to prevent their return to the planet. As the series closes, the main characters all graduate from high school but barely escape an FBI plot to capture them, going on the road in a van, presumably toward further adventures away from Roswell. The romantic subplots are (rather hastily) wrapped up as well. Liz marries Max and goes along with the group, as does Maria, who decides she wants to be with Michael, despite the chaos he brings to her life. Isabel, however, leaves Jess behind, for his own safety.

The mythological material in *Roswell* and the fact that the Roswell aliens have superhuman powers lend a strong element of fantasy to the series, especially for younger viewers. Which teenager, after all, has not at some point fantasized about discovering that he or she is secretly someone special, fated for greatness? In addition, the fantasy elements in *Roswell* point toward the fantasy element that informs the UFO culture as a whole, so nicely captured in the famous *X-Files* declaration, "I Want to Believe!" Longing to believe in something greater than themselves but unable to sustain genuine religious faith, Americans in the decades after World War II have increasingly turned to other options (e.g., UFO mythology), even while clinging to the remnants of traditional religion as well—supplementing traditional Western religions with a sampling of Eastern religions (especially Buddhism).

Teenagers, of course, have particularly powerful longings for the presumed greater spirituality of Eastern religions—and for a general sense of moving beyond the ordinary. One recent series that takes particularly direct advantage of such longings is *Kyle XY*, which premiered on the ABC Family channel in the summer of 2006 and began its third season in the summer of 2008. Although it features some promising ideas, *Kyle XY* is in many ways toned down to make it more acceptable for younger viewers, seriously weakening the ability of the series to explore controversial material. The program still has some violence and some threatening villains, but the actual combat is minimized, while the superhero material is liberally interlaced with heavy doses of "family value" messages. Many of these messages seem aimed especially at teenage viewers (e.g., the importance of abstinence from sex and drugs), who are clearly viewed as the series' principal demographic. *Kyle XY* attempts, in line with other programming on ABC Family, to appeal to viewers of all ages, however. Moreover, the didacticism of the series is fairly subtle, and the show acknowledges that many of the issues that it portrays are complex and multifaceted, even though it ultimately sides with the relatively conventional values that one might expect from a program on this particular Disney-owned channel.

In the first episode of *Kyle XY*, the title character (played by Matt Dallas) awakes naked in a forest outside Seattle, with no memory of his life prior to that point. Physically, he appears to be a normal sixteen-year-old, except for the fact that he has no navel. There seem to be clear hints at this point that Kyle might be an alien. Taken in by the authorities, he is eventually handed over to psychological case-worker Nicole Trager (Marguerite MacIntyre), who decides to take him into her own home. Gradually, Kyle begins to feel that he is a part of the Trager family, which also includes father Stephen Trager (Bruce Thomas), a software designer, and teenage children Lori (April Matson) and Josh (Jean-Luc Bilodeau). At the same time, Kyle also becomes increasingly aware that he has both mental and physical abilities well beyond those of ordinary humans.

Much of the plot of the first season involves Kyle's attempts to discover his origins, which brings him into contact with several shady and potentially dangerous characters. In the meantime, Lori and Josh experience various teen crises, while the Trager parents provide a solid foundation to which their children know they can always return in troubled times. As the first season ends, however, a couple claiming to be Kyle's real parents arrive to take him home with them. It is fairly clear that there is something suspicious about the pair, and there are hints that they might be working for Zzyzx, a sinister group that seems to have a strong interest in Kyle. At the beginning of the second season, however, we learn that these "parents" are in fact working for one Adam Baylin (J. Eddie Peck), the brilliant scientist who founded Zzyzx (apparently with altruistic motives) but is now working against them.

Kyle learns that he is Baylin's laboratory-produced clone, raised under special conditions in a gestation pod, and given abilities potentially even beyond those of the extraordinary Baylin, if he can only learn to use them. Unfortunately, Baylin is (apparently) assassinated by agents of Zzyzx in the early stages of training Kyle. Baylin's lieutenant, Tom Foss (Nicholas Lea), responds by blowing up the Zzyzx laboratory, hoping to destroy the organization, and Kyle returns to Seattle to live with the Tragers. He does not tell them what he has learned about his origins but instead produces a cover story involving the accidental deaths of the "real" parents who took him away earlier. Foss also comes to Seattle and secretly continues Kyle's training. In the meantime, Zzyzx turns out to have been merely a subsidiary of the giant Madacorp, which continues to shadow Kyle, considering him a valuable corporate asset. They assign crack agent Emily Hollander (Leah Cairns) to find and retrieve Kyle, while Hollander employs the aid of Jessi XX (Jaime Alexander), a genetically engineered female produced by Zzyzx and implanted with memories that make her think she is Hollander's younger sister.

Most of the first half of the second season (split into two halves, one airing in the summer of 2007, the other in early 2008) revolves around the ongoing attempts of Madacorp to regain control of Kyle. They view Kyle as a valuable asset, especially because his extraordinary brain might contain conscious or unconscious memories that could be either valuable or extremely damaging to them. Madacorp, using the extensive resources at its disposal, secretly buys out the start-up software firm that Stephen Trager helped to found, subsequently firing Trager, who then finds employment with Madacorp. There the beautiful Hollander undertakes a subtle but unsuccessful program of seduction, hoping to break up the Trager family and remove the support that they provide to Kyle. Because this is the ABC Family Channel, the family triumphs, of course. By the end of the first segment of the season, after several twists and turns (many involving the question of whether Foss is a good guy or a bad guy), the Tragers remain firmly together. Kyle, however, is on the run with Jessi. The series veers into somewhat far-fetched territory as the two discover a high-tech secret room in a seemingly rustic mountain cabin. In the room they find Baylin (or perhaps another clone of Baylin) in an apparent coma. Together Kyle and Jessi are able to rouse "Baylin" long enough for him to warn Kyle that Jessi has betrayed him. As Season 2A ends, Jessi leaps off a cliff, seemingly committing suicide to prevent Madacorp, which has programmed her to do its bidding, from using her against Kyle. Little really happens in Season 2B, which descends mostly into the genre of teen drama, portraying more who will invite whom to the prom than serious questions about the implications of Kyle's posthuman status.

In the case of *Kyle XY*, we are provided with entirely scientific explanations for Kyle's superhuman abilities, so that the program does not involve supernatural elements. Whereas the program vaguely hints that the Tragers are good (but far from fanatical) Christians, religion does not appear to be a huge part of their lives. In fact, it is hardly mentioned, in keeping with the tendency of American commercial television programming to avoid any serious representation of religion. This is not because the networks are dominated by secular-minded atheists who hate religion (or because they are afraid of negative response from atheists), but because they are wary of reactions from religious extremists who might be provoked by any such representation. *Kyle XY*, although it thrives on plot twists that involve reversals of our understanding of whether certain characters are good guys or bad guys, generally relies on fairly well-established polar oppositions between good and evil. For example, the Trager family unit is unequivocally good, no matter what the complications that come into their lives. Conversely, Madacorp is unequivocally evil, serving as a sort of American cultural cliché—the evil corporation, which has been a particular staple of the science fiction genre. Ultimately, the series delivers a positive message about the power of family, reassuring viewers that, whichever dark forces might be afoot in the world, traditional family values (updated a bit to reflect the complexities of the postmodern world) provide a source of strength and goodness that can triumph over evil. In this sense, the series is unusual among superhero stories in that it places primary emphasis on the power of the family, not on the power of the individual hero. Kyle's reliance on the Tragers for support does not differ all that dramatically from the way in which young Clark Kent learns to be the right-thinking hero he will become, largely because of the solid values bestowed on him by Jonathan and Martha Kent.

OUR OTHERS, OUR SELVES: THE MUTANT SUPERHERO

Heroes such as Buffy, Clark Kent, the Roswell aliens, and Kyle XY are outsiders somewhat in the mode of the lonely frontier heroes who struck out into the wilderness partly because of their inability to function within ordinary civilization. These more recent heroes are fundamentally (including biologically) different from other humans, however, and not simply nonconformists who cannot fit in. They are therefore entirely modern figures who look back less to Davy Crockett, Daniel Boone, and Natty Bumpo than to more immediate predecessors, especially those in comic books. Particularly relevant here are Marvel's *X-Men*, a team of mutant superheroes, and an imprint for which *Buffy* creator Whedon has, significantly, served as an author.

The *X-Men* are perhaps the prototypical example of a new direction taken by the outsider hero in the past 50 years, spurred largely by Cold War concerns over radiation-induced mutations. The members of this team stand apart not just from human society but from the human race itself, made genetically different from other humans by a variety of inherited or acquired mutations. This vision of outsider heroism thus addresses several fundamental American anxieties, not just about the danger of nuclear war, but also about race. What if we or our children could suddenly be transformed into members of a different race? How then do we draw the racial line between ourselves and Others, between Us and Them?

The premise of the *X-Men* comics, which first appeared in 1963, was that the world had experienced (since World War II) an explosion in the birth rate of mutants (many of them with superhuman powers), many of whom were now in their teens and beginning to come into their full powers (which typically activate at puberty). Paraplegic mutant telepath Professor Charles Francis Xavier (aka Professor X) gathers together a team of these teenage mutants, trains them to control their powers and use their special abilities to fight evil, especially that represented by the Brotherhood of Evil Mutants, headed by the powerful mutant Magneto. Given the obvious way in which mutations in the *X-Men* comics allegorize American concerns about racial difference, it should come as no surprise that the X-Men would quickly become the most racially diverse team of superheroes in comic book history.

Tellingly, the X-Men also broke the dominance of the two towering superhero figures of Superman and Batman with the release of the highly successful *X-Men* film (directed by Bryan Singer) in 2000, a film that was carefully crafted to attract much of the same youthful audience that had long been crucial to the comics. Although Professor X (Patrick Stewart) and the more mature mutant Wolverine (Hugh Jackman) are the two most important characters in the film, much emphasis is placed on the youthful mutants training at Professor X's school. One of these younger mutants, known as Rogue (Anna Paquin), turns out to be particularly crucial and is instrumental in the defeat of Magneto in the film. Rogue has the ability to absorb the powers of anyone she touches, although by doing so she puts a potentially lethal drain on their system. She thus has the added alienation of not being able to have physical contact with anyone, further complicating her situation as a young woman who must cope both with the usual strains of adolescence and the added responsibilities of having superpowers.

Teenage mutants are even more central to *X2*, the 2003 sequel to *X-Men*, also directed by Singer. The battle lines here are clearly drawn between humans and mutants, so that Professor X and his charges find themselves battling not against other mutants but against xenophobic human foes who seek to exterminate them. Magneto and his group find themselves fighting on the side of the X-Men against the humans, whose attacks include an all-out, commando-style assault on Professor X's school. This leads to an important plot arc in which Wolverine leads a group of teenage mutants on the run after they escape this assault. The fleeing teenagers include Rogue, her boyfriend Iceman, also known as Bobby Drake (Shawn Ashmore), and the rather bitter Pyro, also known as John Allerdyce (Aaron Stanford). The problems of being both an adolescent and a mutant seem particularly difficult for Pyro, whose bitterness toward and mistrust of humans makes him a sort of younger version of

Magneto. Perhaps the most telling scene in their depiction occurs during a visit to Bobby Drake's family, during which he then learns (in a classic coming-out scene) of his mutant abilities. Shocked, his conformist middle-class parents do not handle the news well: Mrs. Drake, without irony, asks Bobby if he has ever considered trying not to be a mutant—much in the way such a parent might encourage a gay teenager to try "not to be gay."

The third *X-Men* film, *X-Men: The Last Stand* (2006, directed by Brett Ratner), introduces still more teenage protagonists, including Kitty Pryde (Ellen Page), who has the ability to walk through walls, and Warren Worthington III, also known as Angel (Ben Foster). Warren has large angel-like wings that allow him to fly, although he is at first tormented by the discovery at the onset of puberty of his sprouting wings—and even tries to cut them off. In response to his child's torment, Warren's father dedicates himself to finding a "cure" for mutantism, in a motif that more clearly than anything else in any of the *X-Men* films resonates with the experiences of gays, lesbians, bisexuals, and transsexuals in our own society. Numerous conservative commentators, ignorant of the realities of human gendering, have quite often viewed any sort of sexuality outside straight heterosexuality to be not only deviant but also a disease for which straight society should seek a cure, thus eliminating "dangerous" sexual misfits. At least the elder Worthington realizes that mutantism is a genetic condition, not a psychological one, and he is able to focus his research on DNA-altering treatments. The crucial discovery of a mutant boy whose powers enable the development of a drug that negates mutantism seems to have been an accident, however.

Many mutants (including Rogue) take the drug voluntarily, seeking to end the torment that their difference from the norm has caused them. Meanwhile, this "cure" for mutantism (essentially designed to wipe out mutants altogether) leads to a climactic struggle in which Magneto responds by raising a mutant army and attempting to kill the boy who produces the drug. Wolverine and Storm (Halle Berry) lead the X-Men (after Professor X is killed) in a battle to save the boy. As the film ends, tensions between humans and mutants have not really been resolved, but the world seems set for a new era of human-mutant cooperation, with mutant Hank McCoy, or Beast (Kelsey Grammar) becoming the new U. S. ambassador to the United Nations.

The *X-Men* films have all been major hits at the box office, both in the United States and abroad, suggesting that their theme of super-powered mutants who have difficulty finding acceptance from ordinary humans has a very wide appeal. The films also feature state-of-the-art special effects and action sequences of a kind that tend to attract large audiences no matter what the themes portrayed. The same is true of the *Spider-Man* sequence of films, although the *Spider-Man* films have been even bigger hits at the box office, drawing audiences so large that the films clearly have an appeal that goes beyond special effects that clearly push the envelope.

The X-Men have become such icons of American popular culture that virtually any narrative featuring mutants immediately asks for comparison with them. A particularly interesting recent example is the television series *The 4400*, which initially began broadcasting (in the summer of 2004 on the USA network) as a miniseries and then was expanded into a regular series, running for four seasons into the fall of 2007. *The 4400* features an intriguing but seemingly straightforward premise: 4400 people who had disappeared over several decades are suddenly returned en masse, seemingly from outer space. The initial implication seems to be that they have been abducted by aliens and now returned for some purpose known only to the aliens, making them a large group of Chosen Ones, though no one knows what they have been chosen *for*. All of the 4400 are initially quarantined in a holding facility where they can be tested for signs of psychological trauma or biological contagion. All of them appear normal, however, seemingly unchanged (and not having aged even if it was decades ago) from the moment of their abduction. Eventually, with no legal grounds on which to hold them, the 4400 are all released, although the government remains extremely wary of them and takes steps to keep close tabs on their whereabouts and actions.

The first few episodes portray the attempts of individual members of the 4400 to resume their lives, even though the people they know and love might have changed greatly (or even died) while they were gone. Things become more interesting, however, when it becomes obvious that the 4400 are, one by one, beginning to display signs of superhuman abilities, such as clairvoyance, telekinesis, or super strength and speed. The series remains episodic as we are introduced on a case-by-case basis to the powers of the various members of the group. This aspect of the series, however, eventually adds more and more complications to an increasingly continuous plot arc as "normal" humans predictably react with suspicion and fear when they learn of these abilities. The government, here depicted as a rather sinister entity, takes steps to control the powers of the 4400, or even to harness them as weapons or other tools.

The premise of *The 4400* allows for (and even requires) the introduction of a fairly large number of characters, although the two most central characters are not members of the 4400 at all. They are Tom Baldwin (Joel Gretsch) and Diana Scouris (Jacqueline McKenzie), who work as agents of the National Threat Assessment Command (NTAC), a division of the Department of Homeland Security. Baldwin and Scouris inevitably recall Mulder and Scully of *The X-Files*, although Gretsch in particular lacks the charisma of David Duchovny as Mulder. Gretsch and McKenzie together fail to generate the level of interpersonal chemistry that made the relationship between Mulder and Scully so special. *The 4400*, in fact, shows several strong *X-File* influences, even after it becomes clear at the end of the first season that the initial alien-abduction theory was erroneous and that the 4400 were actually abducted by humans from earth's future. These humans have now modified them to give them special powers that will help them, once inserted back into the earlier timeline, to change the course of history and hopefully to prevent the baleful events that have made the future earth a virtually uninhabitable wasteland.

The 4400 particularly recalls *The X-Files* in the way in which various discoveries lead to surprising plot twists, forcing viewers continually to revise their assumptions about what is actually going on in the series. Suggestions of shadowy government conspiracies also recall *The X-Files*, although *The 4400* moves into new, highly topical (and potentially very controversial) territory in its exploration of the dynamic between the 4400 and the rest of American society. Some of this dynamic simply involves xenophobic fears on the parts of unmodified humans that they will be endangered or even made obsolete by the 4400 and their powers. In this sense, the series is reminiscent more than anything of the *X-Men* comic books and films, in which mutants with super-human powers must deal with the animosity of nonmutated humans, which clearly becomes a sort of metaphor for racism and discrimination against differences of all kinds. When some of the 4400 (known as the Nova Group), however, turn to terroristic violence in their own defense against exploitation or even possible extermination, the series begins to tread on particularly sensitive territory, given the fears about terrorism in the American mindset in the early twenty-first century. Given that the government often comes off as the villain whereas the terrorists among the 4400 are at least partly sympathetic, the treatment of this motif in the series is unusually bold for American commercial television.

This entire scenario, meanwhile, is further complicated by the rise of billionaire industrialist Jordan Collier (Billy Campbell) as a key leader of the 4400. Collier uses his managerial skills, financial resources, and personal charisma to found an organization dedicated to providing support for the 4400 and helping them to learn to use their powers while learning to function in normal society. Collier's policies, however, run contrary to the more radical positions of the Nova Group, which then moves to have him assassinated by Baldwin's son Kyle (Chad Faust), who shoots and apparently kills Collier in a moment of temporary insanity brought on by the influence of the Nova Group.

Collier mysteriously returns, possibly having arisen from the dead, thus becoming a Christlike figure (now complete with beard and long flowing hair) who becomes even more important as a leader of the 4400. The resurrection of Collier also takes the series into new, seemingly mystical territory, although there is always the chance that his resurrection was somehow engineered by the future humans. They might also have used their time-traveling abilities to seed what appear to be prophecies from the early twentieth century of Collier's rise as a spiritual leader. Meanwhile, it is discovered that the 4400 have apparently gained their abilities through the effects of "promicin," a neurotransmitter that activates previously dormant parts of the brain and that was apparently given to them while they were abducted into the future. In a key twist to the conspiracy element of the series, it is also revealed that the government had already discovered the presence of promicin in the 4400 and had secretly dosed them with a promicin inhibitor while they were in their initial quarantine. This inhibitor greatly limits the development of their powers and also triggers a potentially fatal reaction that begins to kill off members of the 4400 as the second season comes to an end.

The plot takes another turn when brilliant scientist Kevin Burkhoff (Jeffrey Combs) develops an antidote to the inhibitor, which is then distributed to the remaining members of the 4400, enabling the full release of their new powers. In addition, Burkhoff develops a serum that allows promicin to be injected into ordinary humans, giving them abilities like those of the 4400. This technology becomes involved in still another *X-Files*-like subplot, in which the government attempts to use the serum to create an army of supersoldiers with superpowers like those of the 4400. Collier, Burkhoff, and 4400 member Tess Doerner (Summer Glau) manage to foil the supersoldier program by stealing its supply of promicin, while Collier then uses this supply, in the dramatic conclusion of the third season, to begin the distribution of the drug to anyone who wants it, free of charge.

At the beginning of the fourth season, this distribution plan quickly spreads superpowers through the general population. However, the treatment has been banned by the government because it is highly dangerous, causing death in one half of those who take it. Collier and his key followers are forced to go underground to escape arrest, while his movement takes on increasingly religious undertones after he becomes aware that he is apparently fulfilling prophecy. He is, he proclaims, bringing "God" to the world, although he hastens to add that those uncomfortable with "God" can simply consider him to be bringing paradise.

In one of the few instances in which American commercial television has seriously addressed the question of Utopia, Collier sets about building his ideal world, establishing a beachhead in a slum area of Seattle, which he and his followers transform into a pocket paradise, known as Promise City. To demonstrate the ideal future that they offer to humanity, they clean up the blighted area, including turning a heavily contaminated local river into a pristine stream, free of all pollutants. All of this looks very good, although it remains central to Collier's vision that all of humanity must take the promicin treatment, giving one half of them (unpredictable) superpowers, but killing the other half, thus freeing the future of any possible tensions between ordinary humans and transformed superhumans, or promicin "positives." In particular, Collier remains staunchly opposed to the administration of a test, developed by Burkhoff, that will allow people to determine in advance whether the treatment will be safe for them.

Disagreements over this test lead to tensions between Collier and young Shawn Farrell (Patrick Flueger), Collier's former lieutenant and Baldwin's nephew. Farrell still sympathizes with many of Collier's aims but feels that the death of one half of the human race is too high a price to pay to achieve those aims. He thus supports Burkhoff and the development of the test; he and a guerrilla band of "positives" (including Doerner) thus rescue Burkhoff from Promise City after Collier and his followers kidnap the scientist and imprison him there. Meanwhile, these battles and disagreements among the positives are mirrored by complications that arise among the ordinary humans of the series. In a plot twist that echoes such science fiction classics as *Invasion of the Body Snatchers* (1956), these complications become particularly sinister when it is slowly revealed that a group of humans from the future (opposed to the group that created the original 4400) seems to be engineering a plot to derail Collier's plans. They plan to inject several prominent people with nanites, which are designed to allow "elite" members of this future group to control the minds of the injected people. Left with a scar from the procedure, these people come to be known as the "Marked."

Much of the fourth season revolves around the fact that Baldwin himself has become one of the Marked, a situation discovered by both Scouris and NTAC head Meghan Doyle (Jenni Baird), who by this time also happens to have become Baldwin's lover—in one of many (mostly unsuccessful) attempts on the part of *The 4400* to inject a little sexual sizzle into the series. Scouris and Doyle thus work to try to free Baldwin from the control of the nanites, even as "Baldwin" goes about his plot to destroy Collier's utopian project. Collier appears to be a more sympathetic figure next to this possessed (and supposedly evil) Baldwin, although the series is punctuated by swings in the presentation of Collier, who sometimes seems pretty sinister himself. Eventually, "Baldwin" and his cohorts kidnap Collier, planning to mark him and then return him as one of their own agents to destroy the real Collier's plan to build a better posthuman future.

This entire motif is complicated by the fact that the Marked have infiltrated so many high places, including the U.S. government. The plan to kidnap and co-opt Collier is orchestrated by none other than a marked Rebecca Parrish (Penny Johnson Jerald), the Director of National Intelligence for the U.S. government. Parrish is an African American woman, which inescapably suggests parallels with real-world Secretary of State (and former National Security Advisor) Condoleeza Rice. This is particularly true given that so many aspects of *The 4400* seem to invite interpretation within the context of the U.S. government's "war on terror," often in ways that are clearly critical of the xenophobic rhetoric and possibly unconstitutional security measures that have been pursued as part of that "war." In this sense, *The 4400* employs the strategy of *cognitive estrangement,* identified by Suvin as the key to the power of science fiction to comment on social and political practices in our own world by forcing readers and audiences to look at those practices from new perspectives. The particular motif of modified posthumans that is so crucial to *The 4400* places it within a genre the most important founding work of which might be the *X-Men* comics but that also includes such contemporary television series as *Heroes* and *Painkiller Jane*.

Baldwin is eventually cured, and Collier is rescued. As the fourth and final season draws to a close, Sean's brother Danny (Kaj-Erik Eriksen) takes promicin and acquires the ability to create a virus that quickly spreads, making anyone who comes into contact with it promicin positive. One half of those die, of course, whereas the other half suddenly and inadvertently acquire superpowers. The result is complete chaos in Seattle. Amid a complete collapse in authority, Collier and his band of positives suddenly become the only source of stability in the city. Called on by the NTAC to help restore order in Seattle, they succeed in doing so. In fact, they are so successful that, at the end of the season (and the series, as it turned out), for better or worse, they find themselves in complete control of Seattle, which has now effectively become an extended Promise City.

If *The 4400* tries to make its material seem more serious by adding a dark and gritty edge, the recent series *Heroes* is much more willing to revel in its comic-book origins. *Heroes,* which premiered in the fall of 2006 on NBC, went on to become the most successful superhero television series ever—at least for its first season, when it scored consistently high in the Nielsen ratings (especially with the key 18- to 49-year-old demographic). It finished the season ranked twenty-first overall in the ratings (eleventh among 18- to 49-year-olds) and was NBC's top-rated scripted program. Ratings declined only slightly in the second season, leading to renewal for a third season as well.

Created by Tim Kring, *Heroes* employs a complex ongoing plot line with multiple threads that slowly weave together, with numerous twists and turns that frequently change our understanding of the roles played by individual characters. In this, the series seems to have been significantly influenced by *Lost*; on-line chats among fans have frequently suggested links and parallels between the two series, including suspicions of some sort of secret alliance between the two shows (mirroring the various conspiracies and shifting alliances that underlie the plots of both shows), despite the fact that the two shows are on different networks. Of course, other series (*The X-Files* is especially important in this regard) have also provided precedents for the plot structure of *Heroes*. Comic books have long employed similar convoluted, developing plots, making the genealogy of *Heroes* quite complex.

Jeph Loeb is the co-executive producer of *Heroes*; Loeb was a writer and supervising producer on *Lost* and on *Smallville*. He is also an important writer of superhero comic books, and—whatever the influence of *Lost*—the real source of *Heroes* is in these comics, a heritage that the program embraces in several ways. For one thing, the concept of mutations causing superpowers comes almost straight from the *X-Men* comics. In addition, on-screen text in *Heroes* is generally displayed using a font reminiscent of that which one might find in a comic book. (This font was created by comic-book artist Tim Sale, based on his own lettering style.) Several of the series's large and diverse cast of characters (something else it shares with *Lost*) are comic-book readers, and one of the series's numerous superheroes, one Isaac Mendez (Santiago Cabrera), is a comic-book artist, albeit one with the superpower of seeing—and drawing— the future. Mendez also paints the future in large, comic-book-style paintings (which, like all of "Mendez's" artwork that is shown in the series, is actually done by Sale). From the point of view of the series, however, his most important work is the comic *9th Wonders!*, which depicts the future. The comic tells of the future exploits of a Japanese samurai-like warrior who has the power to bend space and time, giving him the ability to travel through time or instantly teleport himself from one place to another. This Japanese hero is Hiro Nakamura (Masi Oka), who happens to be the future self of a young comic-book–reading office worker in Tokyo. When the present-day Nakamura reads of his own future exploits in the comic, he concludes that it is his mission in life to perform the deeds depicted in the book. These deeds include saving New York from a cataclysmic nuclear explosion by killing one Sylar (Zachary Quinto), the main villain of *Heroes*, who will presumably be responsible for the explosion.

Despite the pulp origins of its main plot material, *Heroes* is a slickly produced series, well acted and featuring some of the best special effects in television history. Moreover, it takes its comic-book material absolutely seriously, without a hint of camp and with no concern that its over-the-top plot and characters might seem ridiculous to viewers. The success of the series in its first season suggests that this was a good choice and that viewers, attracted both by the fantasy value of the superpowered characters and by the intricate puzzle-like plot, with its wheels-within-wheels and frequent surprising twists, have no trouble suspending their disbelief and treating the series like a serious drama.

In the beginning, the main cast of *Heroes* consists of a group of eight superheroes, all of whom are just beginning to discover their powers and most of whom are unaware of the others, although one of the key devices of the series is the gradual establishment of an extensive network of connections among the various heroes. In addition to Nakamura and Mendez, these initial heroes include the following:

Claire Bennet (Hayden Panetierre), a high-school cheerleader in Odessa, Texas, who has the ability to regenerate, so that she can spontaneously (and quickly) recover from any wound, and even death.[17]

Matt Parkman (Greg Grunberg), a dyslexic Los Angeles police officer who can hear the thoughts of people in his vicinity.

Nathan Petrelli (Adrian Pasdar), an ambitious New York City assistant district attorney who has the ability to fly, Superman-like, at high speeds. It is eventually revealed that Claire Bennet is Nathan's illegitimate daughter.

Peter Petrelli (Milo Ventimiglia), Nathan's younger brother. Peter works as a male nurse and only gradually understands that he has the ability to take on the superpowers of other heroes with whom he comes into contact. Initially, he loses these acquired powers as soon as the "donor" hero moves away, but ultimately he learns to maintain and control all of the powers he absorbs, an ability that makes Peter potentially the most powerful of all the heroes.

Micah Sanders (Noah Gray-Cabey), a young boy who has an amazing affinity for machines of all kinds, and seems able to communicate with them and get them to do his bidding.

Niki Sanders (Ali Larter), Micah's mother, a beautiful blonde woman who sometimes (especially times of great stress) takes on an alternative personality called Jessica, the name of her dead sister killed by their abusive father. Jessica has superhuman strength and tends to be violent and ruthless in the use of it. The kinder and gentler Niki, meanwhile, devotes most of her energies to trying to take care of Micah.

This initial group of heroes is soon joined by D. L. Hawkins (Leonard Roberts), Niki's husband and Micah's father. Hawkins can "phase shift" and thus pass through solid matter. In prison as the series begins, he uses this ability to escape and rejoin his family, although he is still on the run from the law. Both he and Niki are pursued by the henchmen of one Mr. Linderman (Malcolm MacDowell), a powerful Las Vegas mobster. As the series proceeds, however, we learn that Linderman is in fact himself a mutant, with the ability to heal others. Linderman is also using his considerable resources to spearhead a complex plot to ensure that the destruction of New York *will* happen. The premise for this is that the world is on the brink of total collapse, and this megadisaster will bring the human race together and help to get human civilization back on the right course.

If Linderman is thus a classic case of the villain who thinks he is doing the right thing, Sylar seems to be motivated by pure malice. Growing up as the son of a watchmaker determined to escape the banality of his father's existence (especially because his mother continually admonished him to strive to do extraordinary things), Sylar nevertheless also becomes a watchmaker. He escapes that life, however, when he finds that he has the ability permanently to gain the abilities of mutated superheroes whom he kills by sawing off the tops of their heads. He apparently absorbs their mutations through their exposed brains, which he possibly eats, although that is not made entirely clear. Sylar then sets out to track down and kill as many mutants as possible so that he can gain more and more power and thus do more and more damage—including destroying New York.

This motif of tracking down mutants is crucial to the plot of the first season of *Heroes*, providing a convenient means to gradually connect the various characters and tying together various plot strands. Engaged in a similar quest but motivated by altruistic reasons is Indian geneticist Mohinder Suresh (Sendhil Ramamurthy), who comes to America to pursue his father's research into the genetic origins of the superpowers that seem suddenly to be springing up everywhere. The elder Suresh has developed a formula for identifying the mutation from DNA samples, but he is murdered by Sylar before he can use the formula or convey it to anyone else. Mohinder hopes to decode the formula and to use it to help him locate mutants and help them to deal with their newly found powers.

Still another attempt to track down mutants is undertaken by a shadowy organization, the Company, that employs Noah Bennet (Jack Coleman), Claire's adopted father, as one of its key agents. This agency gave the apparently orphaned infant Claire to Bennet to raise as his adopted daughter, on the suspicion that she might have inherited superpowers from her mutant mother. (They seem unaware that Nathan Petrelli is her father.) Bennet himself has no superpowers but uses the considerable resources of his employers to help to identify and keep track of those who do have superpowers. These resources include mutants who are also employed by the organization, including a mysterious Haitian (Jimmy Jean-Louis) who has the ability to nullify the superpowers of other nearby mutants and who accompanies Bennet on virtually all of his missions. Bennet's organization presumably seeks to help mutants use their powers to do good for the world, including preventing the New York explosion. The organization employs decidedly questionable tactics in its treatment of the mutants, however, and seems to have taken a sinister turn somewhere along the way. Bennet eventually rebels against his employers, partly to protect Claire from his former colleagues and partly so that he can indeed help to prevent the nuclear explosion.

That explosion is the central focus of the entire season, dominating Mendez's visions, motivating Nakamura's mission, and eventually bringing all of the heroes together in New York. Along the way, the plot undergoes numerous twists and turns; at first seemingly evil characters such as Bennet turn out to be good; others, like Linderman, turn out to be more complex than we first thought. Minor characters, such as Angela Petrelli (Christine Rose), the mother of Nathan and Peter, become much more important and much more involved in the action than we first thought. For example, Mrs. Petrelli was involved with Linderman in a plot to ensure that New York is destroyed and that, in the wake of this disaster, Nathan will be elected President, leading the world toward the dawn of a new age.

The plot thickens as we meet still another superhero, Ted Sprague (Matthew John Armstrong), who is somehow charged with nuclear energy and has the power to make himself explode like an atomic bomb. At first, it seems likely that Sprague will be the bomb that destroys New York, but he is killed by Sylar, who assumes his nuclear power. Meanwhile, Peter has met Sprague and taken on that power as well, and much of the plot involves his fear that he will somehow explode and cause the disaster. At the cataclysmic end of Season One, Peter faces off with Sylar in a climactic struggle, seemingly killing the villain but also triggering what will be his own eventual explosion. At the last moment, Nathan, abandoning the plot to become president in the aftermath of the destruction of New York, swoops down and flies with his brother Peter high into the skies over New York. A huge explosion occurs harmlessly in the stratosphere, presumably blowing up both Peter and Nathan. Peter might be able to recover from the blast because he has taken on Claire's power of spontaneous regeneration, however. On-line text informs us that this is the end of Volume One of *Heroes*, which one would expect to close the episode. Instead, in a final surprising twist, the episode immediately cuts to Volume Two (subtitled "Generations"), which begins as the time-traveling Nakamura lands in the middle of a Japanese battlefield just outside Kyoto in the year 1671. Indeed, he finds himself in the midst of a building battle between an army of warriors on one side and a lone samurai on the other. Suddenly, the field goes dark as the sun is blotted out by a total eclipse—forming the logo that is shown at the beginning of each episode.

The second season of *Heroes*, interrupted by the writers' strike, is somewhat fragmented and does not come together as well as the first season. Much of the plot involves the efforts of the two Petrellis and Sylar (all of whom have survived) to recover in the aftermath of the events that closed Season One. Much of the action centers on the research of the Company into the Shanti virus, which threatens to kill off those with superhero mutations. Those genetically chosen to have great power are also chosen to have great vulnerabilities. Several new heroes are introduced as well, making the cast a bit unwieldy and relegating many of the major characters from Season One to secondary roles. *Heroes* is slated to begin a third season in the fall of 2008, this time adding, reportedly, a cast of supervillains who arise to challenge the series' superheroes.

Among other things, the narrative structure of *Heroes* makes particularly clear the close connection between mutant narratives and Chosen One narratives, the Chosen Ones now having been selected by biology rather than some supernatural agency. Meanwhile, if the Chosen Ones of *Heroes* often seem fated for greatness, there are also occasional Chosen One narratives, especially in very recent popular culture, that attempt to keep their Chosen Ones ordinary, even though they may have remarkable superhuman powers. This motif presumably makes it easier for audiences to identify with the Chosen Ones, but also suggests a certain skepticism toward the whole Chosen One premise. One thinks here of the quirky supernatural comedy-drama *Pushing Daisies*, which premiered on ABC in the fall of 2007, to considerable critical acclaim. The brain child of Bryan Fuller, creator of the earlier supernatural series *Wonderfalls* and *Dead Like Me*, *Pushing Daisies* is based on the premise that protagonist Ned (Lee Pace), a professional pie maker, has the ability (for no known reason) to raise the dead (human or animal) simply by touching them. If he touches the resurrected person or animal again, however, it will once again die, this time permanently. Furthermore, if he does not touch (and thereby kill) the resurrected being within 60 seconds, another being of a similar species instantly drops dead, restoring the balance. As the series begins, Ned has found no great uses for his gift, which he uses primarily in his work with private investigator Emerson Cod (Chi McBride) in a scheme whereby they wake recent murder victims, get them to identify their killers, and then put them back to death, using the information gained to catch the killers and collect any available rewards. They are helping to bring about justice and in that sense are on a mission of good, but their primary goal is simply to make money.

Ned's life becomes seriously complicated when his childhood sweetheart Charlotte "Chuck" Charles (Anna Friel) is murdered on a cruise ship. Ned wakes her, but she is unable to identify her killers. He is unable to bring himself to put her back to death, so she stays alive, while the unscrupulous corpse-robbing owner of the funeral parlor in which her body had awaited burial drops dead in her place. Chuck becomes Ned's constant companion, although they are unable to touch, lest she be returned to death. Their relationship thus adds a new twist to the stock motif of unrequited sexual tension that was so central to the success of series such as *The X-Files*. They are able to kiss through Saran wrap, but there is nothing ghoulish here. Far from morbid or zombie-like, the beautiful Chuck is, if anything, a bit too lively, with a perky, talkative charm that often veers dangerously close to the annoying. Ned, Chuck, and Cod subsequently become an unconventional crime-fighting team as they continue the former quest for rewards. All the while, they are themselves investigated by the snoopy Olive Snook (Kristin Chenoweth), a waitress in Ned's pie shop. Olive is in love with Ned, who does not return her feelings. She is also terribly jealous of Chuck and incredibly curious about Chuck's sudden appearance in Ned's life.

The preposterous premise of *Pushing Daisies* is part of the point, as the series strives to create an offbeat, fairy tale–like atmosphere, reminiscent of some of the films of Tim Burton. This off-kilter atmosphere is aided by computer animation, a capricious musical score, and quirky voiceover narration provided by Jim Dale. There is a certain potentially inherent mismatch between the whimsical tone of the series and the subject matter, which is actually quite dark. Initial critical response to the series was strong, although (as with Fuller's other series), audience response was lukewarm. The very fact that such an odd series got on the air suggests a perceived interest on the part of the viewing public in stretching their imaginations beyond the day-to-day world of mundane reality, however. The basic profit motive that drives the supernatural adventures of Ned, Chuck, and (especially) Cod suggests the difficulty of escaping the gravitational pull of consumer capitalism, even within the realm of quirky fantasy.

Although Ned finds a significant personal use for his powers in raising Chuck from the dead, he has no real sense of a greater mission. One might compare here the Fox drama *Tru Calling* (which ran for two seasons, from 2003 to 2005), in which protagonist Tru Davies (*Buffy*'s Eliza Dushku) also has encounters with the recently dead. A technician working the night shift at the city morgue, Tru sometimes finds that corpses seem suddenly to awaken and ask for her help, whereupon she is transported back in time to the beginning of the day of the person's death, which she then works to try to prevent. Tru thus does have a sort of mission, and (as the show's title indicates) her gift is explicitly characterized as a "calling," making her very much a Chosen One. In fact, she is apparently working as the agent of one of two great supernatural powers (*not* God and Satan) that vie with each other to determine the basic texture of human existence.

Tru seems possibly to have inherited her calling from her mother, who apparently had the same power, which suggests that the power has a biological origin. A similar situation occurs in the ABC supernatural legal drama *Eli Stone*, whose protagonist has powers that he might have inherited from his father. Much of the charm of this series (which premiered in January 2008 and ran into April of that year for a thirteen-episode season) involves the winning vulnerability of its eponymous protagonist, played by the likable Jonny Lee Miller. As the series opens, Stone is one of the most effective and ruthless operatives of a prominent San Francisco law firm (whose clients tend to be rich, powerful, and usually in the wrong). Stone, still young, seems on his way to major career success and is a favorite of his firm's senior partner Jordan Wethersby (Victor Garber), to whose beautiful daughter Taylor (Natasha Henstridge) Stone also happens to be engaged. All of this changes, however, when Stone starts to have a series of visions (many involving the erstwhile pop superstar George Michael). These visions (which require considerable interpretation) tend to point him toward specific missions in which he can be a force for good, gradually turning him away from his sharklike quest for money and power and toward a new role as a defender of the oppressed. Stone's transformation also affects those around him. Jordan Wethersby turns from his former quest for higher profits toward doing good works, declaring (in one of the most potentially radical statements ever made on American network television) that Stone has taught him to realize that "capitalism without mercy is tantamount to evil."

Not suprisingly, Stone's new mission as a crusader for justice does not sit well with his firm, getting him into considerable difficulties that are exacerbated by his own erratic behavior, as when his visions strike him in the midst of courtroom proceedings or boardroom meetings. These visions, beginning with George Michael's performance of the song "Faith" in the first episode, tend to be something like music videos, gradually coming to feature his friends and colleagues as the performers, giving them an offbeat quality that is somewhat reminiscent of the lip-synched musical performances in the famed BBC miniseries scripted by Dennis Potter, such as *The Singing Detective*. As such, they are a key aesthetic element of the series and part of its quirky charm, although Stone's visions tend to become nonmusical as the first season proceeds. The series also has a mystery element as well, as both Stone and the audience seek to determine the source and significance of his visions, which appear to be related to an inoperable brain aneurysm. This aneurysm also seems to have been inherited from his father, leading to the elder Stone's own reputation for strange and irresponsible behavior. The visions (and the aneurysm) might have supernatural origins as well, making Stone a sort of modern-day (but very down-to-earth) prophet. Eventually, Stone undergoes surgery to have the aneurysm removed; he nearly dies from the surgery and apparently meets God, who turns out to look (and sing) exactly like George Michael. Stone is then sent back to life because he still has work to do on earth. What exactly we are to make of this remains to be seen in the show's second season, recently given the go-ahead by ABC as of this writing.

Perhaps the most unusual of recent Chosen One television narratives is the series *Reaper*, which began airing on the CW network in the fall of 2007. Here, protagonist Sam Oliver (Bret Harrison) has just turned 21 and is mostly drifting through life; he still lives with his parents and works as a clerk at the Work Bench, a home improvement superstore clearly based on the Home Depot. Sam's friends Ben (Rick Gonzalez) and carefree slacker Bert "Sock" Wysocki (Tyler Labine) also work at the Work Bench, as does beautiful Andi (Missy Peregrym). The friends seemingly mark time until they can figure out what to do with their lives, often getting into comical conflicts with their officious boss, store manager Ted (Donavon Stinson). In many ways, *Reaper* is a fairly straightforward Generation Y comedy, as the young lead characters try to come to grips with the demands of young adulthood in a world that does not necessarily promise them a bright future.

A major complication is introduced into the basic scenario of the series by the fact that Sam's parents made a contract with the Devil (played by Ray Wise) before Sam's birth, stipulating that, in return for curing the father of a serious illness, the Devil would own the soul of their firstborn upon the latter's twenty-first birthday. That firstborn is Sam, who finds on turning 21 years old that he is now a chosen one who is contractually obligated to serve the Devil, portrayed more as a lovable and mischievous rogue than a figure of supernatural evil. In particular, Sam is required to work as a reaper, a sort of supernatural bounty hunter who hunts down souls who have escaped into the world from hell, sending them back whence they came. Given the Devil's power, Sam has little choice but to accept this role, although he does it with great reluctance while continuing to hope to find a loophole in the contract. Meanwhile, this basic plot takes a sudden turn near the end of the first season, when it is revealed that Sam might actually be the son of the Devil, not of his putative human father, and that father might not himself be fully human after all, perhaps as a result of his deal with the Devil.

The humorous characterization of the Devil and the ironic treatment of the Chosen One narrative in *Reaper* can both be taken as signs of a growing postmodern skepticism that makes it harder and harder, in the early years of the twenty-first century, for Americans to take their own national myths seriously, despite wanting to do so. The escaped souls seem universally to be evil (and to have returned to earth to wreak havoc), however, and Sam—although in the service of the Devil—is in fact fighting against evil, albeit reluctantly. Aided by Sock and Ben (but initially keeping his supernatural role a secret from Andi, on orders from the Devil), Sam succeeds in one mission after another. He and his friends generally have no idea what they are doing, however, largely because the Devil chooses to provide very little support or guidance—apparently finding it amusing to watch them stumble through their assignments.

The first episode of *Reaper* was directed by acclaimed filmmaker Kevin Smith, who continued to serve as a creative consultant for the series, which as a whole has some of the energy of Smith's supernatural comedy *Dogma* (1999), with some of the feel of Smith's legendary *Clerks* (1994) tossed in as well. The basic silliness of the series can be a bit off-putting for anyone who might come to *Reaper* in search of supernatural drama, yet there is a reasonable amount of action, and the basic premise can be fairly entertaining once one gets past its ridiculousness. The cast is extremely good: Harrison and Peregrym are likeable and appealing, and Labine provides some spirited comic energy. It is Wise, however, playing the Devil with charming and generally harmless malevolence, who provides the series's best comic moments, and it is certainly telling that this Satanic figure could be represented so winningly on an American television network. Granted, Satan is supposed to be appealing and seductive, but in a misleading and malicious way. Wise's Devil seems genuinely charming and is (despite taking pleasure in tormenting Sam) basically using his considerable supernatural powers to work for the good of mankind throughout the series. The series did not draw particularly large audiences to its early episodes, but it has attracted a substantial amount of positive critical response, suggesting that its high-risk presentation of a likeable Devil has been a success. After all, the series fulfills what might be described as a national longing to believe in the power of Satan, but sugarcoats that image with zany comedy and with assurances that it is all just a joke and that this Satan means no real harm. Apparently, Americans want to believe in Satan, but they don't *really* want to believe in Satan. Or do they?

Three

U.S. VS. THEM: AMERICAN PARANOIA AND THE LONGING FOR EVIL IN AMERICAN HISTORY AND AMERICAN CULTURE

Satan has served as the prototype for the depiction of racial Others as savage and depraved from the initial encounters of European settlers with native Americans onward. For example, Ronald Takaki has convincingly argued that the very notion of strict racial differences is largely a product of the early Puritan association of Native Americans with Satan. For centuries the English had regarded themselves as the epitome of civilization and thus as radically superior to their most important Others, the "primitive" and "barbaric" Irish. Conversely, prior to the seventeenth century, they had regarded these differences as largely cultural rather than biological and had assumed that the Irish could be civilized by proper acculturation. Contacts with Native Americans in the early seventeenth century, however, eventually led the English colonists in New England to believe that their differences from Native Americans were racial and could not be overcome by culture. According to Takaki, "Indians...personified the Devil and everything the Puritans feared—the body, sexuality, laziness, sin, and the loss of self-control" (p. 43).

Among other things, this demonization was part of the Puritan perception of Satan as a palpable entity, giving them a sense of supernatural forces (largely evil) afoot in the world. For the Puritans, Satan was a very real presence who had to be battled every day. The constant vigilance and diligence required by this ongoing battle no doubt made a crucial contribution to the development of the Puritan work ethic; however, it also led to a sense of paranoia that has influenced some of the more negative strains in American history. Writing in the 1960s, the eminent American historian Richard Hofstadter argues, in a well-known essay ("The Paranoid Style in American Politics"), that paranoid visions of conspiracies against the United States and its people by shadowy, evil others have been a part of the texture of American politics throughout U.S. history. For example, the early years of U.S. nationhood were marked by intense concerns about Masonic plots to take over the U.S. government, concerns that peaked during the presidential administration of Andrew Jackson (1829–1837), himself a Mason. By the end of the Jackson administration, rumors of anti-American Catholic conspiracies were already rampant. Hofstadter, having established these precedents, then jumps to the more contemporary example of right-wing McCarthyite visions of communist conspiracies. Of course, it is well known that, in the half century since McCarthy, conspiracy theories (signified by the addition of the term "conspiracy theory" to our national daily vocabulary) have become only more ingrained in the texture of day-to-day life in the United States. The events of September 11, 2001, provided a stunning punctuation to this tendency.

The conspiracy theories discussed by Hofstadter are primarily secular in nature, although they tend to involve religious issues. Moreover, as Hofstadter notes, for paranoid conspiracy theorists, "history *is* a conspiracy, set in motion by demonic forces of almost transcendent power, and what is felt to be needed to defeat it is not the usual methods of political give-and-take, but an all-out crusade" (p. 29). Again, one thinks here of the rhetoric not only of Joseph McCarthy's war on communism but of the more recent war on terrorism of the Bush administration, both of which can be seen as close reimaginings of the vision that drove the Salem witch trials of the seventeenth century.

As Richard Slotkin has demonstrated, the racialized demonization of "savage" enemies has been crucial to the historical formation of the national identity of the United States as the nation that wages "savage war" on such vicious and uncivilized foes. Slotkin's magisterial three-volume study of the role of racial frontier violence in the formation of the American national identity comprises *Regeneration through Violence* (1973), *The Fatal Environment* (1985), and *Gunfighter Nation* (1992). Slotkin demonstrates the crucial role played in the formation of the national identity of the United States by narratives of the taming of the West and the concomitant defeat of Native America. What is especially important for my purposes is Slotkin's indication, especially in *Gunfighter Nation*, of the ways in which, after the actual taming of the West at the end of the nineteenth century, the savage war narrative continued to be central to American culture, as narratives of racial conflict shifted from the real frontier to more symbolic and imaginary ones. Some of these new cultural productions were simple fictionalized recreations of earlier frontier conflicts, leading to the prominence of the Western as a genre in much of the twentieth century. This often suggested a nostalgia for the "good old days," when savage enemies could easily be located within the geographic bounds of the United States. Others were diversions of the energies of the Western in new directions. For example, Slotkin devotes considerable discussion to the popular early-twentieth-century adventure novels of Edgar Rice Burroughs as an illustration of this phenomenon.

More recently, Engelhardt has employed an argument quite similar to that of Slotkin in his elaboration of the importance of what he calls "victory culture" to the development of the national cultural identity of the United States. Patrick Sharp's *Savage Perils* (2007), which features a blurb by Slotkin on the back cover, focuses especially on the use of a racially charged construction of civilization (meaning the United States) versus savagery (meaning the national enemy of the moment) as the basis for a sense of national mission in American history. Sharp particularly relates this phenomenon to the "Darwinist frontier vision" that drove American politics in the nineteenth century but insists on its contemporary relevance as well. Indeed, he identifies the Bush administration's "Axis of Evil" rhetoric as a contemporary reinscription of this strategy, arguing that Bush, in elaborating this concept in his first major post-9/11 speech, "tapped into a rich vein of racism that extended back to the dawn of the United States" (p. 3).

Hofstadter is perfectly right to identify the anticommunist and anti-Soviet hysteria of the peak Cold War years as a leading example of American political paranoia, although his essay also usefully reminds us that this phenomenon was not unique but represented a fairly typical episode in U.S. political history. Among other things, Hofstadter's essay thus helps to explain the seeming disproportion of American Cold War paranoia to the actual threat of communist subversion or Soviet attack. As the distinguished British historian Eric Hobsbawm notes, both sides in the Cold War were understandably worried about the power of the other. Only in America, however, did the tone of Cold War anxieties become absolutely "apocalyptic," and only in the United States did talk of a "communist world conspiracy" become a major part of the political rhetoric of the period (pp. 236–237). Viewed within a larger historical perspective, the vision of apocalyptic conspiracies that so centrally informed American attitudes during the Cold War was a fairly typical example of American political rhetoric. It is no doubt also the case, however, that the then-recent introduction of nuclear weapons gave this vision an unprecedented urgency. After all, the means were now at hand to destroy all of human civilization with just the touch of a couple of buttons.

Given this situation, it was only natural that American culture during the peak Cold War years of the long 1950s (1946–1964) should reflect the apocalyptic anxieties of the period. Whereas American culture had always been centrally populated by evil and savage others against whom virtuous Americans could do righteous battle (Native Americans in the pre-1950s Western are the classic case), such figures became even more prominent during the Cold War. Similarly, the climate of the period made it almost unavoidable that the perfidious activities in which these evil others were engaged tended to be conspiratorial in nature and involve plans for world conquest and domination. The classic case here was the science fiction alien invasion narrative, usually constructed as a fairly transparent allegory about the threat of communist subversion. Narratives such as Don Siegel's 1956 classic *Invasion of the Body Snatchers* (perhaps the best example) often reflected other typical anxieties of the period (e.g., the increasing economic independence of women and the increasing penetration of daily life by a rapidly expanding system of consumer capitalism) as well. Indeed, even as Joseph McCarthy and others attempted to implicate the film industry itself in communist conspiracies, a variety of anticommunist films explicitly depicted fears of communist conspiracies. Anticommunist films—including R. G. Springsteen's *The Red Menace* (1949), Gordon Douglas's *I Was a Communist for the FBI* (1951), and Edward Ludwig's *Big Jim McLain* (1952)—produced during this period can be seen at least in part as an attempt to demonstrate that Hollywood was not dominated by un-American radicals. These films are often so lurid and so extreme that they actually make the McCarthyite anticommunist movement, not communism itself, seem more like a crazed conspiracy.[1] More sophisticated Cold War–inspired films, however, as in the case of John Frankenheimer's *The Manchurian Candidate* (1962), often showed a view of the world that was just as paranoid. The communist conspiracies depicted in these films are secular, but the rhetoric of mainstream anticommunism during the period clearly attributed a Satanic quality to communist strivings. More extreme, fundamentalist visions tended to figure the rise of world communism as a sign of the coming Apocalypse—even as anticommunism itself gained tremendous energies from fears of an impending apocalyptic nuclear confrontation with the Soviet Union.

Not surprisingly, then, fears of communist conspiracies in the 1950s quite often morphed in popular culture into realms beyond the secular and the human. Depictions of genuinely Satanic supernatural conspiracies were probably a bit *too* much for American audiences in the 1950s. Still, the various monster movies and alien invasion movies of the decade no doubt gained considerable energy from the Christian apocalyptic tradition, although this tradition was an even more obvious influence on the emergent science fiction genre of the apocalyptic and postapocalyptic tale, almost all examples of which during this period were directly or allegorically linked to fears of nuclear holocaust.[2]

The various monsters and holocausts that populate the American popular culture of the long 1950s are almost all secular in nature, products more of runaway science than of supernatural evil. Of the pop cultural monsters from the period that have even vaguely supernatural intonations, only the old figure of the vampire remained truly popular in the 1950s, and here largely because vampires are potentially romantic figures who offer a vision (however negative and frightening) of escape from the routine of gray-flanneled conformity. The popularity of vampires (and of the horror genre in general) in the 1950s probably owed less to millenarian anxieties than to the simple fact that such films have a special appeal for the young audiences that became more and more crucial to the film industry during this decade, attending films for dating and other social purposes, whereas older viewers got more and more of their entertainment from television. In particular, Christopher Lee's turn as Dracula for England's Hammer Films was a highlight of the decade, launching Lee on one of the most successful acting careers in horror-film history. After all, Lee's Dracula was a highly sexual monster, providing subtly titillating material for date films, even while (in keeping with the surface prudishness of the decade) avoiding overt mention of actual sex. Cyndy Hendershot thus notes that the Hammer films restored some of Dracula's erotic mystique, providing a sort of escapist fantasy from the daily routine of 1950s life. In American films of the 1950s even vampires were somewhat routinized, reformulated evil Others typical of the kind generally associated with communism or creatures of science rather than the supernatural (pp. 43–54).

ROSEMARY'S BABY AND THE HORROR BOOM OF THE 1970S

The depiction of supernatural evil in American popular culture entered a dramatic new phase with the release of Roman Polanski's chilling *Rosemary's Baby* in 1968. Among other things, this film was a watershed in American cultural history because it was a self-consciously *good* film, artfully constructed by an A-list director and featuring top-notch actors. This film demonstrated that horror films could be subtle psychological dramas; here, in a film with no bloodshed, no special effects, and essentially no actual portrayal of violence, Polanski creates a slow and gradual accumulation of terrifying minor details, culminating in the final revelation that the baby just given birth by young Rosemary Woodhouse (Mia Farrow) is in fact the child of Satan, come to claim dominion over the earth. If the American horror genre as a whole has numerous links with the early Puritan fascination with Satan as an ever-present threat, here Satan at last emerges as a major player in the popular culture of modern consumerist America.

Even here Satan remains in the background—as someone so sneaky might be expected to do. As the plot (in both senses of the word) gradually un-folds, Polanski manages to play, in a masterful way, on any number of central modern fears, building to this climax. Early in the film, Rosemary and her ac-tor husband Guy Woodhouse (John Cassavetes) move into an old New York apartment building that has long been plagued by rumors of strange (and pos-sibly supernatural) goings on among its inhabitants. These hints, along with certain oddities about the apartment they rent, introduce a haunted-house motif that helps to prepare an atmosphere in which other minor peculiarities that the Woodhouses notice about the building and their neighbors take on an added weight and air of suspicion. These neighbors at first seem to be merely a collection of oddballs, but this atmosphere (and the generic character of the film) suggest to us that their eccentricities might have a sinister side.

This fear of neighbors (especially in big-city apartment buildings, where they live close but are not generally well known) is a typical modern experi-ence. In the context of modern capitalism, even one's most intimate acquain-tances seem alien, and Rosemary's concerns about the neighbors are soon en-hanced by concerns that Guy himself might be in league with the strange tenants, introducing a fear of intimate Others of a kind that is central to such films as *I Married a Monster from Outer Space* (1958). Such fears are much more disturbing after Rosemary becomes pregnant (as a result of a supernat-ural rape in which Guy and the neighbors are complicit), placing her in a vulnerable position that produces anxieties under the best of circumstances. If a pregnant woman cannot trust her own husband to help protect her and her unborn baby (which she believes is Guy's) from harm, whom can she trust? Conventionally, of course, the answer might be her physician. One of the most effective moves introduced by Polanski is to make the prominent ob-stetrician Abraham Sapirstein (Ralph Bellamy), who treats Rosemary during her pregnancy, an obvious member of the conspiracy, leaving poor vulnerable Rosemary essentially no recourse.

The vulnerability of the waifish, big-eyed Rosemary as the central object of the Satanic plot of the film is also a key to the success of the film, even as it raises important questions about gender stereotyping. Rosemary is the object of little physical violence (the most frightening physical assaults shown are the two moments in which Sapirstein forceably injects her with a sedative to secure her docility when she begins to resist the conspiracies). Otherwise, however, she is precisely the sort of pretty, small, frail, blonde woman victim to whom Buffy Summers would later emerge as a rejoinder in *Buffy the Vampire Slayer*. Still, *Rosemary's Baby*, by building on so many fundamental modern fears, almost needs such a prototypical victim at its center, besides which such victims were not quite the clichés in 1968 that they would later become. Meanwhile, Polanski carefully avoids making Satan (or even the Satanic child) the focus of the film by never showing either on the screen. This is not merely a tactic based on the supposition that "the devil you don't know is more frightening than the devil you do know." It is very much the reverse. The focus is not on Satan but on Guy, Dr. Sapirstein, and the neighbors, creating a conspiracy of the ordinary that is far more frightening than Satan to modern viewers, who must deal with such ordinary others on a daily basis. In this case, hell really is other people.

Perhaps the most striking aspect of *Rosemary's Baby* is the way it downplays both the role of Satan and the apocalyptic role that is about to be played by Satan's son. These are, after all, abstractions. What is really terrifying in the world of late capitalism is the day-to-day horror of each against all, and *Rosemary's Baby* picks up on this horror perhaps better than any other American film. Moreover, the film's ending, suggesting that Rosemary herself will join the conspiracy, is more horrifying than the possibility that has loomed all along that she will be destroyed by it. In a world saturated with evil, who can hope to escape contamination? The saturation of the commonplace by supernatural evil is a key ingredient of *Rosemary's Baby*, which thus might be at its most terrifying in its implication that even the supernatural does not provide a thrilling (if horrifying) escape from the banal, because here the supernatural *is* banal.

Of course, it is a virtual cliché of the horror film that the innocent are the preferred victims of evil, but seldom are the innocent won over to the side of evil without any real coercion. In the case of Rosemary, she seems more seduced by her natural mother's love for her own baby (however Satanic he might be) than by the traditionally seductive wiles of the baby's father. Although various individual characters certainly conspire against Rosemary, the mundane focus of the film gives this conspiracy a small, localized quality that lacks the paranoia of later visions in American culture of Satanic plots to bring about the Apocalypse. Such paranoid visions, in fact, really begin only in the 1970s, no doubt partly because of the fallout of the Watergate scandal, which also triggered a spate of paranoid thrillers involving political conspiracies, such as Alan J. Pakula's *The Parallax View* (1974) and *All the President's Men* (1976), Francis Ford Coppola's *The Conversation* (1974), and Sydney Pollack's *Three Days of the Condor* (1975).

The beginnings of this move toward more of a focus on Satanic plots can be found in William Friedkin's *The Exorcist* (1973). Satan (or at least an ancient evil spirit—that apparently emerges from Iraq, no less) here seems more interested in making particular persons really miserable than in bringing about a universal Apocalypse. To that end, the spirit possesses the body of an innocent young girl, Regan MacNeil (Linda Blair). The consequent actions of the possessed girl (who spends most of the second half of the film tied down in her bed for her own safety) represent some of the most memorable scenes in all of American film: Regan's head spins around backward on her neck; she projectile vomits a torrent of green liquid onto a priest; she levitates into the air; she performs a number of shocking sexual gestures, including a lewd demand to be fucked by a priest and a violent attack on her own genitals using a crucifix as a weapon.[3] These various scenes are so distinctive that they have frequently become the object of parodies over the years, so much so that (at least to me) much of their original shocking effect has been removed.

Shock is clearly the strategy of *The Exorcist*, a film that centrally deals with our lack of preparation, in the skeptical modern world, to deal with genuine supernatural threats when they confront us. Regan's mother, film actress Chris MacNeil (Ellen Burstyn), spends most of the first half of the film taking her daughter to various doctors and hospitals, seeking a medical explanation for the girl's increasingly bizarre behavior.[4] That there is no such explanation is one point of the film, which argues that there are more things in heaven and earth than are dreamt of in the rationalizing philosophy of modern science. In the meantime, the film is also (like *Rosemary's Baby*) able to draw on the inherently frightening experience of modern medical treatment, even as it maneuvers to posit an evil that goes completely outside the realm of medicine.

With science and other modern institutions, such as the police, unable to come to Regan's aid, what is left is the church, specifically the Catholic Church, Satan's old nemesis. The two priests, Father Karras (Jason Miller) and Father Merrin (Max von Sydow), who come to Regan's aid do not seem well equipped to do so either, despite their taking Satanic possession seriously and supposedly having a preestablished method for dealing with it. Merrin, an experienced exorcist, is also an archaeologist, whereas Karras is a psychiatrist, trained at all the best schools. They therefore bring both scientific and mystical expertise to the task of banishing the demon that has possessed Regan, but they are still not up to that task. Merrin quickly dies (possibly killed by the possessed girl), and Karras ultimately dies as well, although his is a sacrificial death that ostensibly sets Regan free of the demon, which jumps from her body to that of Karras just before the priest leaps to his death. The question remains: What scars will Regan have suffered, despite suggestions that she mercifully remembers nothing?

Although many of the scenes in *The Exorcist* were genuinely chilling until familiarity robbed them of some of their shock effect, the film is also inherently less terrifying than *Rosemary's Baby* precisely because it does focus more on supernatural evil as a threat. Even so, the film's demon does not seem so much bent on a conspiratorial effort at world conquest or triggering the holocaust as on making a few peoples' lives genuinely miserable. The domestic focus of the film, concentrating on the attempts of a mother to shield her daughter from outside threats, provides an avenue that most audiences can identify with. In a review of the 2000 Director's Cut of the film, Roger Ebert suggests that one of the film's strengths is the way it sets its horror in the mundane by embedding "the sensational material in an everyday world of misty nights, boozy parties and housekeeping details, chats in a laundry room, and the personal lives of the priests." Of course, one is tempted to view the possession, which occurs in Regan's early adolescence, as a sort of metaphor for puberty, making Regan's plight something of an analog for the emergence of feminine sexuality (if one focuses on her gender) or just an analog for the famously crazed behavior of teenagers in general (if one focuses on her age). Mostly though, *The Exorcist* is such a powerful and visceral assault that it is rather pointless to attribute any meaning beyond what appears on the screen. In many ways, it is more the forerunner of the later turn to slash and gore in the horror film than the successor to the more thoughtful effort of *Rosemary's Baby*.

Rosemary's Baby was one of the most important American films of the late 1960s, successful both critically and commercially, a genuinely frightening supernatural thriller that was also a well-crafted work of cinematic art. *The Exorcist* comes close in importance as a touchstone in the history of American popular culture. Among other things, these films are important because they were so influential on the genre of the horror film, spawning a number of imitations and knockoffs and virtually creating their own demon-child subgenre of the horror film. This subgenre—which includes such entries as *It's Alive* (1974), *The Omen* (1976), *Audrey Rose* (1977), *Demon Seed* (1977), and *The Brood* (1979)—was one of the most important phenomena in American horror films of the 1970s, a decade that was particularly rich for horror cinema. Of these, Richard Donner's *The Omen* (which triggered its own chain of direct sequels, as well as a 2006 remake), is probably the most successful and important.

The Omen, which focuses on the birth of the Antichrist (and the subsequent threat of an Apocalypse) carries particularly strong religious/eschatological resonances. The film begins as the rich and powerful Robert Thorn (Gregory Peck) gets the bad news from a priest that his newborn son has died. The priest then urges Thorn to accept an orphaned newborn as a substitute, a fact that they agree to hide from his emotionally fragile wife Katherine (Lee Remick). They then raise the boy, Damien (played in most of the film by Harvey Stephens), as their own, though the mother gradually becomes concerned that there is something strange and dangerous about the child.

These hints of strangeness gain focus when his governess commits a very public and spectacular suicide during an elaborate birthday party for the boy, driven to do so to allow the devil's servant, Mrs. Baylock (Billie Whitelaw), to step in to become the boy's new nanny. From that point on, the boy grows increasingly odd and withdrawn, always shadowed by Mrs. Baylock and a mysterious black dog that seems to appear whenever something really bad is about to happen. Eventually, another priest tells Thorn (now the U.S. ambassador to England) that his adopted son is the spawn of Satan. Thorn is suspicious of the priest but checks out the warnings nevertheless, eventually discovering that his biological son had been murdered at birth so that Damien could be substituted for him. The plan is that the boy will grow up and inherit the wealth and power of his adoptive father, who is a friend of the current president of the United States and a leading candidate to become a future president in his own right. Eventually, convinced that Damien is evil, Thorn attempts to kill the boy but is shot down in the process by police. With Katherine having already been murdered by Mrs. Baylock, the boy is orphaned. He lands on his feet, however, and the film ends with the joint funeral of the Thorns, attended by Damien holding the hand of the president. This ending suggests that the president will adopt the boy, putting him in a position of great power and placing the locus of conspiratorial evil in the Oval Office, in what can be taken as a direct nod to the then-recent Watergate scandal. *The Omen* ends before the actual Apocalypse, but it looks ominous—paving the way for the sequels.

This ending, however, is more fun than terrifying, providing a little frisson of delightful fear reminiscent of the endings of older monster movies when the monster, presumably killed or at least incapacitated, suddenly arises again. Granted, *The Omen* takes all of its material with absolute seriousness, even solemnity, although (as is usually the case with this genre) its most chilling effects surely derive not from the big picture eschatology, but from the basic personal drama of parents (especially the frail and vulnerable mother) being threatened by their own evil child. Various other common parental fears come into play as well, including anxieties about taking home the wrong child from the hospital or even about accidentally handing one's child over to sinister child-care workers. The very fact that such mundane concerns trump the film's fundamental end-of-the-world premise suggests that American audiences are better at imagining personal tragedy than large-scale disaster, and that these audiences, by and large, aren't really all that seriously worried about the Apocalypse, however consistent such worries are with the religious beliefs that most Americans claim to hold.

Nevertheless, the popular culture of the 1970s, with the twin specters of Watergate and Vietnam hovering in the background, is filled with a new sort of anxiety that goes beyond the relatively simple and easily definable fears of the peak Cold War years. Now the conspiratorial forces that threaten America and Americans are becoming increasingly shadowy and nebulous, us-versus-them narratives becoming blurred by the increasing difficulty of distinguishing between *us* and *them*. Now, rather than defend the American way of life from evil, savage foes who would destroy it, Americans begin very seriously to wrestle with the proposition that the greatest evil that threatens them is the American way itself, at least to the extent that this way has been co-opted by secret, sinister forces in the U.S. government, in large corporations, or both.

Given the long penchant of American culture to express conspiratorial fears in supernatural terms, it should come as no surprise that the 1970s were a boom decade not only for paranoid political thrillers but also for horror films. Arguing that horror in the 1970s became "the most important of all American genres and perhaps the most progressive," Robin Wood characterizes this decade as a period of "extreme cultural crisis and disintegration" in which the rise to prominence of the horror genre was "entirely logical, even inevitable" (pp. 63, 76). Conversely, perhaps because of the intensity of the cultural crisis that informed the 1970s, the horror films of that decade tend to be informed more by a sense of chaos and confusion than by a sense of large-scale, carefully constructed plots to do evil. In the 1970s, Satan is a disrupter and not a maker of plans.

Thus, although *Rosemary's Baby* involves a conspiratorial plot, it is localized and small scale, dealing centrally with the subornation of Rosemary and making the possibility of a coming Apocalypse a mere afterthought. Meanwhile, most of the horror films of the decade after *Rosemary's Baby* are so rooted in that troubled period that they have not been able to overcome the built-in prejudice against horror as a disreputable genre to become lasting monuments of American cinema. Brian De Palma's *Sisters* (1973), described by Wood as "perhaps the most brilliant of all 70s horror films," is hardly remembered at all and then only as a minor early Hitchcock-inflected effort in De Palma's long and prolific career (p. 85). Larry Cohen's *It's Alive* (1974) and *It Lives Again* (1978), both also much admired by Wood, have their followers among horror film aficionados but are otherwise regarded as marginal and somewhat tawdry efforts—although still marketable enough to warrant a 2008 remake.

Of the horror films of the 1970s, only *The Exorcist* (1973) rivals *Rosemary's Baby* in its prominence in American cinema. One could argue that George A. Romero's relatively crude, low-budget zombie films—beginning with *Night of the Living Dead* (1968) and *Dawn of the Dead* (1978)—have had at least as much impact on American popular culture as either of these glossier efforts, however. Romero's stumbling, staggering, but insatiable zombies—emblems, among other things, of the status to which ordinary consumers are reduced under late capitalism—are among the most iconic images of recent American culture and remain the central figures of what has become a booming zombie subgenre. What is particularly powerful about Romero's version of the zombie narrative, of course, is the fact that here zombies—who could be seen as the ultimate other, as estranged from humanity as one who has ever been human could possibly become—are not really others at all. In Romero's films, the zombies are what the mainstream population of America has become in the era of late capitalism. They are the norm, and those who resist the mindless conformity of consumerism are the strangers in the strange land of "post-zombification" America.

Romero's zombies are also pretty much entirely secular, losing the mystical dimension that zombies once had in their Voodoo origins and thus also becoming emblems of the increasing secularization of the supernatural in American popular culture. They also represent a new twist on the old conspiracy theme. Rather than an evil plot masterminded by a superintelligent villain (or villains), the zombies become a sort of mindless plague, sweeping across the face of the earth in an inexorable wave of colonization. Like capitalism itself, they become an unstoppable force that consumes everything in its path, even without any sort of well-crafted plan to guide its expansion. Thus, the suggestion of a coming zombie Apocalypse that lies at the center of all of Romero's zombie narratives is particularly frightening because it refuses to provide the two basic comforts that make apocalyptic narratives popular in the first place: the attribution of evil to a recognizable other who can be confronted and potentially defeated, and the simple suggestion that all the bad things in the world are part of an order and a plan that, however nefarious, ultimately make sense.

Romero's troubling narratives were somewhat out of phase with the Reaganite 1980s, in which the simple moral universe of the *Star Wars* films rose to the fore as part of a U.S. national desire to put the troubles and confusions of the 1970s in the past. A central theme of the Reagan years was moving forward into a new era of prosperity in which the American national narrative of the

Cold War years could be restored by breathing new life into the old concept of communism as an "Evil Empire," making the United States once again a champion of good. Little wonder, then, that Romero's only zombie narrative of the decade, *Day of the Dead* (1985), was probably his weakest effort or that it brought his zombie cycle to an end. The zombie theme was resurrected (like zombies themselves) with a vengeance in 2005 with the release of *Land of the Dead*, which appropriately updated the satire of the earlier films for the era of globalization. This film added new layers of meaning that made it possible to read the zombies now as the masses of poor worldwide, encircling the wealth of the denizens of the luxury high-rise Fiddler's Green, which now stands for the United States and other localized concentrations of prosperity amid a generally impoverished world.[5] The glimmers of intelligence that the zombies in this latter film begin to display can surely be taken as a sign that the masses of poor that encircle the globe are beginning to understand what lies behind their fate, with ominous implications for the wealthy.

Given the horror boom in American film in the 1970s, it is not surprising that horror increasingly made its way onto television screens in that decade, although television had not previously been particularly fruitful territory for the genre. Indeed, one of the most memorable horror series in television history was already on the air when the decade began, having premiered in 1966: that is, the daytime soap opera *Dark Shadows*, which still has a cult following and is the only long-running American soap opera to have been released in its entirety on home video. *Dark Shadows* features a panoply of supernatural events and creatures, most important being the vampire Barnabas Collins (Jonathan Frid). Collins first appeared about a year into the run of the show, which (after a relatively conventional beginning) began to move more and more into supernatural territory. In 1970, horror also broke into prime time with the premier of *Night Gallery*, hosted by Rod Serling. This series attempted to capture some of the magic of Serling's earlier anthology, *The Twilight Zone*, but in a darker mood and with more of an emphasis on horror. Serling, however, left the series after three years as he became increasingly disgruntled at network attempts to tone down the show, keeping it safely within the banal bounds of the commercial television mainstream.

The difficulties experienced by Serling with *Night Gallery* are indicative of the obstacles faced by horror in commercial television, where executives tend to be averse to controversy of any kind. With the specter of the widespread controversies over 1950s horror comics (especially those, such as the notorious *Tales from the Crypt*, produced by E.C. Comics[6]) still haunting the memory of American popular culture, it should thus come as no surprise that the broadcast networks in particular have been squeamish about beaming horror stories into American homes.[7] Horror thus made only modest inroads into network television in the 1970s, as in *The Norliss Tapes* (1973), a TV movie that has gained something of a cult following, although the series for which it was the pilot was never produced. *The Norliss Tapes* features Roy Thinnes as a writer whose investigations into the supernatural reveal shocking truths. As such, it has much in common with the most successful supernatural horror series of the 1970s, *The Night Stalker* (also called *Kolchak: The Night Stalker*), which remains one of the cult favorites of 1970s TV, despite the fact that it ran for only one twenty-episode season in 1974 and 1975. The series followed the TV movies *The Night Stalker* (1972) and *The Night Strangler* (1973), both written by the much-acclaimed novelist and scriptwriter Richard Matheson. In the first movie, rumpled newspaper reporter Carl Kolchak (Darren Mc-Gavin) traces a series of Las Vegas murders to a deadly vampire. In the second, Kolchak discovers that a similar series of murders in Seattle have been committed by a nineteenth-century surgeon who has developed an immortality serum, the effects of which must be renewed every 21 years with the blood of young girls. In the series, Kolchak settles in Chicago, investigating a series of bizarre and grisly crimes that always turn out to have supernatural or science fictional perpetrators.

Diminishing audiences and the unhappiness of star McGavin with his role led to the cancellation of the series before it had completed the run of its first season. McGavin, however, was terrific in the role, and the ongoing popularity of the series in reruns and on DVD is probably due mostly to his quirky turn as Kolchak, which helped to spice the dark subject matter of the series with humor. Kolchak is a sort of stock reporter figure, really a comic and less tough variation on the hard-boiled detective. McGavin's performance gives Kolchak a unique charm, vaguely along the lines of Peter Falk's Columbo. In this, he is something of a forerunner of Mulder in *The X-Files*, which should come as no surprise given that *X-Files* creator Chris Carter has identified *The Night Stalker* as one of his personal favorites and as a major influence on *The X-Files*. McGavin ultimately made multiple guest appearances on *The X-Files* as FBI agent Arthur Dales, who turns out to have founded the FBI's X-Files project back in the 1950s. His character thus becomes the predecessor to Mulder and Scully, just as *The Night Stalker* preceded *The X-Files*.

THE X-FILES AND THE POSTMODERN CONSPIRACY NARRATIVE: MAPPING THE APOCALYPSE

One of the iconic images of *The X-Files* was a poster that adorned the cluttered FBI office of agent Fox Mulder, showing a flying saucer and displaying the caption "I Want to Believe," a mantra that joined "The Truth Is Out

There" as the two slogans of the program. The gradually unfolding (and re-folding) mytharc plot of the series then involved both its protagonists and its viewers in a never-ending quest to discover this truth and to find this belief, even if the news thus obtained was often bad. This almost paranoid process of attempting to connect the dots to find order and make sense of an otherwise chaotic reality is another of the many ways in which *The X-Files* was a landmark series of its time, followed by numerous other programs that tried (mostly unsuccessfully) to achieve the same effect. Many of these subsequent programs also resembled *The X-Files* in placing the locus of this elusive "truth" somewhere beyond contemporary reality, in what might be interpreted as an almost desperate attempt to transcend the confusion of the mundane by breaking through into another realm, where things make more sense.

The X-Files has been immensely influential, both in its dark, noirish look and in the way its protagonists (and viewers) must slowly piece together patterns of connections that almost make sense but never quite completely come together. One can thus see *The X-Files* as the progenitor of the modern genre of "paranoid" television, which includes the proliferation of such successful recent serial dramas as *Lost* and *Heroes*. Granted, other 1990s science fiction programs—both *Babylon 5* (1993–1998) and *Star Trek: Deep Space Nine* (1993–1999)—actually began broadcasting a few months before *The X-Files* and used continuous plot arcs as well, but it was *The X-Files* that perfected the use of a continuous plot gradually unfolding to develop hints of vast conspiracies. Actually, however, *The X-Files* employs a complex plot structure that is not fully continuous. Most of the episodes are stand-alone "monster-of-the-week" shows in which Mulder and fellow agent Dana Scully (Gillian Anderson) battle against an array of paranormal criminals, most of whom are taken straight from urban legend or popular folklore, including vampires, witches, werewolves, and other supernatural creatures.[8]

Because these monster-of-the-week episodes are meant to stand alone, they typically involve no real elements of supernatural conspiracy, although the accumulated experience of Mulder and Scully in encountering a seemingly endless string of such monsters suggests that some sort of wider phenomenon might be at work. *The X-Files* becomes really interesting, however, in its so-called mytharc episodes, a collection (usually six to eight episodes per season) of episodes that together make up a continuous plot that mainly involves alien plans to colonize the earth and the conspiratorial efforts of a shadowy group of mysterious persons within and beyond the U.S. government either to counter this invasion or to facilitate it for their own selfish purposes.

The X-Files was genuinely unprecedented in the extent to which, within the realm of commercial broadcast television, it suggested the complicity of the U.S. government in far-ranging and potentially apocalyptic conspiracies.

Then again, the time was apparently right for such suggestions to be made in American popular culture. After all, one of the most prominent works of that culture in the years just before the premiere of *The X-Files* in 1993 was Oliver Stone's highly controversial *JFK* (1991). *JFK* is a film that lays out an elaborate and detailed theory of a conspiracy between the Mafia and the CIA to assassinate President John F. Kennedy, largely because his policies were interfering in the desires of both organizations to do business in Cuba.[9] Many aspects of the conspiracy plot of *The X-Files* are highly reminiscent of *JFK*, which became a sort of prototype for conspiracy-based narratives of the 1990s, although *JFK* itself clearly owes much to its predecessors among the paranoid political thrillers of the 1970s, especially *All the President's Men*.

Of course, *The X-Files* had television predecessors in its delineation of nefarious alien invasion plots (the most important influence is probably *The Invaders*, which ran from 1967 to 1969), but *The X-Files* went far beyond other alien invasion series in the cynicism and paranoia with which it treated this motif. In *The Invaders*, protagonist David Vincent (Roy Thinnes) could never convince the authorities that an invasion was under way; in *The X-Files*, the authorities not only know about the invasion plot but are part of it. *The X-Files* takes popular suspicions that the government is involved in a campaign to cover up evidence of UFOs to a whole new level, suggesting that the government not only hides such evidence but might even be complicit in the alien invasion. Indeed, the series is unremittingly cynical about the government, which appears capable of any and all dastardly activities. As a result, the protagonists never know whom to trust ("trust no one" is an underlying theme of the series) and are even unaware of certain dark secrets about themselves and their own pasts.

Although gifted with boyish charm and a wise-cracking sense of humor, Mulder is something of a fanatic, dedicated to unraveling the mysteries of the X-Files at any cost. He is also a brilliant Oxford-educated psychologist, although his abiding interest in paranormal phenomena (triggered supposedly by childhood trauma caused by his sister Samantha's alien abduction) has caused him to be regarded as something of a kook, earning him the nickname "Spooky." Meanwhile, Mulder's fierce dedication to his offbeat investigations leads the FBI to assign Scully to work with him and to keep an eye on him. A trained medical doctor with a reputation for dispassionate scientific objectivity, Scully is seen as a counter to Mulder's potential for excess—but also as a way of keeping tabs on him to prevent him from probing into areas that are better left alone. One of the crucial premises of the series is that many of the cases in the X-Files involve a vast international conspiracy carried out by The Syndicate, a mysterious group that includes officials highly placed in the U.S. government. Other mysterious figures in the government (and even within The Syndicate) sometimes lend aid and support to Mulder and Scully, further complicating the picture. As the series proceeds, Scully remains the voice of conventional reason, but she also begins to grant that Mulder's theories might have more validity than she first believed, whereas Mulder himself experiences occasional bouts of skepticism. In the meantime, Mulder and Scully become genuine friends as well as professional allies, their bonding and mutual respect providing one of the key elements of the series. The relationship (complete with growing sexual tensions) between the two protagonists was a key to the success of the series, as was the basic attractiveness of the protagonists themselves. Ultimately, the fact that they can trust no one else drives Mulder and Scully to trust each other all the more, leading to one of the most compelling intercharacter relationships in the history of commercial television.

By the end of the series, Mulder and Scully are a couple on the run from the authorities. They have even given birth to an infant whose alien DNA gives him superhuman powers and makes him a sort of Chosen One, although his powers have apparently been negated and he has been given away to live with another family for his own safety. Mulder and Scully have been expelled from the FBI and are now being hunted by that organization, even as they also still hope somehow to strike a blow against the final alien invasion, now stipulated to be scheduled for December 22, 2012.[10]

In terms of plot, the heart of *The X-Files*—what made it a special phenomenon in television history—is the conspiracy motif that binds together the mytharc episodes and leads to this ominous, if open, conclusion. In addition to the basic plot elements involving the alien invasion, these episodes often deal with conspiracy in other ways, sometimes in ironic ways that call into question the basic paranoia that drives all conspiracy theories. For example, in "Musings of a Cigarette Smoking Man" (November 17, 1996) we learn that the shadowy and sinister villain of the episode title (played by William B. Davis) might have been involved in several key conspiracies in modern U.S. history, in addition to the central plot involving aliens and The Syndicate. He seems to have been the actual assassin of both John F. Kennedy and Martin Luther King and might have been instrumental in rigging the famous 1980 Olympic Gold Medal hockey game, in which the United States team scored an unlikely victory over the heavily favored Soviets. This episode also reveals the Cigarette Smoking Man's ambition to be a writer of fiction, and it is possible to interpret his musings on his shocking past as mere fantasy. This episode addresses (even if in a tongue-in-cheek way) the possibility that virtually all of recent history is the result of one giant conspiracy.

More seriously, the conspiracy themes in *The X-Files* sometimes touch on important political issues. For example, in the episode "Talitha Cumi" (May 17, 1996), the "good" alien Jeremiah Smith (Roy Thinnes) is held captive by the Cigarette Smoking Man after he uses his superhuman powers to heal some gunshot victims, thus threatening to draw media attention. Smith's captivity leads to the following exchange:

Smoker: "Have you any idea what the cost of your actions is? What their effect might be? Who are you to give them hope?"

Smith: "What do you give them?"

Smoker: "We give them happiness, and they give us authority."

Smith: "The authority to take away their freedom under the guise of democracy."

Smoker: "Men can never be free because they are weak, corrupt, worthless, and restless. The people believe in authority. They've grown tired of waiting for miracle and mystery. Science is their religion. No greater explanation exists for them. They must never believe any differently if the project is to go forward."

This conversation captures many of the central ideas of *The X-Files*, including the contempt of those in power for democracy and for ordinary people, and the sense of the powerful that they can best maintain their power if ordinary people have extremely limited imaginations. In an optimistic view, then, *The X-Files* as a whole can be seen as a concerted attempt to spur the imaginations of viewers and to encourage them to believe in realms of experience that go beyond the everyday world of science and rationality. The success of the show, meanwhile, can be seen as evidence that this attempt matches a collective desire among the audience members. Like Mulder, they want to believe in something more than what they observe in their daily lives—even when this something might prove disastrous, as in the coming alien Apocalypse envisioned by the series. Of course, it helps that viewers know the show is fictional, which makes the various threats that it narrates less frightening. One could also argue that the real attraction of such shows is that they divert audience attention from seemingly insoluble real-world problems to the more manageable (however complex) problems posited by their fictional scenarios. Pushing this interpretation just a bit farther, *The X-Files* and similar works of fiction provide just enough relief from the combined confusion and rationalization of the real world to make life in the real world more bearable, thus decreasing the already small likelihood that members of the audience might attempt to take real political action to improve the conditions under which they live.

There are any number of ways in which *The X-Files* was perfectly in tune with the American mood in the 1990s. Indeed, it was fairly predictable that the 1990s would see a considerable upswing in popular interest in the idea of vast evil conspiracies potentially leading to an all-out Apocalypse. For one thing, the Iran-Contra scandal of the late 1980s had made it seem to many, as the 1990s began, that Watergate was not an isolated event but that, instead, the U.S. government routinely engaged in conspiratorial actions. Moreover, the relative lack of public outrage at the revelations of the investigation into this affair (which showed the Reagan administration to have been extensively involved in illegal international arms dealing in the Middle East to fund its plans to overthrow a legally elected sovereign government in Nicaragua) made it clear that, by this time, few were shocked that the U.S. government could be involved in such nefarious dealings.

As the 1990s began and the end of the millennium neared, apocalyptic visions received a predictable boost, even if the most compelling of these was the entirely secular "Y2K" computer scare. For another, with the Cold War over and the easily identifiable "Evil Empire" of the Soviet bloc no longer available as an anchor to stabilize the popular American vision of global politics, the world looked more complex and confusing than ever. The fascination with conspiratorial and evil others that runs throughout American history suggests that there has always been something comforting about the sense of order supplied by the perceived existence of specific forces at work to promulgate the evils of the world. This comforting aspect of the idea of vast evil conspiracies surely gained in power as an alternative to the chaotic global politics of the post–Cold War era. There is a sense, then, in which the desire for order that is manifested in the contemporary popular fascination with conspiracy narratives can be seen as the result of a utopian longing, produced by what Fredric Jameson has compellingly described in *Postmodernism* as a much deeper loss of the ability to perform "cognitive mapping." Jameson argues that contemporary postmodern subjects find themselves increasingly entangled in the web of a global capitalist system that is changing more and more rapidly, all the while becoming more and more complex and seemingly incomprehensible, making it virtually impossible for individual people to have a sense of how the system works or what their place in the system might be.

Mulder and Scully in *The X-Files*, very much like the viewers of *The X-Files*, are engaged precisely in an extended exercise in cognitive mapping. Many of the programs that were directly influenced by this aspect of *The X-Files*—such as the 1990s remake of *The Night Stalker* and the short-lived 2003 ABC series *Miracles*—were canceled so quickly that they never really had a chance to provide their viewers with the same sorts of satisfactions. Viewed as exercises in cognitive mapping, however, it is clear that a long-form medium such as the television series potentially has much more to offer than a feature film, which simply does not have enough time to build the intricate networks of connections that this process requires. Although it was inevitable that apocalyptic supernatural thrillers would make something of a comeback in the late 1990s as the millennium change neared, none of these end-of-the-century works were able to achieve the success of earlier works such as *Rosemary's Baby* and *The Exorcist*. These earlier works, after all, had been fueled by anxieties that nefarious conspiracies might be afoot in the world. By the end of the 1990s, few filmgoers doubted the existence of such conspiracies, so suggestions of them of the abbreviated type available to the feature film were not very alarming and could do little to provide that frisson of fear that is so crucial to the pleasure of the horror film.

One example of the turn-of-the-millennium supernatural thriller, Kevin Smith's *Dogma* (1999), even treats the Apocalypse as an occasion for slapstick comedy. Alternatively, the 1999 supernatural thriller *Stigmata* takes quite seriously the notion that, were Christian mythology literally true, the texture of our world would be transformed into that of a horror film. Meanwhile, the film shows its postmodern cynicism by depicting the Catholic church, in its ruthless quest for wealth and power, as part of the problem, engaged in conspiracies of its own. However cynical it might be about the church, *Stigmata* is ultimately a sort of romance in which the good guys win and all is right with the world. As the film ends, the protagonist (having left the priesthood) seems well on his way to getting the girl, while Christ Himself emerges as a heroic down-home God, shedding the trappings of organized religion in favor of delivering His message of love directly to the people.

A more serious effort to create a sense of apocalyptic threat can be seen in the 1999 film *The Ninth Gate*, in which, more than three decades after *Rosemary's Baby*, director Polanski returned to the genre of the supernatural thriller. *The Ninth Gate* stars Johnny Depp as Dean Corso, a dealer in rare books who is commissioned by wealthy collector Boris Balkan (Frank Langella) to try to determine the authenticity of the world's only three existing copies of a seventeenth-century volume entitled *The Nine Gates*. This volume is supposed to give its user the power to summon Satan to appear on earth, but Balkan has already determined that his own copy of the book does not appear to work. Most of the film is essentially a detective story in which Corso tracks down the other two copies of the book and attempts to unravel the mystery of their magic, eventually determining that only three of the nine illustrations in each book are actually authentic, so one must collect the proper illustrations (drawn by Satan himself and signed "LCF," for Lucifer) to conjure up Satan. In the end, with Balkan having been killed while trying to prove that he is fireproof after thinking he has taken on Satan's power, Corso himself summons Satan, who appears to be about to emerge on earth just as the film ends. Unfortunately, however, this film never achieves the sinister atmosphere of supernatural dread that informs *Rosemary's Baby*, while Depp's turn as Corso is perhaps his most lackluster film performance.

If even the team of Polanski and Depp could not produce a genuinely frightening supernatural thriller on the verge of a millennium change, it might be because (reported poll results about the astounding level of belief in the supernatural among Americans notwithstanding) by the end of the twentieth century, most Americans could no longer generate genuine fear of supernatural evil. Moreover, it was simply the case that Americans, now accustomed to the notion of shadowy conspiracies, no longer found them as frightening as the alternative possibility that there were *no* conspiracies and no order in the world at all. If popular culture is any barometer of the popular mood, Americans by the end of the 1990s were more fascinated with and less frightened by conspiracies than ever before. They were so much so that the real pleasures to be derived from conspiratorial apocalyptic narratives were to be found in television programs such as *The X-Files* that allowed viewers to participate in the gradual unraveling of the complex plots of these narratives. Several such programs were, in fact, directly related to potential millenarian anxieties, making it clear that conspiracy narratives and apocalyptic narratives had now effectively collapsed into the same genre.

APOCALYPTIC TELEVISION AT THE TURN OF THE MILLENNIUM

The constant threat of apocalypse that drives the narratives of *Buffy* and *Angel*, as well as the alien apocalypse of *The X-Files*, had already prepared the way for several apocalyptic television series that appeared just before and just after the turn of the last century. Whereas all of these apocalyptic narratives derive at least some energy from the Christian apocalyptic tradition, they tend to treat the Apocalypse as a narrative device rather than a genuine reality. As a result, they employ the concept of apocalypse with considerable irony and use it largely as a device to generate tension and thus entertainment. The use of apocalyptic motifs for sheer entertainment value can be seen even in works that take the Christian apocalypse quite seriously, as in the "Left Behind" series of novels by Tim LaHaye and Jerry B. Jenkins, which began appearing in 1995. In these books the narratives follow quite closely the Biblical prophecy of the coming of a dark period of rule on earth by the Antichrist, followed by the Second Coming of Christ and a titanic struggle between good and evil, culminating in the triumph of good, the punishment of sinners, and the reward of the faithful in an everlasting life on earth in the New Jerusalem. It is clear, however, that the highly successful "Left Behind" novels are intended less as a means of Christian inspiration and education than as a source of high-voltage entertainment in which the faithful can take (rather gruesome) comfort in assurances that they will receive infinite rewards for their vigorous efforts as Christ's soldiers, while (perhaps even more important) the nonfaithful will suffer infinite pain and torment.

Of course, the "Left Behind" series treats its themes far more seriously than most recent works in the apocalyptic genre, which might account for the almost total lack of success of the film adaptations of that series. The lampooning of the series in the *Simpsons* episode "Thank God It's Doomsday" (May 8, 2005) can be taken as an expression of a far more mainstream attitude toward the Apocalypse. Even when treated seriously, most works of recent popular culture portray only the first stage of the Christian Apocalypse: the destruction of the world as we know it in the coming of a global reign of evil. Among other things, this situation suggests that these works grow out of the nuclear fears of the Cold War more directly than out of the Christian apocalyptic tradition, although of course the two are related. The strength of Christian apocalyptic thought provides at least one clue to the historical puzzle of why the fear of nuclear holocaust reached levels of hysteria in the United States greater than those anywhere else in the world.

This first stage of the apocalypse simply makes for a narrative structure that is much more easily adapted to the needs of television and film than does the full multistage process. Although the full Biblical Apocalypse is ultimately (for the faithful) a good thing that merely involves an unfortunate early stage, the Apocalypse as represented in recent American popular culture is unequivocally bad news, providing a very clear good-versus-evil plot structure in which a protagonist or group of protagonists must galvanize their efforts to prevent the looming catastrophe from occurring at all.

Elizabeth Rosen, noting the tendency of recent apocalyptic narratives to leave out the utopian New Jerusalem stage of the Apocalypse, sees this characteristic as an aspect of the oft-touted postmodernist skepticism toward "grand metanarratives," of which the apocalyptic myth is a classic case. For Rosen, whereas postmodern writers and filmmakers have shown a fascination with narratives of apocalypse, they have rejected the "absolutism" of religious versions of the apocalyptic myth, often using such narratives to "challenge, explode, or undermine the belief system or assumptions underlying this particular grand narrative" (p. *xx*). Rosen seems to underestimate the postmodern skepticism of recent apocalyptic narratives, perhaps because she focuses mostly on novels, with a side glance at films, but essentially ignores television. On television, the apocalyptic myth is treated as a pastiche rather than parody (in the sense meant by Jameson in his discussion of postmodernism). Apocalyptic television series neither endorse nor really challenge the belief system that lies behind the Christian apocalyptic tradition; they simply use that tradition as a source of material.

Series that have taken the Christian apocalyptic tradition relatively seriously have generally failed to attract much of an audience, perhaps because true believers do not find this venue appropriate for the exploration of their beliefs. One thinks here of the short-lived *Point Pleasant*, which lasted a mere eight episodes when it aired on the Fox Network in early 2005, although a total of thirteen episodes were made and are now available on DVD. Executive produced by Marti Noxon, one of the principal creative forces behind *Buffy*, *Point Pleasant* features a protagonist who is a teenage girl with special supernatural powers. Otherwise, however, it has very little in common with *Buffy*. For one thing, the show includes virtually no humor or hip pop cultural references; for another, it relies quite heavily on *Melrose Place*–style soap opera plot lines to drive its supernatural premise forward. This premise is an intriguing one, however. As the series begins, protagonist Christina Nickson (Elisabeth Harnois) washes up on the beach in Point Pleasant, New Jersey, and is rescued by lifeguard Jesse Parker (Samuel Page). Soon afterward, the rather sinister Lucas Boyd (Grant Show) comes to town, further complicating the already complex relations among the town's locals. It is only gradually revealed that Christina is the daughter of Satan by a human woman and that Boyd is a minion of Satan sent to ensure that Christina develops in the proper directions to enable her to become the Antichrist and bring about the Apocalypse. Jesse seems to be a chosen minion of God, sent to stop Christina, whether by killing her or by helping her to overcome her evil side and become good is never made entirely clear, especially because the early cancellation of the series never really gave this promising plot line time to develop.

The New Testament vision of a coming Apocalypse is particular central to *Revelations*, a six-part miniseries that aired on NBC in the spring of 2005. *Revelations* was the brain child of *Omen* screenwriter David Seltzer, and there are numerous similarities between the two works. Taking its title directly from a book of the Bible, the miniseries presents an apocalyptic vision derived fairly directly from that book and from Catholic traditions deriving from it. The various signs of the coming Armageddon are depicted as occurring just as the Bible had predicted, and the Apocalypse does seem set to occur. It is averted, however, through the heroic actions of Sister Josepha Montafiore (Natascha

McElhone), a rogue nun, and Professor Richard Massey (Bill Pullman), a Harvard astrophysicist. Of course, the Apocalypse still appears inevitable at the end of the film (both Christ and the Antichrist have been born into the world), but at least the protagonists have bought some time for humanity to get its act together and to come off a bit better when Armageddon does occur. Massey, a former scoffer at all things supernatural, has learned that there are things his scientific philosophy cannot explain. Indeed, science and medicine come off rather poorly in this series, which seems to tout religious faith as a preferable way of dealing with the world, but all in all the series simply comes off as a bit silly—excellent cast and high production values aside.

Whereas *Buffy* in particular pokes self-conscious fun at the way its world is constantly on the verge of the Apocalypse, the typical Apocalypse-without-God scenario of apocalyptic television series does not necessarily result in humor. The late-1990s television series that was tied most directly to apocalyptic fears related to the millennium was the tellingly titled (and extremely serious) *Millennium*, which ran on the Fox network from October of 1996 until May of 1999. The brain child of *X-Files* creator Chris Carter, *Millennium* bears many family resemblances to its older sibling, although it is altogether grimmer and darker (yet ultimately less compelling) than *The X-Files*. Like *The X-Files*, *Millennium* swerves through numerous plot twists and mood changes; however, whereas the peripatetic nature of the former adds energy to the conspiracy motif, involving viewers in the protagonists' attempts at cognitive mapping, *Millennium* at times just seems to be stumbling about in search of its own identity. Nevertheless, at its best, *Millennium* could be quite effective, chillingly capturing the deep-seated fears of its era.

Millennium features Frank Black (Lance Henriksen), a psychological profiler whose intense understanding of the criminal mind is furthered by the fact that he has vague psychic powers that allow him to see flashing visions of recent violent crimes simply by visiting the crime scene. As the series opens, Black has retired from the FBI, traumatized by the terrible things he has seen as a profiler specializing in investigations of serial killers. He has moved with his wife Catherine (Megan Gallagher) and young daughter Jordan (Brittany Tiplady) to an idyllic yellow house in suburban Seattle. There Black hopes to shelter his family from the horrors of the outside world. Immediately after the Blacks move to Seattle, however, someone begins sending Frank anonymous letters bearing Polaroids of Catherine and Jordan, making it clear that the family is being watched and might be in great danger.

Much of the first season of *Millennium* reads essentially like an episodic crime series; each week Black, now working as a freelance consultant, is called in to help catch a different serial killer, using his special skills, which are only gradually revealed to be psychic in nature. In addition to the common theme of serial killings, several threads do tie the episodes of the first season together. The plot is really more cumulative than sequential, as one horrifying crime after another gradually leads to a building sense that something is seriously wrong with American society. In the episode "Blood Relatives" (December 6, 1996), Catherine (a psychological counselor) bemoans to Frank that so many children in American are growing up in institutions, abandoned by their families and receiving no real love. These neglected children then often grow up to commit brutal crimes, typically designed to disrupt the family lives of others. "They're out there, Frank," Catherine tells her husband. "People with holes in them."

Moments such as this one clearly address widespread contemporary fears about both crime and the decline of the American family. Black's own family is crucial here, as it becomes increasingly obvious that their retreat to the yellow Seattle house can shield them neither from violent crime nor from the psychic consequences of Frank's work, which make it more and more difficult for him to maintain normal human relationships. Black himself becomes one of America's walking, psychically damaged wounded. He loves Catherine and Jordan deeply but cannot overcome his frustration at being unable to protect them or his fear that his work is putting them in jeopardy. It is important that although Frank's work and special abilities set him apart from the mainstream, the series clearly suggests that the alienation and psychic fragmentation from which he increasingly suffers is a condition pandemic to the American population. No one, in fact, is safe from the impending crisis, as is made especially clear in episodes such as "Weeds" (January 24, 1997), in which violent crime intrudes even into an affluent, high-security, gated community.

This theme of an America increasingly threatened by an underclass of soulless and merciless criminals is the crucial one of the first season, although the latter part of the season begins to attribute the brokenness and emptiness of the American psyche less and less to social and institutional causes and more and more to supernatural ones. In particular, the series begins to point toward the possibility that the impending crisis is related to the Biblical Apocalypse, just as Black's foes gradually shift from human criminals to demons and spirits. The first clear sign that the evil stalking America is supernatural in origin occurs in the episode "Lamentation" (April 18, 1997), in which the criminal of the week, Lucy Butler (Sarah-Jane Redmond), turns out to be an immortal demonic entity. There is also a human serial killer in this episode, but he assures Frank that his evil pales in comparison to the greater supernatural evil that is now loose in the world. This latter evil intrudes directly into Frank's world as well, as Butler (who becomes a recurring character throughout the rest of the series), gruesomely murders Frank's friend, police lieutenant Bob Bletcher (Bill Smitrovich), in the basement of the yellow house.

The first season ends as Catherine is abducted by a serial killer, whom Frank then kills in the first episode of Season Two, thereby saving his wife, but creating further trauma that leads Black to move out of the yellow house into a place of his own. Most of the second season is punctuated by the personal loneliness and anguish experienced by Frank, who desperately wants to be with Catherine and Jordan but cannot overcome his personal demons so that he can manage a genuine relationship. He battles other demons throughout this season as well, as the series drifts more and more into supernatural territory. A further element is introduced into the series in this second season in the evolving depiction of the Millennium Group, the organization for which Frank does most of his consulting work. Originally described as an organization of former law enforcement officers who have banded together to make their considerable skill and experience available to local law enforcement in especially difficult cases, the group gradually becomes more and more mysterious as the series proceeds. Eventually, we learn that the group has ancient origins and that it has long been involved in an attempt to prepare humanity for the Biblical Apocalypse (often thought to be associated with the end of a historical millennium), beginning with a run-up to the year 1000 (with hints that the group helped prevent an Apocalypse in that year) and now continuing with the approach of the year 2000.

Questions about the secretive Millennium Group proliferate through the second season, in which it slowly becomes clear that the group is not what it appears to be and that its purposes might not be entirely benevolent. The series thus moves deeper into the conspiracy territory of *The X-Files*, suggesting plots within plots in the workings of both the Millennium Group and its foes. We also learn that the group is not a monolithic entity but contains subgroups that differ dramatically in their attitudes. In particular, the group turns out to be made up of two main factions: the Roosters, who believe that a Biblical Apocalypse is indeed imminent, and the Owls, who believe that humanity should be preparing for a more secular disaster related to an astronomical phenomenon expected to occur in the 2060s.

Eventually, the in-fighting between these two factions seems virtually to destroy the Millennium Group in this season, although it inexplicably reappears as a powerful conspiratorial force in Season Three. Meanwhile, the usually unmitigated darkness of the series is punctuated in the second season by the inclusion of two self-parodic ludic episodes, much as such comic episodes had provided some of the most memorable highlights of *The X-Files*. Indeed, both of these comic *Millennium* episodes—"Jose Chung's Doomsday Defense" (November 21, 1997) and "Somehow, Satan Got Behind Me" (May 1,

1998)—were scripted by Darin Morgan, who had written such ludic *X-Files* episodes as "Clyde Bruckman's Final Repose," "War of the Coprophages," and "Jose Chung's *From Outer Space.*" In these ludic episodes the similarities between *The X-Files* and *Millennium* become most clear, including the fact that a key character, popular writer Jose Chung (Charles Nelson Reilly), crosses over from one series to the other in the episodes with titles that include his name. The character is finally but humorously killed off in "Jose Chung's Doomsday Defense," an episode whose comedy is largely derived from the contrast between its intentional silliness and the typically heavy seriousness of *Millennium*. There is some fine comic acting from the usually grim Henriksen, whose deeply lined face perfectly reflects the usual sense of carrying the weight of the world on one's shoulders.

"Somehow, Satan Got Behind Me," is even funnier, mercilessly lampooning *Millennium* itself as a group of four demons gather at a coffee shop to swap humorous anecdotes about their attempts to ruin humanity. This lighthearted episode also makes some serious satirical points, however. Perhaps the most important of these involves the complaint of one demon that it is virtually impossible to rob humans of their souls because that has already been done by the soul-stealing, mind-numbing routinization of life under modern capitalism. As he puts it, virtually quoting Max Weber, "Mankind has progressed to a point in its dim-witted history where life has been drained of all its enchantment." The demon then discourses on the banality of everyday life in modern America, where mankind has been enslaved and rendered soulless by inventions such as alarm clocks and practices such as the regimentation of life in the workplace.

Such comic interludes suggest that the makers of *Millennium* were beginning to find it harder and harder to take their own vision of impending supernatural doom seriously. One could also argue, however, that they feared that this vision was beginning to hit too close to home with the approach of the actual millennium, thus making viewers a bit too uncomfortable. It is no surprise, then, that the series again changed directions in Season Three, now reinventing itself as a conspiracy-oriented political thriller, with touches of the supernatural thrown in for good measure. The Millennium Group here emerges as a sinister conspiratorial force involved in a variety of secret shenanigans, often with the support of the U.S. government. The most sinister of these is their apparent involvement in biological weapons research, including the release of a deadly experimental virus in Seattle at the end of Season Two, leading to the deaths of 70 people, including Catherine Black.

In Season Three, a white-haired and noticeably aging (presumably from stress and Catherine's death) Frank has moved back to Virginia with Jordan and is working for the FBI as a consultant. Through this work he hopes to be able to counter the nefarious activities of the Millennium Group, which now seems involved in almost entirely secular conspiracies, although there are hints that these activities might be influenced by supernatural evils they once battled. Frank also has a new partner in the person of FBI agent Emma Hollis (Klea Scott), but there is little chemistry between the two and the partnership never really clicks. *Millennium* never achieved the success of *The X-Files* partly because Frank, a tormented loner, never had much chemistry with any of his partners, including wife Catherine and his second-season partner from the Millennium Group, fellow psychic Lara Means (Kristen Cloke). Ultimately, *Millennium* unraveled in its third season, as the series found it harder and harder to establish its own tone and themes. Its cancellation at the end of that season was thus not surprising, although the season does end with something of a cliffhanger as Frank and Jordan go on the run to attempt to escape from the Millennium Group, which now seems increasingly dangerous. The group has by this time turned the focus of its research to the development of a brain chemistry treatment to produce a new race of advanced humans, presumably able to build a better society and avoid the coming Apocalypse—although all they are able to do is produce custom-designed serial killers.

This ending places *Millennium* within the context of "posthuman" science fiction—the branch of contemporary science fiction that envisions techno-logical advances that lead to fundamental changes in the human body and mind. Genetic engineering is the most obvious form of this science fiction, although electronic and computer technology can be important as well, as in the development of electronic implants to supplement the normal function-ing of the human brain. *Millennium* thus bounces between supernatural and superhuman themes throughout its run, although it is always concerned with the notion of an apocalyptic crisis and with the fact that dramatic and sudden changes are on the horizon for the human species. The series leaves room for doubt whether these changes are for good or ill, but the bulk of the series is informed by a decided anxiety that these changes at best will be difficult for humans to assimilate, and at worst they could wipe out the human species altogether.

Although the series ends without closure, *Millennium* was wrapped up to some extent in the "Millennium" episode of *The X-Files*, which first aired on November 28, 1999, just on the verge of what most people thought of as the coming of the new millennium. (Scully, ever the scientist, points out in this episode that, strictly speaking, the new millennium actually starts on January 1, 2001, not January 1, 2000. Mulder, however, dismisses this technicality. "Nobody likes a math geek," he tells her.) In this episode, Mulder and Scully are called in to investigate a sudden rash of suicides among FBI agents, all of whom have been resurrected as zombies. When the involvement of the Millennium Group is suspected, Mulder and Scully turn to Frank Black for advice but find that Black is now recuperating in a mental hospital, trying to get his life together and put all thought of the Millennium Group behind him so that he can regain custody of Jordan, now living with Catherine's parents. As a result, Black refuses to get involved in the case but of course ultimately does get involved, helping Mulder and Scully to destroy the zombies and prevent them from attempting to trigger the Apocalypse, which was apparently their purpose.

Whether the zombies could have triggered the Apocalypse (and exactly how they might have done it) is left open to speculation. As it is, the episode ends on a high note. Frank and Jordan are reunited, at least temporarily, while Mulder and Scully share a tender moment at the stroke of midnight on December 31, 1999. In fact, they even share their first kiss, after years of building sexual tension. In a masterstroke of multiple meaning, Mulder smiles at Scully after the kiss and says, "The world didn't end," referring both to the thwarted apocalypse and to the fact that the kiss did not itself mean the end of the world for the kissers. It was, however, all downhill after that for *The X-Files*, which Duchovny (Mulder) left a few months later at the end of that season.

One particularly interesting recent apocalyptic series is *Carnivàle*, which ran for two seasons (24 episodes) on HBO from September 2003 to March 2005. Created by Daniel Knauf, the series exemplifies the high production values and sophisticated content for which HBO's original series have justifiably become famous. *Carnivàle* is an elaborate period piece, set in the mid-1930s and replete with costumes and other details from that crucial time, one of the most important and recognizable eras in American history. In the main plot line, a traveling carnival moves about the American Southwest, encountering grim poverty wherever they go. Much of what they encounter is pretty much what one would expect, but the focus on this carnival, with its roster of freaks and outcasts, gives *Carnivàle* a distinctive point of view on Depression-era America, which is thus viewed from the margins, much in the tradition of the picaresque novel.

The carnival setting is also self-reflexive; just as the carnival itself provides a vague (if degraded) element of exoticism and romance to the impoverished lives of the townspeople they entertain, so too does the series itself include supernatural elements that potentially add magic to the routinized lives of its viewers. The carnival includes a cast of psychics and freaks that place it outside the ordinary, giving the series an offbeat flavor that has reminded many of David Lynch's notorious *Twin Peaks*, except that *Twin Peaks* is often quite humorous, whereas *Carnivàle* is deadly serious. There is at least one direct link between *Twin Peaks* and *Carnivàle*: the carnival itself is run by one Samson, a dwarf who had formerly worked in the carnival as a miniature strongman. This character is played by Michael J. Anderson, who had had an important recurring role in *Twin Peaks*. Adding further strangeness to *Carnivàle*, Samson appears to take his orders from a mysterious (possibly supernatural) personage known as "Management," whom only he has ever seen. The carnival moves farther into supernatural territory when young Ben Hawkins (Nick Stahl) a poor farm boy whose mother has just died and whose farm in dust bowl Oklahoma has just been repossessed joins them. It soon becomes clear that Ben is a special young man indeed, possessed of supernatural powers, the nature and extent of which are revealed only gradually in the course of the series. Much of what drives the rather desultory and slowly developing plot is the search for the secret of Ben's powers and his mysterious past, neither of which is ever fully revealed, owing to the early cancellation (after the second season) of the series. Originally envisioned by Knauf as a six-year epic with a continuous plot arc, *Carnivàle* was to have followed a plan similar to that of J. Michael Straczynski for the 1990s science fiction series *Babylon 5*.

The plot involving the carnival is supplemented by a secondary plot that centers on Brother Justin Crowe (Clancy Brown), a seemingly devoted Methodist minister in California. Crowe has no apparent relationship with the carnival; however, it soon becomes clear that he too has certain supernatural powers and that there is some sort of connection between his powers and those of Ben Hawkins. For example, the two of them share certain visions and appear in each other's dreams. As the series proceeds, Crowe runs afoul of his official church when he insists on founding and operating a second church. This church was designed to minister to the needs of the poor migrant workers who have come to California looking for work, like the Joad family from John Steinbeck's Depression-era classic *The Grapes of Wrath*, a clear influence on the series. Crowe's alternative church for the migrants is burned down (apparently by the locals), killing six small children who are living there. In response, the distraught Crowe leaves his official ministry and goes on the road.

Ultimately, it is revealed that Crowe's alternative church was actually set ablaze by Crowe's sister Iris (Amy Madigan), who hoped that the burning of the church (and killing of the children) would win sympathy for her brother's cause. It does so, especially after Crowe becomes a prominent radio personality, taking his message to the airwaves in a mode that is somewhat reminiscent of the real-world Depression-era radio preacher Father Coughlin. Eventually, Crowe founds a Christian community, New Canaan, to which 15,000 of his followers flock to start new lives as part of his ministry. It becomes clear, however, that Crowe is anything but the saintly figure he appears to be. In fact, he is the "Usher," an embodiment of pure evil, roughly synonymous with Satan, although that identification is never made absolutely. Meanwhile, we learn that Ben Hawkins is the "Prince," an embodiment of good (roughly synonymous with Christ) and that the young man has been charged with the mission of tracking down and killing Crowe before he can conquer the human race and establish his reign of hell on earth.

The series is filled with vague hints that all of these supernatural goings-on are closely related to human history. It is suggested (but never elaborated) that the baleful events of the 1930s, such as the Depression and the rise of fascism, are somehow related to the rise of evil in the person of Crowe. Meanwhile, many of Hawkins's supernatural visions involve the explosion of an atomic bomb (apparently at the Trinity test site), suggesting that the development of nuclear weapons is a by-product of Crowe's project as well. It becomes clear that the titanic battle between good and evil that underlies the series has been raging since the beginning of time and that Crowe and Hawkins are only the latest (perhaps last) figures in a long line of such figures. For example, Management turns out to be one Lucius Belyakov, who is not only the father of Crowe (whose real name is Alexei Belyakov), but also the predecessor to Hawkins, essentially playing John the Baptist to Hawkins's Christ. Hawkins eventually learns that he is the son of one Henry Scudder (John Savage), who turns out to be the predecessor to Crowe.

This switch from good to evil from generation to generation not only suggests that good and evil are inextricably intertwined but also that the line between the two is not as clear as one would like to believe. A similar complication arises from the fact that the embodiment of evil in the series is a Christian minister, whereas Hawkins, the embodiment of good, turns out to be an escaped murderer. This suggestion of a complex and mutually implicated relationship between good and evil differs dramatically from the stark distinction between good and evil that is central to conventional Christianity, even though the mythology of the series draws so heavily on Christian precedents. Although *Carnivàle*'s story of an impending apocalypse draws heavily on the Book of Revelation, its principal mythology is supposedly set forth in the marginal Gospel of Matthias, an actual apocryphal New Testament text that has long been lost but copies of which exist within the world of *Carnivàle*.

The depiction of Crowe as a sort of supernatural con man can be taken as a critique of conventional organized religion, especially of the media-oriented evangelical kind. In the final episode, Samson tells Crowe, "You know, in a way, you and me in the same business," suggesting that Crowe, as an evangelical minister, is just as much a huckster as is Samson, who employs trickery, theft, and virtually any other means at his disposal to fleece the various rubes they encounter on their travels and to keep his ragtag carnival afloat in the difficult economic climate of the 1930s. Many elements of the series appear to be supernatural. However, the series frequently seems to suggest that conventional Christianity is just as inadequate as science as a description of the supernatural aspects of the world. As does *Millennium*, *Carnivàle* depicts a vaguely Christian cosmos without ultimately endorsing the Christian understanding of that cosmos.

Potential critiques of religion aside, the main thrust of *Carnivàle* seems to suggest that there are elements at work in human history that go far beyond the understanding of rational science. Indeed, the series itself was apparently beyond the understanding of many viewers, who found it so strange as to be incomprehensible, leading to a decline in viewership and early cancellation. The series does provide several aids to viewers, however. Each season begins with a prologue, delivered by Samson, that sets the stage for the coming episodes, providing viewers with at least some explication of the events to follow. The first season, for example, begins with a brief explanation of the role of avatars of good and evil in the ongoing battle between good and evil throughout human history. Noting the ancient origins of the battle, Samson declares, "There was magic then, nobility, and unimaginable cruelty. So it was, until the day that a false sun exploded over Trinity, and man forever traded away wonder for reason."

After the mention of the Trinity site (where a test explosion of the first atomic bomb was carried out in July 1945), the series contains many hints that part of Hawkins's mission in destroying Crowe is to prevent the development of nuclear weapons and thus to avert the biblical Armageddon. We know that such weapons were developed, suggesting that Hawkins fails in his mission, although the series as it stands leaves the possibility that Hawkins's actions still prevented a nuclear apocalypse. Meanwhile, Samson's first-season prologue once again addresses the theme of rationalization and routinization, suggesting that the development of nuclear weapons usurped powers that should have remained beyond the human, and announcing a final victory of science over magic, accompanied by a resulting impoverishment in human experience—and possibly by the destruction of the human race.

Near the end of the final episode of *Carnivàle*, Hawkins succeeds in killing Crowe, and Sofie (Clea Duvall), a young woman aligned with the carnival who has been kidnapped by Crowe, is saved by Clayton Jones (Tim DeKay), the foreman of the carnival's roustabouts and Hawkins's chief ally. The main plot line thus seems, momentarily, to have been resolved; however, this seeming resolution quickly unravels in the last few minutes of the episode. Shockingly,

Sofie (who turns out to be the biological daughter of Crowe, who raped her mother) turns a gun on Jones and shoots him down. She then goes to the cornfield where Crowe seemingly lies dead and attempts to resurrect him. Hawkins himself lies near death from his battle with Crowe, while the carnival quickly spirits him away from New Canaan. The series thus ends on a cliffhanger that was never to be resolved.

FINDING THAT SPECIAL PLACE: THE STRANGE ENCLAVE NARRATIVE FROM *TWIN PEAKS* TO *LOST*

Millennium (with Frank Black's yellow house) and *Carnivàle* (with the community of New Canaan) both explore the possibility that there might be special locations that are free of the chaos and corruption that reign in the world at large. In both of these cases, this hope is not fulfilled. Evil invades the yellow house, and New Canaan is a product of evil in the first place. This fascination with special places that stand apart from the rest of the world is frequently dramatized in contemporary American popular culture, in what I have termed the "strange enclave" narrative. Moreover, these narratives are closely related to the longing for successful cognitive mapping that is crucial to narratives of conspiracy and apocalypse. If a utopian desire to find order and meaning in the world—and to combat the collapse of cognitive mapping that is, for Jameson, a key symptom of the postmodern era—is crucial to contemporary conspiracy and apocalyptic narratives, this same phenomenon also provides a basis for understanding the contemporary popular fascination with the strange enclave narrative. If the concept of a vast evil conspiracy at least gives some shape to the chaos of contemporary reality, then the strange enclave vision of protection from evil (or even concentrations of evil) in special locations suggests that some places are different from others, an idea that also offers the possibility of a mapping of contemporary reality that overcomes the complete entropy of total homogenization.

Homogenization is one of the key cultural phenomena of our era. Jameson's notion of postmodernism as the "cultural logic" of late capitalism places special emphasis on capitalist globalization as a driving force behind the phenomenon of postmodernity; among other things, he notes that this globalization is gradually leading to a homogenization (which to a large extent means Americanization and emphatically does *not* mean economic equalization) of world culture. Such homogenization seems especially intense in America itself, partly because Americans have been a rather rootless nation of travelers from the beginning and partly because capitalist postmodernity is most advanced in the United States.

In his recent book *Country of Exiles*, historian William Leach notes that one particularly American consequence of the general instability and insubstantiality of everything under modern capitalism is the gradual dissolution of any conventional sense of place. One result of this dissolution is increased mobility among Americans who, freed (or deprived, depending on one's point of view) of any real connection to any particular place, could move about the country (or the world) in search of whatever they were seeking. Another consequence, Leach notes, is the unique fascination of Americans with invented environments (e.g., theme parks or the fictional settings of movies), which stand in for any real sense of place. This fascination, Leach also notes, is highly "subversive to taking seriously a sense of place, or the world people actually lived and died in" (p. 13).

Other observers have also noted the decline of "place" in contemporary America, often (as in the case of Jameson) diagnosing a gradual homogenization of place as a key symptom of the postmodern condition. If (as Leach and Jameson claim), this loss of a sense of distinct places with distinct and different identities deprives people of a connection with the world that is crucial to their psychic health, then the fascination with invented places that Leach also notes can be seen as the result of a utopian desire somehow to recover the loss of real places. I would argue that this phenomenon is very much a part of the same movement that leads to a fascination with magic and the supernatural in American culture as a result of the removal of magic from everyday life in the real world. It should come as no surprise, then, that a fascination with special invented places in American culture is quite often entangled with a fascination with magic and the supernatural. It is not for nothing that the best-known invented place in America is probably Disney's Magic Kingdom, the heart of both Disneyland and Disney World (a "unique" place that exists in duplicate, thus indicating its manufactured and commodified nature).

This fascination with invented places (which are special and thus escape the general homogenization of place in the United States) is closely related to the recent popularity of the strange enclave genre of supernatural culture. When invented places are entangled with the supernatural, they generally become loci for strange and often sinister goings on that involve phenomena that would not normally be observable outside this one particular location. Frequently, these phenomena cause the invented place to be sealed off from normal contact with the outside world. That is why I have chosen to call such places "strange enclaves." Such special enclaves exist in a variety of forms in American culture, from the idyllic magical Utopia of Shangri-La in Frank Capra's 1937 film *Lost Horizon*, to the sinister enclave in the suburban Connecticut of the 1975 film *The Stepford Wives*, even to the rundown Radiator

Springs of the Pixar animated film *Cars* (2006), a home of traditional values and unalienated social relations (thanks to the fact that it does not lie on the Interstate highway system). Of course, much of the success of works such as the *Lord of the Rings* franchise depends on the compelling nature of the invented places in which the action takes place. Strange enclaves have become particularly important in recent American supernatural television. *Buffy the Vampire Slayer* could not work as a series were Sunnydale not a strange enclave situated over a Hellmouth. Similarly, the narrative of *Smallville* depends greatly on the special character of its titular small town (with its high incidence of supervillain "meteor freaks" and heavy concentration of kryptonite).

In its current form, the strange enclave subgenre can cite the near-legendary *Twin Peaks* as its founding work. Perhaps the most written- and talked-about series of the early 1990s, *Twin Peaks* became an immediate sensation after its premiere on ABC in April 1990. By the spring of 1991, however, the show (which might have been *too* strange for a mainstream audience) had lost much of its viewership and found itself canceled. The show's reputation as one of the most unusual and innovative series ever to appear on American commercial television remains strong to this day, however, and the series has also exerted a substantial influence on successors such as *The X-Files*.

Twin Peaks combined striking, often jazz-based music with unusual, out-of-whack visuals to create an atmosphere of strangeness that greatly enhanced its weird plot, itself derived from a combination of a variety of genres, most obviously the detective story and the soap opera. The series is also marked by the presence of a large ensemble cast of mostly eccentric characters, although the main character, in many ways, is the town of Twin Peaks, Washington— the strange enclave of the series. The basic premise of the series seems fairly simple. As the series begins, FBI Special Agent Dale Cooper (Kyle MacLachlan, who had also starred in Lynch's *Dune* and *Blue Velvet*) is sent to Twin Peaks to investigate the murder of local teen queen Laura Palmer (Sheryl Lee). Cooper's investigation provides the main detective-story plot of much of the series, although his methods are highly unusual and deviate significantly from established FBI procedures (eventually leading to his suspension and nearly to prosecution). Much of his insight comes from dreams and visions, accompanied by numerous hints that he has a special sensitivity to the supernatural shenanigans that are very much a part of life in Twin Peaks. As the investigation proceeds, we learn that Laura had not been living the idyllic life that most residents of the community had imagined. The golden girl of Twin Peaks High School, she had been the daughter of a prominent local attorney, who provided her with a pleasant suburban home and other accoutrements of upper-middle-class affluence. Virtually a walking stereotype of the "popular" girl in high school, Laura had been the girlfriend of Bobby Briggs (Dana Ashbrook), the quarterback of the high school football team. She had also been secretly seeing the working-class James Hurley (James Marshall), however, and living a much more shocking secret life involving drugs and prostitution as well.

As the show proceeds, we also meet various other local characters and learn a great deal about their extensive eccentricities. Finally, we learn that the town itself would be a virtual embodiment of 1950s-style small-town American values were it not for the fact that it is threatened by numerous evil forces (many of them supernatural) from both within and without. These forces, more than the colorful inhabitants, make Twin Peaks a truly strange enclave. The series itself, with its sometimes weird look, odd mixing of genres, and sudden switches in tone, was itself a sort of strange enclave amid the "vast wasteland" of American commercial television.

The mood of *Twin Peaks* can change in a heartbeat, as if to ensure that viewers can never settle into a comfortable, passive mode of reception. One scene might feature Cooper and local Sheriff Harry S. Truman (Michael Ontkean) trying to solve a gruesome and abject murder; the next might feature the bumbling comic antics of characters such as Deputy Andy Brennan (Harry Goaz) and Lucy Moran (Kimmy Robertson), whose very names evoked two of the greatest stars of the television sitcom, Andy Griffith and Lucille Ball. Truman, meanwhile, is one of the "straightest" and most "normal" characters in *Twin Peaks*, yet his intrusive name contaminates even his relatively ordinary activities with a corrosive irony. The characters themselves are similarly impure, and not merely because many of them tend to be morally depraved. They also change their basic characteristics from one moment to the next, exhibiting surprising behavior that is completely inconsistent with their prior characterization, much in the mode of the schizophrenic characters discussed by Fredric Jameson as typical of postmodernism.

For example, Laura Palmer is not the only citizen of Twin Peaks to have a secret life. Bobby Briggs might be the high school quarterback, but he is also a drug dealer and a killer. Briggs might be Laura's boyfriend, but he is also having an affair with Shelley Johnson, the wife of Leo Johnson (Eric Da Re), who is one of his key drug suppliers. James Hurley, meanwhile, is an outsider who looks something like a juvenile delinquent but turns out to be a paragon of virtue, at least relative to almost everyone else in Twin Peaks. In the course of the series, various other characters behave in complex and contradictory ways as well, as when Audrey Horne (Sherilyn Fenn), in a kind of reversal of Laura's behavior, first appears as a sultry high school vixen and bad girl, only to turn out by the end of the series to be a virgin, a paragon of virtue, and an environmental activist. Characters suddenly change age (at least in their own minds), as when 35-year-old Nadine Hurley (Wendy Robie) becomes a teenager again—not to mention suddenly being blessed with comically super-human strength. They also change gender, as when David Duchovny makes a memorable (especially in retrospect, after his *X-Files* fame) appearance as cross-dressing DEA agent Denis(e) Bryson. The scheming Catherine Martell (Piper Laurie) goes one better, changing both race and gender by assuming the identity of Mr. Tojamura, a Japanese businessman. Speaking of Asians, there is the completely unreadable Josie Packard (Joan Chen), a beautiful Chinese woman from Hong Kong, who constantly flip-flops between positions of good and evil, innocence and depravity.

The main source of mystery in the series, however, is the town of Twin Peaks itself, stipulated to be a site where strange forces converge to bring about strange events. As Sheriff Truman tells Agent Cooper early in the series, "Twin Peaks is different, a long way from the world." Truman means this largely as praise for life in Twin Peaks, but he admits that this situation has a "back end," which consists of the fact that "there's a sort of evil" that resides in the woods surrounding the town. "Call it what you want," he goes on. "A darkness. A presence. It takes many forms, but it's been out there for as long as anyone can remember." Meanwhile, of course, the strangeness that separates the town of Twin Peaks from the outside world is mirrored in the offbeat strangeness of the series itself, which thus resides a long way from the world of run-of-the-mill popular culture.

If this strangeness clearly contributed to the quick demise of *Twin Peaks*, other strange enclave narratives, such as *American Gothic* (created by Shaun Cassidy and executive produced by Sam Raimi), have similarly struggled to find an audience. *American Gothic*, the tale of a small Southern town terrorized by a corrupt sheriff backed by evil supernatural powers, lasted only a single season on CBS from 1995 to 1996. The Sci Fi channel series *Eureka* has fared a bit better (but only by the standards of cable networks), beginning its third season in the summer of 2008. *Eureka* focuses on a small Washington town of that name. Eureka is a sort of think-tank town, the residents of which in-clude some of the world's greatest scientific geniuses, brought together to pool their knowledge and talent in the interest of science. As a result, the town is a sort of high-tech Utopia, with several cutting-edge technological advances, far beyond what would be available anywhere outside of Eureka, having already been implemented there in what one might call beta-test versions.

If the town in *Eureka* is quirky rather than sinister (the series is really more like *Northern Exposure* than *Twin Peaks*), the more sinister version of the strange enclave narrative has proved capable of major commercial success in recent years. Learning lessons from the convoluted mytharc plotting of

The X-Files, but also strongly echoing the strange enclave aspects of *Twin Peaks* (without the offbeat humor), the ABC television drama *Lost* debuted in September 2004, and quickly became one of the next big things in American popular culture, drawing more far more viewers than *Buffy*, *Angel*, or *The X-Files* ever had, although ratings did decline over time. The immediate commercial success of the program (along with that of *Desperate Housewives* and *Grey's Anatomy*) reversed the flagging fortunes of the ABC network. In addition, *Lost's* combination of this success with critical acclaim made it one of the most influential series of its era (in the world of American commercial television, an "era" is usually five years or less).

On first examination, the two most striking features of *Lost* are its large ensemble cast and its complex, continuous plot line (punctuated by numerous flashback segments that fill in the oddly intertwined—and often surprising—backgrounds of its various characters). Ensemble casts and continuous plots can also be found in *Desperate Housewives* and *Grey's Anatomy*, but the offbeat soap-based *Desperate Housewives* is set in the mundane world of suburbia, whereas *Grey's Anatomy* is a reasonably realistic medical drama (with added comic and sometimes soap-opera ingredients). What sets *Lost* apart from these two sister series (and looks back to predecessors such as *The X-Files*, *Buffy*, and *Angel*) is the extra spice added by its frequent (almost teasing) hints of science fiction or supernatural elements.[11]

The basic premise of *Lost* involves the crash of an intercontinental jetliner (en route from Australia to the United States) on a remote island, where a group of approximately seventy crash survivors struggle to stay alive while hoping eventually to find a way off the large island. The supernatural elements begin to kick in as they gradually explore the island, with one startling discovery after another, causing them (and the audience) continually to revise their assessment of the nature of the strange environment in which they find themselves. For one thing, the island seems oddly cut off from the rest of the world in ways that go beyond mere geographical remoteness. For another, it is apparently populated by a variety of surprising inhabitants, including ghosts, polar bears, a weird (murderous) black cloudlike entity, and a mysterious group of human inhabitants, whom the survivors come to know as the Others. Furthermore, the swarming cloudlike entity seems to be an avatar of the (possibly sentient) island itself. The island is also sprinkled with strange relics, such as underground research stations, which are left over from the earlier efforts of an organization known as the "Dharma Initiative," apparently destroyed by the Others. Perhaps strangest of all, however, is the fact that the laws of nature seem to operate differently on the island than in the rest of the world. Wounds, for example, heal inexplicably quickly, and the island has other restorative powers as well. Thus, one of the survivors, John Locke (Terry O'Quinn), long confined to a wheelchair, finds that he is able to walk normally after the crash. The island also seems to have negative effects on the human body, as when it becomes clear that women who have become pregnant on the island have invariably died midway through the pregnancy. Finally, frequently there are hints that the island and events there have a unique significance and might be crucial to the survival of the rest of the world, introducing an apocalyptic element to the series.

In addition to Locke (whose role in the series is particularly complex), the most important members of the main group of crash survivors include spinal surgeon Jack Shephard (Matthew Fox), good-girl-gone-bad Kate Austen (Evangeline Lilly), and con man James Ford (Josh Holloway), who has adopted the name "Sawyer." Also important are Hugo "Hurley" Reyes (Jorge Garcia), a lottery winner who otherwise seems to have been cursed with bad luck; Sayid Jarrah (Naveen Andrews), a former Iraqi Republican Guardsman, presented as courageous, capable, and honorable; Charlie Pace (Dominic Monaghan), a British former one-hit-wonder rock star trying to kick a drug habit; and Claire Littleton (Emilie de Ravin), a pregnant Australian woman who gives birth soon after the crash. Rounding out the central cast are Sun-Hwa Kwon (Yunjin Kim) and Jin-Soo Kwon (Daniel Dae Kim), a Korean couple with a checkered past. In fact, all of these characters seem to have unusually checkered pasts that have intersected with one another in all sorts of complex ways, cumulatively suggesting that some sort of large, mysterious (possibly mystical) force has been at work in bringing them all together on the island. In addition, the premise of the series allows for some major characters to die off (because there are plenty more) and for new characters to be introduced. These new characters sometimes emerge as survivors not previously featured on the series, although they also include people who have come to the island by means other than the plane crash. The most important of these are the Others, some of whom become important characters, especially beginning in Season Three, when interactions between the survivors and the Others increase considerably. The leader of the Others (although he himself seems to take orders from a ghostly entity known simply as "Jacob") is Benjamin Linus (Michael Emerson), a former lowly member of the Initiative who conspired with the "indigenous" inhabitants of the island (who seem, however, to be of mostly European ancestry) to destroy the Initiative. Linus is often quite ruthless in pursuing his agenda (which is generally hard to identify), ostensibly because he believes the fate of the world might depend on his efforts. Another crucial Other is Dr. Juliet Burke (Elizabeth Mitchell), formerly a Miami fertility researcher, who (apparently) switches allegiance and joins the crash survivors at the end of Season Three, partly because of her growing attraction to Shephard.

Jack is attracted to both Juliet and Kate (who is attracted to both Jack and Sawyer), making potential romantic connections in the series almost as complex as the interconnections in the overall plot arc. We also learn in the course of things that Jack and Claire surprisingly have the same father, as do Locke and Sawyer, as the various entanglements among the crash survivors proliferate wildly. Both of these interconnections and the overall plot of *Lost* are far too convoluted to summarize here, but these convolutions seem largely to be the point, as the various revelations and sudden twists pile up week after week, creating an active engagement on the part of viewers, who join the characters in the struggle to solve the puzzle. Meanwhile, the slowly evolving network of interconnections that marks the series helps to give viewers—firmly held, in their own lives, in the grip of a late capitalist system in which it becomes progressively more difficult to connect anything to anything—a reassuring albeit paranoid sense that there is an understandable order at work in the world, or at least in the world of *Lost*.

These interconnections become even more convoluted at the end of the Third Season (and throughout the fourth), as the series's frequent flashbacks are joined by flash-forwards that show many of the characters in the *future*, after they have been rescued from the island. This further complication to the time flow of the series goes hand in hand with the science fictional time-travel plot that also becomes an important part of the series in Season Four. In this season, a ship bearing both scientists involved in time-travel research and heavily armed mercenaries arrives in the vicinity of the island and even discovers a pathway to the almost unreachable island itself. Although the castaways initially greet the new arrivals as rescuers, it soon becomes clear that rescue is not part of the mission of the ship, which has been sent by mysterious magnate Charles Widmore, who hopes to use the special powers associated with the island for his own obscure, apparently cynical purposes. He also has apparently ordered the mercenaries to capture Linus and to kill everyone else on the island. Linus, however, is aware of Widmore's plans and has placed a spy aboard the ship in the person of Michael Dawson (Harold Perrineau), a former member of the castaways on the island.

This season is punctuated with frequent flash-forwards showing the experiences of the "Oceanic Six," six of the survivors (Jack, Kate, Sun, Sayid, Hurley, and Claire's son) who have been rescued from the island, although the circumstances of their rescue are not made clear until the last episode of the season. The mercenaries are defeated, and the special properties of the island (now revealed as possibly related to the existence there of a pocket of "negatively charged exotic matter") allow it to be moved to a new location, saving those who are still there, for the time being, from Widmore. This exotic matter apparently warps both space and time, giving us a possible scientific explanation for the strangeness of the island, although Locke, in this same episode, also provides a mystical theory by declaring, "This is not an island. This is a place where miracles happen." In any case, the season then ends with a flash-forward involving the sudden appearance of the ever-mysterious Linus, who warns Shephard that he and all the others must return to the island to avoid horrific consequences. This leaves open the possibility that their return to the island in Season Five (of what is projected to be a six-season story arc) might somehow warp time and negate much of what seems to have occurred in Season Four.

The end of this season thus leaves the plot of *Lost* more unresolved than ever—so much so that the producers of the series were issuing press notices to reassure viewers that they had a plan and that all questions would be answered in the show's final two seasons. Mysteries are all well and good, but audiences involved in trying to piece together the intricate interconnections that underlie *Lost* are clearly involved in an exercise in cognitive mapping. The very fact that so many such interconnections exist and can be identified serves as a sort of utopian compensation for the difficulty of connecting up the various loose ends that constitute contemporary reality. As a result, it is important that making connections *within* the show not be *too* difficult.

Lost represents an especially obvious combination of the strange enclave narrative with the conspiracy narrative, with liberal hints of possible Apocalypse thrown in as well—just as *Heroes* combines the superhero narrative with conspiracy and apocalyptic narratives. Such multigeneric programs thus potentially provide viewers with the sorts of satisfactions that are typically offered by all of these genres in which they participate. They also illustrate some of the ways in which their component genres (and the satisfactions they provide) are interrelated, making especially clear that different genres can offer their audiences similar compensations, such as exercises in successful cognitive mapping. The question that remains is whether these exercises in turn help viewers to develop cognitive strategies and skills that can be applied to the world at large or whether the satisfactions provided by these genres simply provide comforts that make the confusion of real life more bearable. If the latter, they actually act to discourage viewers from actively seeking to cognitively map their places in the real world. Similar questions in fact pertain to all of the works discussed in this text—and perhaps to all of contemporary culture. Such questions are inherently difficult to answer because of the contradictory nature of the works of popular culture discussed in this book, which are designed both to provide a utopian release from the excessive rationalization of life under late capitalism and to help audiences make sense of an increasingly confusing (although increasingly rationalized world). Such contradictions and the problems that they pose for viewers are addressed in the final chapter of this volume.

CONCLUSION: THE CONTRADICTORY
COMPENSATIONS OF POPULAR CULTURE

Critical commentaries on popular culture have generally fallen into one of two camps. On the one hand, we have the tradition of seeing popular culture as a vast and powerful corporate system that holds its consumers in thrall, bombarding them with such a constant stream of procapitalist ideological messages that they have no ability to think anticapitalist thoughts. This tradition, in its current form, can trace its genealogy directly to the description of the American Culture Industry by Max Horkheimer and Theodor Adorno in the 1940s. Concerns about the possible negative impact of the rise of mass culture were rampant in the United States as early as the 1920s, and by the 1930s, even producers of what could be called popular culture were straining against its mind-numbing effects, as in the attempts of hard-boiled novelists such as Hammett and Chandler to wrest the detective fiction genre from the perceived morass of mass culture.[1] Concerns about the mind-numbing effects of mass culture grew even stronger in the 1950s, as critics such as Dwight MacDonald railed against the anti-intellectual consequences of the new medium of television. More recently, critics began to read against the grain and to emphasize the potential for audiences to wrest control of the messages embedded in popular culture from their corporate roots, turning these messages into subversive antiauthoritarian statements. Crucial elements of this tradition have included such contributions as Dick Hebdige's work on the subversive potential of subcultural styles, Michel de Certeau's elaboration of the notion of cultural "poaching" by ordinary people, and John Fiske's insistence on the ability of television audiences to resist dominant meanings and creatively produce their own. Such readings of the positive potential of popular culture clearly owe much to the countercultural energies that arose in the 1960s. As a result, such work is called into question by the recent work of critics such as Thomas Frank or Heath and Potter, which seriously doubts that the "counterculture" really runs counter to mainstream consumerist ideologies at all.

That astute observers could draw diametrically opposed conclusions about the implications of popular culture for consumers is a testament to the complex and dialectical nature of that culture. Of course, most popular culture is produced not from below but from above, by huge corporate media giants who have no interest in challenging the status quo other than perhaps to insinuate consumerist ideas even further into the popular consciousness. Just as it is quite obvious that the central goal of commercial television programming is to attract viewers to the commercials that advertise the products marketed by its sponsors, it is also surely the case that popular culture in general both feeds on and attempts to promote consumerist desires that attract audiences to the culture itself and encourage them to become active participants in the consumer capitalist system. Conversely, capitalist ideology itself is extremely complex and often contradictory, so that conveying this ideology through popular culture is by no means a simple enterprise. American consumers in particular have been exposed to so much in the way of consumer messaging that they are by now fairly sophisticated consumers of those messages, which means that the messages (and the pop cultural products that convey them) must be equally sophisticated. As a result, the products of contemporary American popular culture are easily complex enough to allow for multiple, even diametrically opposed, interpretations.

Such complexities and contradictions are built into the capitalist system itself; thus we have Marx's insistence on the necessity of dialectical analysis when dealing with any aspect of that system. They are also therefore an intrinsic characteristic of the cultural products of the capitalist system, and therefore there is Jameson's insistence, in *The Political Unconscious*, on the need for a double—critical and utopian—hermeneutic when discussing those products. I would argue, however, that the kinds of popular culture I have been discussing in this volume are particularly complex and especially given to variant interpretations. Thus, the longing for adventure that I discuss in Chapter One of this volume can be seen both as a utopian response to the routinization and rationalization of everyday life under capitalism and as a longing for community of a kind unavailable amid the rampant alienation of the capitalist world. The successful completion of the quests undertaken in such works as *The Wizard of Oz* or *The Lord of the Rings* (or even *Harry Potter, Pirates of the Caribbean,* and *Shrek*) requires in each case the group efforts of a band of adventurers, no one of whom could have completed the task alone. All of these fantasy adventures feature central hero figures, from the ordinary Dorothy Gale and Frodo Baggins, to the Chosen One Harry Potter, to the antiheroic Captain Jack Sparrow and Shrek the Ogre. They thus simultaneously answer the longing for individual distinction that is central to the ideology of capitalism and that is a key driving force behind the narratives of heroism that I discuss in Chapter Two. Although the contemporary longing for heroes allows consumers, through identification, to experience individualist fantasies of their own uniqueness, the typically superhuman nature of the heroes discussed in Chapter Two also responds to a quasi-religious desire to believe in someone or something greater than oneself that might enable one to handle problems and dangers far too great for ordinary people to surmount. Finally, if all of the narratives in Chapters One and Two answer a desire for some dimension of existence beyond the humdrum rationalization of daily life as a cog in the capitalist machine, the longing to believe in vast evil conspiracies responds both to this same desire and to a contrary longing to believe in some sort of patterns that make sense amid a situation in which that capitalist machine has become so vast and complex as to seem incomprehensible, with even cogs in the machine having no idea quite where they fit into the works.

All of the longings to which these works respond can be described as desires (however unconscious and unarticulated on the part of individual consumers) for something *more*, which of course is precisely the dynamic of desire that drives consumer capitalism, which depends on the longings of consumers to acquire more and more, regardless of how much they already have. This sense that there must, or at least should, be more to life than the daily struggle for money and the commodities it can buy is no doubt one reason for the notorious religiosity of Americans. At the same time, the religious backgrounds of American culture (as in the enormous influence on the New England Puritans in building the national identity of the United States) must surely contribute to the dissatisfaction of Americans with the purely material comforts offered by capitalism. The work of Weber offers an important caution to those who would see an absolute opposition between Protestant spiritualism and capitalist materialism. If both Protestant religion and the longing for the supernatural in the cultural products described in this volume can be seen as responses to the psychic shortcomings of capitalism, they can nonetheless also be seen as perfectly congruent with the psychic structure of consumerism. There is something inherently problematic about the superhuman and supernatural motifs that are central to the culture discussed in this volume, something inherently ungraspable, unmanageable, and resistant to rationalized capitalist administration. For one thing, these motifs point, more than do the central motifs in the typical television sitcom, to inadequacies in the current capitalist system and to its inability to fulfill certain basic human psychic needs. For another thing, by their very nature, superhuman and supernatural motifs are open ended, not bounded by the laws of physics or the limits of rationalist thought.

If the longing for something more that drives supernatural and superhuman popular culture is structurally similar to the never-ending desire to consume that drives contemporary capitalism, it is also true that this longing for something more than what is available in the present resembles the striving for the "not yet" that drives the thought of Ernst Bloch, probably the past century's greatest anticapitalist utopian philosopher. By definition, Bloch's version of Utopia, like consumer fulfillment, is never reached, but it can be worked toward; utopian thought is always thought that reaches beyond the real. For Bloch, genuine utopian thought is shot through with concrete possibility, its goal being the transformation of reality and not an escape from it. Bloch's vision, however poetic it might sometimes appear, is resolutely historical. Furthermore, his vision of thinking beyond the present is always oriented toward the future and not the past. Utopian thought, for Bloch, must reach toward the "Not-Yet-Conscious . . . towards the side of something new that is dawning up, that has never been conscious before, not, for example, something forgotten, something rememberable that has been" (*Principle*, p. 11).

In this sense Bloch's utopianism differs dramatically from consumer capitalism, which also reaches constantly toward the future, spurring constant new consumption, but does so in ways that discourage the imagination of systemic alternatives to capitalism and that thus work against, rather than toward, the transformation of society. The consumerist message is clear: Capitalism is a wonderful system, and you too can be happy, if you only work a little harder to be able to consume a little more, and more, and more. Thus, if the rhetoric of consumerism is ultimately designed to convince individual subjects that life is fine despite all evidence to the contrary, Bloch's conception of Utopia is a prescription for surviving current hard times by imagining better ones in the future. In particular, Bloch recommends that people seek sources of hope to help them cope with the exigencies of life under late capitalism, with this hope functioning as an antidote to the fear that Bloch sees as the principal emotional experience under capitalism.

Whether the works discussed in this volume tend more toward the reinforcement of consumerist desire (and thus really support the capitalist status quo despite their suggestion of a need for something more) or whether they urge their consumers to strive for the "not yet thought" in the mode of Bloch (and thus potentially to challenge the current capitalist system) is a question with no single or simple answer. With the exception of certain prosocialist messages encoded in Miéville's *Un Lun Dun*, there is little in the way of overtly anticapitalist content in any of the works described in this text, unless one counts things like Tolkien's *Lord of the Rings* novels, which are only anticapitalist in the sense of their preference for an idealized version of the *precapitalist* world and therefore cannot serve a progressive purpose per the vision of Bloch. Still, virtually all of the works discussed herein can be seen as responding to perceived shortcomings in contemporary reality, even if they do not articulate this perception as systemic critiques of capitalism.

Ultimately, the impact of superhuman and supernatural motifs in popular culture on consumers of that culture may depend on whether those motifs are able to trigger thoughtful analysis in their audiences by encouraging those audiences to make critical comparisons between the real world in which they live and the superhuman and supernatural worlds presented to them in popular culture. In short, the impact of superhuman and supernatural culture on audiences is a question of whether it can trigger cognitive estrangement in those audiences of the kind associated by Suvin with science fiction. For example, if the various patterns of connections that gradually emerge in a series such as *The X-Files* or *Lost* provide viewers with entertaining comfort that discourages them from seeking such patterns in the real world, then those series are politically regressive. If the emergence of patterns in such series encourages the viewers of those series to seek such patterns in the real world as well (and to ask critical questions about those patterns and the forces at work to both build and obscure them), then those series potentially serve a progressive political function. Similarly, if the supernatural forces that arise in *Harry Potter* or *Buffy* provide mere escapist entertainment, then they tend to discourage potentially subversive political thought. If the depiction of these forces causes audiences to stand back and to make critical comparisons between them and the forces that drive the global system of late capitalism, then cognitive estrangement has been achieved.

Whether this cognitive estrangement can occur, of course, depends not just on the structure and content of individual cultural works, but on whether audiences are willing and able to undertake the difficult work it requires, foregoing some of the pleasures offered by popular culture in favor of a quest for enlightenment and understanding. That those pleasures are largely designed precisely to discourage such critical work certainly makes it less likely that such work will be undertaken. The corporate entities that produce popular culture are not likely to introduce products that are intentionally subversive of the capitalist system that feeds them, and we have certainly not yet reached the day when most consumers of popular culture are likely to be able to turn that culture against the entities that produce it. The consistent production of works of popular culture that indicate longings for aspects of existence currently suppressed in the world of late capitalism certainly offers entry points where sufficiently alert consumers can begin to make the first faltering steps toward the kinds of critical analysis that can turn that culture against itself and to use it as a force for, rather than an obstacle to, change.

NOTES

INTRODUCTION

1. Music, at least since the 1960s, has been even more international as a phenomenon than have other forms of popular culture. Crossover between popular American and British music is particularly strong, to the point that in many contexts, it makes little sense to differentiate between the two in discussions of popular music.

2. Other executive producers of *Supernatural* include Kim Manners, who had served as a director, producer, and executive producer on *The X-Files*.

CHAPTER ONE

1. This phenomenon is no doubt related to the closing of the American frontier in the late nineteenth century, but it can also be related to the explosive growth of consumer capitalism from the 1890s to the beginning of the Depression of the 1930s. This sense of the colonization of the American dream by burgeoning corporate interests, leading to the rapid commodification of every aspect of American life, is perhaps best captured in John Dos Passos's magisterial *U.S.A. Trilogy*.

2. For a particularly grim account of the destructive effects of the European colonization of the Americas, see Stannard.

3. For a reading of Baum's book as a populist parable critical of capitalism, see Littlefield.

4. For an account of the repressive turn in American society in conjunction with the U.S. involvement in World War I, see David Kennedy's *Over Here*. U.S. involvement

in the war also plays a pivotal role in the death of the American dream, as narrated in Dos Passos's *U.S.A. Trilogy*.

5. See my essay "The Politics of *Star Trek*" for a fuller discussion of the complex politics of this series.

6. Note, however, Jameson's argument that, if *The Godfather* points back to the utopian potential of older social formations, *The Godfather: Part II* "unmasks" these formations as based in "archaic forms of repression and sexism and violence," while the introduction of the motif of the Cuban Revolution points forward to the possibility of a utopian socialist future" (*Signatures*, p. 34).

7. For example, he noted in a letter describing his intentions that "I had a mind to make a body of more or less connected legend … which I could dedicate simply: to England; to my country. It should possess the tone and quality that I desired, somewhat cool and clear, be redolent of our 'air' (the clime and quality of the North West, meaning Britain and the hither parts of Europe; not Italy or the Aegean, still less the East), and, while possessing (if I could achieve it) the fair elusive beauty that some call Celtic …, it should be 'high,' purged of the gross, and fit for the more adult mind of a land long steeped in poetry" (*Letters*, p. 144).

8. See Marguerite Krause for an especially strong argument about the lack of God (or religion) in the world of Harry Potter.

9. Some critics have found this aspect of the series troubling; thus, Tammy Turner-Vorbeck argues that the books represent "an aggregation of quintessential, hegemonic, hierarchical middle-class social and cultural values (p. 20). She finds that the books and the marketing that surrounds them infringe on and manipulate children's lives by commodifying childhood itself in the interest of corporate hegemony.

10. Indeed, Peter Appelbaum argues that the *Harry Potter* series commodifies magic itself, making it into a form of technology in ways that fit in nicely with our current information economy by making magic something that can be learned through the acquisition of specific skills and expertise. One might compare here the "thaumaturgy" that underlies the Bas-Lag trilogy of novels by Rowling's British contemporary, China Miéville.

11. Disney itself took a cue from the success of these films, introducing its own postmodern update of the classic Disney tales in 2007 with the release of *Enchanted*. In this film, an animated fairy tale princess goes to real-world New York, becomes a live-action character (played by Amy Adams), and experiences considerable comic culture shock. The saccharine *Enchanted* lacks the edge of the *Shrek* films, however, and was only a moderate box-office success.

CHAPTER TWO

1. Although Barnum had been a successful showman for decades, he did not establish the circus for which he is best known until 1871, shortly before Cody turned to show business.

2. See my book *The Post-Utopian Imagination*.

3. The chapters on the 1950s form the heart of Bradford Wright's excellent cultural history of comic books, *Comic Book Nation*.

4. Newman, who had also played the role of Butch Cassidy, was perhaps the central figure in this turn toward charming antiheroes in American film in the 1960s and 1970s, starring in any number of films in which he played such a character. For example, if, in *Buffalo Bill* and *Butch Cassidy*, he created antihero protagonists for the Western (and, in the latter case, the biopic), he did the same for film noir in such films as *The Hustler* (1961) and *Cool Hand Luke* (1967).

5. See my discussion of *Superman* and *Star Wars* in "*May Contain Graphic Material*" (pp. 7–10).

6. It is significant that Jewett and Lawrence, in their extensive discussion of the mythic role of superheroes in American culture, mention Batman and Spider-Man only once each, in passing, without addressing the fact that they do not really support the thesis that superheroes are essentially religious icons in American culture.

7. Significantly, this appellation was first used by Joe Eszterhas in his book *American Rhapsody*, a work of cultural history that was (tellingly) written not by an historian but by a screenwriter, perhaps best known for scripting the notorious films *Basic Instinct* (1992) and *Showgirls* (1995).

8. On such monsters as emblems of capitalism, see Newitz.

9. Rice's later disavowal of vampire fiction because of her conversion to devout Catholicism—seen as many fans as a sort of betrayal—is actually quite consistent with her fascination with vampires, demonstrating the extent to which this fascination is related to the religious longing that informs American culture as a whole.

10. *Angel* has only recently begun to attract the kind of serious critical attention that *Buffy* has mustered for some time now. See the collection *Reading Angel*, edited by Stacey Abbott.

11. For that matter, Angel fed on Buffy's blood to restore his strength in "Graduation Day (2)" the finale of Season Three (July 13, 1999). Here, however, a close tie between the two had already been established.

12. The closest that American popular culture gets to a female vampire protagonist is in the film *BloodRayne* (2005), in which the central character, Rayne (Kristanna Loken), is a half-human, half-vampire who declares war on her evil vampire father (Ben Kingsley). Unfortunately, this ultra-bloody effort (based on a similarly bloody video game) never really gets off the ground, and despite repeated attempts to emphasize Rayne's torments, the central character is just not very interesting.

13. Lynda Carter's Wonder Woman, the protagonist of the 1970s television series of that title, was the principal female superhero on television before the 1990s. She was an admirable and formidable figure but also served largely as eye candy.

14. Peter Coogan has argued that Buffy is not a superhero because her narrative derives too directly from the tradition of vampire narratives, distinctly different from the superhero genre (p. 48). This argument, however, does not pay sufficient attention

to the multigeneric nature of the *Buffy* narratives. I tend therefore to agree more with Roz Kaveney's declaration that "Buffy is a superhero; it is one of the most obvious things about her" (*Superheroes,* p. 204).

15. This event actually occurs within an alternative reality, one of many such instances of that motif in *Buffy*. Here there is an *It's a Wonderful Life* scenario in which we see what Sunnydale might have been like had Buffy never come there. In the mainstream "reality" of the series, of course, Buffy kills the Master at the end of Season One.

16. See, for example, Yurguis. Also see Nina Auerbach's *Our Vampires, Our Selves* for an extended argument that representations of vampires in popular culture serve as excellent reflections of the concerns, fascinations, and anxieties of contemporary culture from the nineteenth century forward. See also the collection edited by Gordon and Hollinger for some particularly good insights into the metaphorical role played by vampires in our contemporary culture.

17. This ability is very similar to that of the comic-book superhero Painkiller Jane (Kristanna Loken), the central character in a short-lived television series of that title that ran on the Sci Fi channel for a single season in 2006 and 2007. *Painkiller Jane,* however, is a virtual reversal of *Heroes,* in that the principal characters, including Jane, work for a government organization that hunts down and attempts to neutralize "neuros," enhanced humans with powerful (and potentially dangerous) psychic abilities. The series complicates any easy assignment of good-guy or bad-guy status to either side, but the focus is definitely on the hunters of neuros rather than on the neuros, who roughly correspond to the mutants of *Heroes.*

CHAPTER THREE

1. For more on these films, see my *From Box Office to Ballot Box* (pp. 65–71).

2. For more on the science fiction of the 1950s, see my *Monsters, Mushroom Clouds, and the Cold War.*

3. Still another stunt, in which Regan spider-walks up the wall and onto the ceiling of her bedroom, is added for the 2000 Director's Cut version of the film that was released to DVD.

4. This part of the film is usefully enhanced in the 2000 version, which otherwise is probably inferior to the original.

5. Romero did, however, have some mainstream success with the 1982 horror anthology film *Creepshow* (1982), based on five stories by horror maven Stephen King, who also wrote the screenplay. This film, which is something of an homage to the classic E.C. horror comics of the 1950s, was successful enough to give birth to a horror anthology television series, *Tales from the Darkside,* which Romero produced and which ran in syndication from 1983 to 1988.

6. The economic structure of the film industry allows filmmakers to be more adventurous than television producers, as in the 1972 horror film *Tales from the Crypt,* overtly based on the E.C. comic of the same title. In television, cable networks are

typically less averse to controversy than are broadcast networks (because of being less dependent on large audiences and the good graces of advertisers). HBO thus also went for an overt link to E.C. comics in its anthology series *Tales from the Crypt*, which ran from 1989 to 1996.

7. For an excellent succinct discussion of the controversies over comic books in the 1950s, see Wright (pp. 154–179).

8. Mulder and Scully are not superheroes, although they might have some alien DNA, and they are dependably virtuous and courageous. They do, however, ultimately mate to produce a super child who is a version of the Chosen One.

9. In the later science fiction television miniseries *Wild Palms* (1993), which aired just a few months before the premiere of *The X-Files*, we learn (in a narrative set in 2007) that all the conspiracy theories set forth in *JFK* have now been proved to be factual. *Wild Palms* was co-produced by Stone himself. This miniseries, by the way, involves several conspiracies itself, including an attempt legally to limit the civil liberties of Americans by a "Liberty Bill" passed in response to the perceived threat of terrorist attacks, thus anticipating the Bush-era Patriot Act.

10. The date is taken from Mayan mythology, which stipulates this as the date of the end of the world.

11. In this, *Lost* also looks back to the early-1990s "science fiction Western" *The Adventures of Brisco County, Jr.*, co-created by Carlton Cuse, co-show runner of *Lost*.

CONCLUSION

1. On these efforts, See McCann.

WORKS CITED

Abbott, Stacey, ed. *Reading* Angel: *The TV Spin-Off with a Soul*. London: I. B. Taurus, 2005.

Agee, James. *Agee on Film*. Vol. 1 of 2. New York: Grosset and Dunlap, 1958.

Appelbaum, Peter. "Harry Potter's World: Magic, Technoculture, and Becoming Human." In *Critical Perspectives on Harry Potter*. Ed. Elizabeth Heilman. New York: Routledge, 2003. 25–51.

Auerbach, Nina. *Our Vampires, Ourselves*. Chicago: University of Chicago, 1997.

Bacon, Francis. *New Atlantis*. 1626. Ed. Alfred B. Gough. Oxford: Clarendon P, 1915.

Baum, L. Frank. *The Wonderful Wizard of Oz*. 1900. New York: Signet, 2006.

Behn, Aphra. *Oroonoko*. 1688. London: Penguin, 2004.

Bellamy, Edward. *Looking Backward: 2000–1887*. 1888. New York: Oxford UP, 2007.

Benjamin, Walter. *Illuminations*. Trans. Harry Zohn. Ed. Hannah Arendt. New York: Harcourt, Brace, and World, 1955.

Billson, Anne. *Buffy the Vampire Slayer*. London: British Film Institute, 2005.

Bloch, Ernst. *The Principle of Hope*. Vol. 1. Trans. Neville Plaice, Stephen Plaice, and Paul Knight. Cambridge, MA: MIT P, 1995.

Booker, M. Keith. *From Box Office to Ballot Box: The American Political Film*. Westport, CT: Praeger, 2007.

———. *"May Contain Graphic Material": Comic Books, Graphic Novels, and Film*. Westport, CT: Praeger, 2007.

———. *Monsters, Mushroom Clouds, and the Cold War: American Science Fiction and the Roots of Postmodernism, 1946–1964*. Westport, CT: Greenwood, 2001.

———. "The Politics of *Star Trek*." *The Essential Science Fiction Television Reader*. Ed. J. P. Telotte. Lexington: UP of Kentucky, 2008. 195–208.

———. *The Post-Utopian Imagination: American Culture in the Long 1950s*. Westport, CT: Greenwood, 2002.

———. *Science Fiction Television*. Westport, CT: Praeger, 2004.

———. *Strange TV: Innovative Television Series from* The Twilight Zone *to* The X-Files. Westport, CT: Greenwood, 2002.

Brecht, Bertolt. *Life of Galileo*. 1947. London: Penguin, 2008.

Burroughs, Edgar Rice. *A Princess of Mars*. 1911. London: Penguin, 2007.

———. *Tarzan of the Apes*. 1914. New York: Penguin, 1990.

Certeau, Michel de. *The Practice of Everyday Life*. Berkeley: U of California P, 2002.

Coogan, Peter. *Superhero: The Secret Origin of a Genre*. Austin, TX: MonkeyBrain Books, 2006.

Defoe, Daniel. *Robinson Crusoe*. 1719. London: Penguin, 2003.

Degh, Linda. *American Folklore and the Mass Media*. Bloomington: Indiana UP, 1994.

Diamond, Jared. *Guns, Germs, and Steel: The Fates of Human Societies*. New York: W. W. Norton, 1999.

Dos Passos, John. *U.S.A.* 1930, 1932, 1936. New York: Library of America, 1996.

Dyer, Richard. "Entertainment and Utopia." *Hollywood Musicals, The Film Reader*. Ed. Steven Cohan. London: Routledge, Taylor, and Francis Group, 2002. 19–31.

Ebert, Roger. Review of *The Exorcist* (2000 Version). Available on-line at http://rogerebert.suntimes.com/apps/pbcs.dll/article?AID=/20000922/REVIEWS/9220302/1023.

Elster, Charles. "The Seeker of Secrets: Images of Learning, Knowing, and Schooling." *Critical Perspectives on Harry Potter*. Ed. Elizabeth Heilman. New York: Routledge, 2003. 203–220.

Engelhardt, Tom. *The End of Victory Culture: Cold War America and the Disillusioning of a Generation*. New York: Basic Books, 1995.

Eszterhas, Joe. *American Rhapsody*. New York: Knopf, 2000.

Fiske, John. *Television Culture*. London: Routledge, 1999.

Frank, Thomas. *The Conquest of Cool: Business Culture, Counterculture, and the Rise of Hip Consumerism*. Chicago: U of Chicago P, 1997.

Frey, Charles H. *Experiencing Shakespeare: Essays on Text, Classroom, and Performance*. Columbia: U of Missouri P, 1988.

Gaiman, Neil. *American Gods*. 2001. New York: HarperCollins, 2003.

Gordon, Joan, and Veronica Hollinger, eds. *Blood Read: The Vampire as Metaphor in Contemporary Culture*. Philadelphia: U of Pennsylvania P, 1997.

Greenblatt, Stephen. *Marvelous Possessions: The Wonder of the New World*. Chicago, U of Chicago P, 1992.

Grossman, Lev. "Feeding on Fantasy." *Time* (Dec. 2, 2002). Available on-line at http://www.time.com/time/magazine/article/0,9171,1101021202-393752,00.html.

Heath, Joseph, and Andrew Potter. *Nation of Rebels: Why Counterculture Became Consumer Culture*. New York: HarperBusiness, 2004.

Hebdige, Dick. *Subculture: The Meaning of Style*. London: Methuen, 1979.

Hendershot, Cyndy. *I Was a Cold War Monster: Horror Films, Eroticism, and The Cold War Imagination*. Bowling Green, OH: Bowling Green State U Popular P, 2001.

Hirsch, Foster. *Detours and Lost Highways: A Map of Neo-Noir*. New York: Limelight Editions, 1999.

Hobsbawm, Eric. *The Age of Extremes: A History of the World, 1914–1991*. New York: Pantheon, 1994.

Hofstadter, Richard. *"The Paranoid Style in American Politics" and Other Essays*. Cambridge, MA: Harvard UP, 1964.

Horkheimer, Max, and Theodor W. Adorno. *Dialectic of Enlightenment*. Trans. John Cumming. New York: Seabury P, 1972.

Jameson, Fredric. *The Political Unconscious: Narrative as a Socially Symbolic Act*. Ithaca, NY: Cornell UP, 1981.

———. *Postmodernism, or, The Cultural Logic of Late Capitalism*. Durham, NC: Duke UP, 1991.

———. *Signatures of the Visible*. New York: Routledge, 1992.

Kaveney, Roz, ed. *Reading the Vampire Slayer: An Unofficial Critical Companion to* Buffy *and* Angel. London: Tauris Parke, 2001.

Kaveney, Roz. "'She saved the world. A lot': An Introduction to the Themes and Structures of *Buffy* and *Angel*." In Kaveney, *Reading* 1–36.

———. *Superheroes: Capes and Crusaders in Comics and Films*. London: I. B. Taurus, 2008.

Kennedy, David M. *Over Here: The First World War and American Society*. 25th Anniversary Edition. New York: Oxford UP, 2004.

King, Neal. "Brownskirts: Fascism, Christianity, and the Eternal Demon." In South 197–211.

Krause, Marguerite. "Harry Potter and the End of Religion." *Mapping the World of Harry Potter: Science Fiction and Fantasy Writers Explore the Bestselling Fantasy Series of All Time*. Dallas: BenBella Books, 2006. 53–68.

Jewett, Robert, and John Shelton Lawrence. *The Myth of the American Superhero*. Grand Rapids, MI: Wm. B. Eerdmans, 2002.

Leach, William. *Country of Exiles: The Destruction of Place in American Life*. New York: Pantheon, 1999.

———. *Land of Desire: Merchants, Power, and the Rise of a New American Culture*. New York: Vintage-Random House, 1993.

Littlefield, Henry. "The Wizard of Oz: Parable of Populism." *American Quarterly* (Spring 1964): 47–58.

Luckhurst, Roger. *Science Fiction*. London: Polity, 2005.

MacDonald, Dwight. *Against the American Grain: Essays on the Effects of Mass Culture*. New York: Vintage, 1962.

Magoulick, Mary. "Frustrating Female Heroism: Mixed Messages in *Xena, Nikita,* and *Buffy. The Journal of Popular Culture* 39.5 (2006): 729–755.

Marx, Karl, and Friedrich Engels. *The Marx-Engels Reader.* Ed. Robert C. Tucker. 2nd ed. New York: Norton, 1978.

Mathews, Richard. *Fantasy: The Liberation of Imagination.* London: Routledge, 2002.

McCann, Sean. *Gumshoe America: Hard-Boiled Crime Fiction and the Rise and Fall of New Deal Liberalism.* Durham, NC: Duke UP, 2000.

Melville, Herman. *Moby-Dick or, The Whale.* 1851. New York: Penguin, 2002.

Miéville, China. *Un Lun Dun.* London: Macmillan, 2007.

Miller, Frank. *Batman: The Dark Knight Returns.* 1986. New York: DC Comics, 1997.

Miller, Mark Crispin. *Boxed In: The Culture of TV.* Evanston, IL: Northwestern UP, 1988.

Moore, Alan. *Batman: The Killing Joke.* 1988. New York: DC Comics, 2008.

More, Sir Thomas. *Utopia.* 1516. Norton Critical Edition. Ed. Robert M. Adams. New York: Norton, 1992.

Morris, William. *News from Nowhere, or an Epoch of Rest.* 1890. London: Routledge and Kegan Paul, 1970.

———. *The Well at the World's End.* 1896. West Valley City, UT: Waking Lion P, 2006.

———. *The Wood Beyond the World.* 1894. New York: Ballantine, 1969.

Nabokov, Vladimir. *Lolita.* 1955. New York: Penguin, 1998.

Nesbit, Edith. *The Enchanted Castle.* 1907. New York: Puffin-Penguin, 1995.

Newitz, Annalee. *Pretend We're Dead: Capitalist Monsters in American Pop Culture.* Durham, NC: Duke UP, 2006.

O'Brien, Daniel. *Robert Altman: Hollywood Survivor.* New York: Continuum, 1995.

Pasley, Jeffrey L. "Old Familiar Vampires: The Politics of the Buffyverse." In South 254–267.

Pender, Patricia. "'I'm Buffy, and You're … History': The Postmodern Politics of *Buffy.*" In Wilcox and Lavery, 35–44.

Quart, Alissa. *Branded: The Buying and Selling of Teenagers.* New York: Basic Books, 2003.

Reynolds, Richard. *Super Heroes: A Modern Mythology.* Jackson: UP of Mississippi, 1992.

Rice, Anne. *Interview with the Vampire.* 1976. New York: Ballantine, 1997.

Rosen, Elizabeth K. *Apocalyptic Transformation: Apocalypse and the Postmodern Imagination.* Lanham, MD: Lexington-Rowman and Littlefield, 2008.

Rowling, J. K. *Harry Potter and the Deathly Hallows.* New York: Scholastic, 2007.

———. *Harry Potter and the Philosopher's Stone.* London: Bloomsbury, 1997.

———. *Harry Potter and the Order of the Phoenix.* New York: Scholastic, 2003.

Savage, Jon. *Teenage: The Creation of Youth Culture.* New York: Viking, 2007.

Seelye, John. Introduction to *Tarzan of the Apes* by William S. Burroughs. New York: Penguin, 1990. vii–xxviii.

Shakespeare, William. *The Tempest*. 1611. New York: Washington Square P, 2004.

Sharp, Patrick. *Savage Perils: Racial Frontiers and Nuclear Apocalypse in American Culture*. Norman: U of Oklahoma P, 2007.

Slotkin, Richard. "Buffalo Bill's 'Wild West' and the Mythologization of the American Empire." *Culture of United States Imperialism*. Eds. Amy Kaplan and Donald E. Pease. Durham, NC: Duke UP, 1993. 164–181.

———. *The Fatal Environment: The Myth of the Frontier in the Age of Industrialization, 1800–1890*. 1985, Norman: U of Oklahoma P, 1998.

———. *Gunfighter Nation: The Myth of the Frontier in Twentieth-Century America*. 1992. Norman: U of Oklahoma P, 1998.

———. *Regeneration through Violence: The Mythology of the American Frontier, 1600–1860*. 1973. Norman: U of Oklahoma P, 2000.

South, James B., ed. *Buffy the Vampire Slayer and Philosophy: Fear and Trembling in Sunnydale*. Chicago: Open Court, 2003.

Stannard, David E. *American Holocaust: The Conquest of the New World*. New York: Oxford UP, 1993.

Suvin, Darko. *Metamorphoses of Science Fiction: On the Poetics and History of a Literary Genre*. New Haven, CT: Yale UP, 1979.

Swift, Jonathan. *Gulliver's Travels*. 1726. London: Penguin, 2003.

Takaki, Ronald. *A Different Mirror: A History of Multicultural America*. Boston: Little, Brown, 1993.

Todorov, Tzvetan. *The Conquest of America: The Question of the Other*. Trans. Richard Howard. New York: Harper and Row, 1983.

Tolkien, J.R.R. *The Hobbit*. 1937. Boston: Houghton Mifflin, 2002.

———. *Letters*. Selected and edited by Humphrey Carpenter, with the assistance of Christopher Tolkien. Boston: Houghton Mifflin, 1981.

———. *The Lord of the Rings: The Fellowship of the Ring*. 1954. Boston: Houghton Mifflin, 2005.

———. *The Lord of the Rings: The Return of the King*. 1955. Boston: Houghton Mifflin, 2005.

———. *The Lord of the Rings: The Two Towers*. 1954. Boston: Houghton Mifflin, 2005.

Turner-Vorbeck, Tammy. "Pottermania: Good, Clean Fun or Cultural Hegemony?" In *Critical Perspectives on Harry Potter*. Ed. Elizabeth Heilman. New York: Routledge, 2003. 13–24.

Weber, Max. *The Protestant Ethic and the Spirit of Capitalism*. 1904–1905. Trans. Talcott Parsons. 1930. London: Routledge, 1995.

Wertham, Fredric. *Seduction of the Innocent*. New York: Rinehart, 1954.

Wilcox, Rhonda, and David Lavery, eds. *Fighting the Forces: What's at Stake in* Buffy the Vampire Slayer. Lanham, MD: Rowman and Littlefield, 2002.

Wilcox, Rhonda. "When Harry Met Buffy: Buffy Summers, Harry Potter, and Heroism." In Wilcox, *Why Buffy Matters*. London: I.B. Tauris, 2005.

Wilcox, Rhonda. *Why Buffy Matters: The Art of "Buffy the Vampire Slayer."* London: I. B. Tauris, 2005.

Wood, Robin. *Hollywood from Vietnam to Reagan.* Expanded and revised edition. New York: Columbia UP, 2003.

Wright, Bradford W. *Comic Book Nation: The Transformation of Youth Culture in America.* Baltimore: Johns Hopkins UP, 2003.

Yurguis, Katia. "The Dark Gift: Vampires in the AIDS Era." *Discoveries* (Fall 2002): 9–21.

FILMS CITED

2001: A Space Odyssey. Dir. Stanley Kubrick, 1968.

300. Dir. Zack Snyder, 2007.

The Adventures of Buckaroo Banzai Across the Eighth Dimension. Dir. W. D. Richter, 1984.

The Adventures of Robin Hood. Dir. Michael Curtiz and William Keighley, 1938.

Æon Flux. Dir. Karyn Kusama, 2005

Air Force One. Dir. Wolfgang Petersen, 1997.

Alien. Dir. Ridley Scott, 1979.

Alien³. Dir. David Fincher, 1992.

Alien: Resurrection. Dir. Jean-Pierre Jeunet, 1997.

Aliens. Dir. James Cameron, 1986.

All the President's Men. Dir. Alan J. Pakula, 1976.

The Andromeda Strain. Dir. Robert Wise, 1971.

Angel Heart. Dir. Alan Parker, 1987.

Audrey Rose. Dir. Robert Wise, 1977.

Basic Instinct. Dir. Paul Verhoeven, 1992.

Batman. Dir. Tim Burton, 1989.

Batman Returns. Dir. Tim Burton, 1992.

Bedknobs and Broomsticks. Dir. Robert Stevenson, 1971.

Ben-Hur. Dir. William Wyler, 1959.

Beowulf. Dir. Robert Zemeckis, 2007.

Big Jim McClain. Dir. Edward Ludwig, 1952.

The Blackboard Jungle. Dir. Richard Brooks, 1955.

Blade. Dir. Stephen Norrington, 1998.

Blade II. Dir. Guillermo del Toro, 2002.

Blade: Trinity. Dir. David S. Goyer, 2004.

Blade Runner. Dir. Ridley Scott, 1982.

The Blob. Dir. Irwin S. Yeawroth, Jr., 1958.

BloodRayne. Dir. Uwe Boll, 2005.

Blue Velvet. Dir. David Lynch, 1986.

Boogeyman. Dir. Stephen T. Kay, 2005.

Braveheart. Dir. Mel Gibson, 1995.

The Brood. Dir. David Cronenberg, 1979.

Buffalo Bill and the Indians, or Sitting Bull's History Lesson. Dir. Robert Altman, 1976.

Buffy the Vampire Slayer. Dir. Fran Rubel Kazui, 1992.

Butch Cassidy and the Sundance Kid. Dir. George Roy Hill, 1969.

Captain Blood. Dir. Michael Curtiz, 1935.

Cars. Dir. John Lasseter, 2006.

Catwoman. Dir. Pitof, 2004.

Chinatown. Dir. Roman Polanski, 1974.

The Chronicles of Narnia: The Lion, the Witch, and the Wardrobe. Dir. Andrew Adamson, 2005.

The Chronicles of Narnia: Prince Caspian. Dir. Andrew Adamson, 2008.

Clerks. Dir. Kevin Smith, 1994.

A Clockwork Orange. Dir. Stanley Kubrick, 1971.

Close Encounters of the Third Kind. Dir. Steven Spielberg, 1977.

Conan the Barbarian. Dir. John Milius, 1982.

Conan the Destroyer. Dir. Richard Fleischer, 1984.

The Conversation. Dir. Francis Ford Coppola, 1974.

Cool Hand Luke. Dir. Stuart Rosenberg, 1967.

Coraline. Dir. Henry Selick, 2009 (projected).

Creepshow. Dir. George A. Romero, 1982.

Crouching Tiger, Hidden Dragon. Dir. Ang Lee, 2000.

Daredevil. Dir. Mark Steven Johnson, 2003.

Dave. Dir. Ivan Reitman, 1993.

Davy Crockett, King of the Wild Frontier. Dir. Norman Foster, 1955.

Davy Crockett and the River Pirates. Dir. Norman Foster, 1956.

Dawn of the Dead. Dir. George A. Romero, 1978.

Day of the Dead. Dir. George A. Romero, 1985.

Demon Seed. Dir. Donald Cammell, 1977.

Dogma. Dir. Kevin Smith, 1999.

Double Indemnity. Dir. Billy Wilder, 1944.

Dr. No. Dir. Terence Young, 1962.

Dune. Dir. David Lynch, 1984.

Elektra. Dir. Rob Bowman, 2005.

Enchanted. Dir. Kevin Lima, 2007.

E.T. the Extraterrestrial. Dir. Steven Spielberg, 1982.

The Evil Dead. Dir. Sam Raimi, 1981.

The Exorcist. Dir. William Friedkin, 1973.

Fallen. Dir. Gregory Hoblit, 1998.

Fantastic Four. Dir. Tim Story, 2005.

Fantastic Four: Rise of the Silver Surfer. Dir. Tim Story, 2007.

Frankenstein. Dir. James Whale, 1931.

From Dusk Till Dawn. Dir. Robert Rodriguez, 1996.

The Godfather. Dir. Francis Ford Coppola, 1972.

The Godfather Part II. Dir. Francis Ford Coppola, 1974.

Gold Diggers of 1933. Dir. Mervyn LeRoy, 1933.

The Golden Compass. Dir. Christ Weitz, 2007.

The Great Train Robbery. Dir. Edwin S. Porter, 1903.

The Greatest Story Ever Told. Dir. George Stevens, 1965.

Harry Potter and the Chamber of Secrets. Dir. Chris Columbus, 2002.

Harry Potter and the Goblet of Fire. Dir. Mike Newell, 2005.

Harry Potter and the Order of the Phoenix. Dir. David Yates, 2007.

Harry Potter and the Prisoner of Azkaban. Dir. Alfonso Cuarón, 2004.

Harry Potter and the Sorceror's Stone. Dir. Chris Columbus, 2001.

Heaven's Gate. Dir. Michael Cimino, 1980.

Highlander. Dir. Russell Mulcahy, 1986.

A History of Violence. Dir. David Cronenberg, 2005.

The Hustler. Dir. Robert Rossen, 1961.

I Know What You Did Last Summer. Dir. Jim Gillespie, 1997.

I Married a Monster from Outer Space. Dir. Gene Fowler, 1958.

Independence Day. Dir. Roland Emmerich, 1996.

Interview with the Vampire: The Vampire Chronicles. Dir. Neil Jordan, 1994.

Invasion of the Body Snatchers. Dir. Don Siegel, 1956.

It Lives Again. Dir. Larry Cohen, 1978.

It's Alive. Dir. Larry Cohen, 1974.

It's a Wonderful Life. Dir. Frank Capra, 1946.

I Was a Communist for the FBI. Dir. Gordon Douglas, 1951.

I Was a Teenage Frankenstein. Dir. Herbert J. Strock, 1958.

I Was a Teenage Mummy. Dir. Ralph C. Bluemke, 1962.

I Was a Teenage Werewolf. Dir. Gene Fowler, 1957.

JFK. Dir. Oliver Stone, 1991.

Kill Bill: Vol. 1. Dir. Quentin Tarantino, 2003.

Kill Bill: Vol. 2. Dir. Quentin Tarantino, 2004.

King of Kings. Dir. Nicholas Ray, 1961.

King Kong. Dir. Merian C. Cooper and Ernest B. Schoedsack, 1933.

Labyrinth. Dir. Jim Henson, 1986.

Land of the Dead. Dir. George A. Romero, 2005.

Lawrence of Arabia. Dir. David Lean, 1962.

Logan's Run. Dir. Michael Anderson, 1976.

Lola rennt. Dir. Tom Tykwer, 1998.

The Lord of the Rings. Dir. Ralph Bakshi, 1978.

The Lord of the Rings: The Fellowship of the Ring. Dir. Peter Jackson, 2001.

The Lord of the Rings: The Return of the King. Dir. Peter Jackson, 2003.

The Lord of the Rings: The Two Towers. Dir. Peter Jackson, 2002.

Lost Horizon. Dir. Frank Capra, 1937.

The Manchurian Candidate. Dir. John Frankenheimer, 1962.

M*A*S*H. Dir. Robert Altman, 1970.

The Matrix. Dir. Andy Wachowski and Larry Wachowski, 1999.

McCabe and Mrs. Miller. Dir. Robert Altman, 1971.

Mirrormask. Dir. Dave McKean, 2005.

Mission to Moscow. Dir. Michael Curtiz, 1943.

Monster's Ball. Dir. Marc Forster, 2001.

Murder in the Air. Dir. Lewis Seiler, 1940.

Nashville. Dir. Robert Altman, 1975.

The Neverending Story. Dir. Wolfgang Petersen, 1984.

Nick Knight. Dir. Farhad Mann, 1989.

Night of the Living Dead. Dir. George A. Romero, 1968.

The Night Stalker. Dir. John Llewellyn Moxey, 1972.

The Night Strangler. Dir. Dan Curtis, 1973.

Nikita. Dir. Luc Besson, 1990.

The Ninth Gate. Dir. Roman Polanski, 1999.

The Norliss Tapes. Dir. Dan Curtis, 1973.

The North Star. Dir. Lewis Milestone, 1943.

The Omega Man. Dir. Boris Sagal, 1971.

The Omen. Dir. Richard Donner, 1976.

The Parallax View. Dir. Alan J. Pakula, 1974.

The Passion of the Christ. Dir. Mel Gibson, 2004.

Pinocchio. Dir. Hamilton Luske and Ben Sharpsteen, 1940.

Pirates of the Caribbean: The Curse of the Black Pearl. Dir. Gore Verbinski, 2003.

Pirates of the Caribbean: Dead Man's Chest. Dir. Gore Verbinski, 2006.

Pirates of the Caribbean: At World's End. Dir. Gore Verbinski, 2007.

Planet of the Apes. Dir. Franklin J. Schaffner, 1968.

Point of No Return. Dir. John Badham, 1993.

The Polar Express. Dir. Robert Zemeckis, 2004.

Poltergeist. Dir. Tobe Hooper, 1982.

The Princess Bride. Dir. Rob Reiner, 1987.

The Professionals. Dir. Richard Brooks, 1966.

Psycho. Dir. Alfred Hitchcock, 1960.

Queen of the Damned. Dir. Michael Rymer, 2002.

The Red Menace. Dir. R. G. Springsteen, 1949.

Red River. Dir. Howard Hawks, 1948.

Red Sonja. Dir. Richard Fleischer, 1985.

Resident Evil. Dir. Paul W. S. Anderson, 2002.

Resident Evil: Apocalypse. Dir. Paul W. S. Anderson, 2004.

Resident Evil: Extinction. Dir. Russell Mulcahy, 2007.

Rollerball. Dir. Norman Jewison, 1975.

Rosemary's Baby. Dir. Roman Polanski, 1968.

Scream. Dir. Wes Craven, 1996.

Scream 2. Dir. Wes Craven, 1997.

Scream 3. Dir. Wes Craven, 2000.

Sheena. Dir. John Guillermin, 1984.

Showgirls. Dir. Paul Verhoeven, 1995.

Shrek. Dir. Andrew Adamson and Vicky Jensen, 2001.

Shrek 2. Dir. Andrew Adamson, Kelly Asbury, and Conrad Vernon, 2004.

Shrek the Third. Dir. Chris Miller and Raman Hui, 2007.

Silent Running. Dir. Douglas Trumbull, 1972.

Sisters. Dir. Brian De Palma, 1973.

Snow White and the Seven Dwarfs. Dir. David Hand, 1937.

Song of Russia. Dir. Gregory Ratoff, 1943.

Soylent Green. Dir. Richard Fleischer, 1973.

Spider-Man. Dir. Sam Raimi, 2002.

Spider-Man II. Dir. Sam Raimi, 2004.

Spider-Man III. Dir. Sam Raimi, 2007.

The Spiderwick Chronicles. Dir. Mark Waters, 2008.

Stagecoach. Dir. John Ford, 1939.

Star Trek: The Motion Picture. Dir. Robert Wise, 1979.

Star Wars. Dir. George Lucas, 1977.

Star Wars: Episode I—The Phantom Menace. Dir. George Lucas, 1999.

Star Wars: Episode II—Attack of the Clones. Dir. George Lucas, 2002.

Star Wars: Episode III—Revenge of the Sith. Dir. George Lucas, 2005.

Star Wars: Episode V—The Empire Strikes Back. Dir. Irvin Kershner, 1980.

Star Wars: Episode VI—Return of the Jedi. Dir. Richard Marquand, 1983.

Stardust. Dir. Matthew Vaughn, 2007.

The Stepford Wives. Dir. Bryan Forbes, 1975.

Stigmata. Dir. Rupert Wainwright, 1999.

Superman: The Movie. Dir. Richard Donner, 1978.

Superman II. Dir. Richard Lester, 1980.

Superman III. Dir. Richard Lester, 1983.

Superman IV: The Quest for Peace. Dir. Sidney J. Furie, 1987.

Tales from the Crypt. Dir. Freddie Francis, 1972.

Teenagers from Outer Space. Dir. Tom Graeff, 1959.

The Ten Commandments. Dir. Cecil B. DeMille, 1956.

The Terminator. Dir. James Cameron, 1984.

Terminator 2: Judgment Day. Dir. James Cameron, 1991.

Three Days of the Condor. Dir. Sidney Pollack, 1975.

Ultraviolet. Dir. Kurt Wimmer, 2006.

Underworld. Dir. Len Wiseman, 2003.

Underworld: Evolution. Dir. Len Wiseman, 2006.

Wall Street. Dir. Oliver Stone, 1987.

The Wild Bunch. Dir. Sam Peckinpah, 1969.

Willow. Dir. Ron Howard, 1988.

The Wizard of Oz. Dir. Victor Fleming, 1939.

Wizards. Dir. Ralph Bakshi, 1977.

X-Men. Dir. Bryan Singer, 2000.

X-Men: The Last Stand. Dir. Brett Ratner, 2006.

X2. Dir. Bryan Singer, 2003.

TELEVISION SERIES CITED

The 4400. USA, 2004–2007.
The Adventures of Brisco County, Jr. FOX, 1993–1994.
The Adventures of Superman. Syndication, 1952–1958.
Alias. ABC, 2001–2006.
American Gothic. CBS, 1995–1996.
Angel. WB, 1999–2004.
The Avengers. ITV, 1961–1969.
Babylon 5. PTEN, 1994–1997. TNT, 1998.
Battlestar Galactica. ABC, 1978–1979.
Battlestar Galactica. Sci Fi, 2004– .
Beauty and the Beast. CBS, 1987–1990.
Bewitched. ABC, 1964–1972.
The Bionic Woman. ABC, 1976–1977. NBC, 1977–1978.
Blood Ties. Lifetime, 2007– .
Buffy the Vampire Slayer. WB, 1997–2001. UPN, 2001–2003.
Carnivàle. HBO, 2003–2005.
Charmed. WB, 1998–2006.
Danger Man. ITV, 1960–1968.
Dark Angel. FOX, 2000–2002.
Dark Shadows. ABC, 1966–1971.
Dead Like Me. Showtime, 2003–2004.
The Dead Zone. USA, 2002–2007.
Desperate Housewives. ABC, 2004– .

The Dresden Files. Sci Fi, 2007.

The Dukes of Hazzard. CBS, 1979–1985.

Eli Stone. ABC, 2008– .

Eureka. Sci Fi, 2006– .

Farscape. Sci Fi, 1999–2003.

La Femme Nikita. USA, 1997–2001.

Forever Knight. CBS, 1992–1993. Syndicated, 1994–1996.

Ghost Hunters. Sci Fi, 2004– .

The Ghost Whisperer. CBS, 2005– .

Grey's Anatomy. ABC, 2005– .

Hercules: The Legendary Journeys. Syndication, 1995–1999.

Heroes. NBC, 2006– .

Highlander: The Series. Syndication, 1992–1998.

The Invaders. ABC, 1967–1968.

Joan of Arcadia. CBS, 2003–2005.

John from Cincinnati. HBO, 2007.

Journeyman. NBC, 2007.

Lois & Clark: The New Adventures of Superman. ABC, 1993–1997.

Lost. ABC, 2004– .

The Man from U.N.C.L.E. NBC, 1964–1968.

Medium. NBC, 2005– .

Melrose Place. FOX, 1992–1999.

Millennium. FOX, 1996–1999.

Miracles. ABC, 2003.

Mission: Impossible. CBS, 1966–1973.

Moonlight. CBS, 2007–2008.

Moonlighting. ABC, 1985–1989.

New Amsterdam. FOX, 2008.

Night Gallery. NBC, 1970–1973.

The Night Stalker. ABC, 1974–1975; 2005–2006.

Northern Exposure. CBS, 1990–1995.

Painkiller Jane. Sci Fi, 2007.

Paranormal State. A&E, 2007– .

Point Pleasant. FOX, 2005.

The Prisoner. ITV, 1967–1968.

Pushing Daisies. ABC, 2007– .

Reaper. CW, 2007– .

Revelations. NBC, 2005.

Roswell. WB, 1999–2001. UPN, 2001–2002.

The Saint. ITV, 1962–1969.

Saving Grace. TNT, 2007– .

The Simpsons. FOX, 1989– .

Smallville. WB, 2001–2006. CW, 2006– .

Star Trek. NBC, 1966–1969.

Star Trek: Deep Space Nine. Syndicated, 1993–1999.

Star Trek: The Next Generation. Syndicated, 1987–1994.

Star Trek: Voyager. UPN, 1995–2001.

Stargate SG-1. Showtime, 1997–2002. Sci Fi, 2002–2007.

Supernatural. WB, 2005–2006. CW, 2006– .

Tales from the Darkside. Syndicated, 1983–1988.

Teen Titans. Cartoon Network, 2003–2006.

Touched by an Angel. CBS, 1994–2003.

Tru Calling. FOX, 2003–2005.

The Twilight Zone. CBS, 1959–1964.

Twin Peaks. ABC, 1990–1991.

The West Wing. NBC, 1999–2006.

Wild Palms. ABC, 1993.

Wonderfalls. FOX, 2004.

Xena: Warrior Princess. Syndicated, 1995–2001.

The X-Files. FOX, 1993–2002.

INDEX

In the Extraordinary World series

Superpower: Heroes, Ghosts, and the Paranormal in American Culture
M. Keith Booker

The Coming of the Fairies
Sir Arthur Conan Doyle
Introduced by John M. Lynch

Scientists and Scoundrels: A Book of Hoaxes
Robert Silverberg

To order or obtain more information on these or other University of Nebraska Press titles, visit www.nebraskapress.unl.edu.